To the Bottom of the Sea

To the Bottom of the Sea

True Accounts of Major Ship Disasters

JOHN PROTASIO

A Lyle Stuart Book
Published by Carol Publishing Group

Copyright ©1990 by John Protasio

A Lyle Stuart Book
Published by Carol Publishing Group

Editorial Offices
600 Madison Avenue
New York, NY 10022

Sales & Distribution Offices
120 Enterprise Avenue
Secaucus, NJ 07094

In Canada: Musson Book Company
A division of General Publishing Co. Limited
Don Mills, Ontario

Manufactured in the United States of America

Library of Congress Cataloging-in-Publication Data

Protasio, John.
    To the Bottom of the sea : true accounts of major ship disasters /
by John Protasio.
    p. cm.
    "A Lyle Stuart book."
    ISBN 0-8184-0530-9 : $18.95
    1. Shipwrecks. I. Title.
G525.P83   1990   90-38405
363.12'3—dc20   CIP

TO ALL THOSE WHO DIED AT SEA

". . . Summoned to the deep
Thou, thou and all thy mates,
to keep an incommunicable sleep."
—Wordsworth

Contents

Foreword

In 1911, James Bisset, an officer in the Cunard Line, overheard two old seamen discussing the new twin luxury liners of the White Star Line. One was impressed by the ships while the other was skeptical.

"She'll be a floating palace," the one said.

"Floating boarding-house, you mean," the other replied. "Not like going to sea at all."

"But think of all the work and wages—a thousand men working for two years building her."

"That's in Belfast, not here. A waste of money."

"And think of all the work for her people. She'll carry a crew of a thousand—seamen, firemen, trimmers, stewards."

"They'd be better on shore. She's so big, she'll bump into summat."

"She's unsinkable."

"My eye and Betty Martin! No ship's unsinkable!"

A year later, on April 10, 1912, one of the twins embarked on her maiden voyage. On the way over that ship, the R.M.S. *Titanic*, struck an iceberg and sank with the loss of more than 1,500 lives. The following are accounts of her sinking and of the sinkings of other ships that have plunged to the bottom of the sea.

1 ■ SEPTEMBER 27, 1854

The *Arctic*
The Ship "Worthy of Neptune"

THE SEA has long been important to man. It has provided him with both fisheries and a means of transportation. Yet for all its gifts, the sea has also been man's mortal enemy. At times, seafaring men find themselves in a life or death struggle against ice, storms and fog. Occasionally the sea has taken its toll.

One such example was the Collins Line's *Arctic*. Launched in 1850, this American vessel became one of the most popular transatlantic steamers of her day. She had all the beauty and comforts that a mid-19th century liner could offer. Passengers were spared the discomfort of cold weather by an elaborate heating system which distributed heat from the boilers to various parts of the ship. The grand salon was filled with magnificent mirrors, carpets, armchairs, sofas, and other luxuries that rivaled even her British counterparts. The *Arctic* was so beautiful that one of her passengers described her as "worthy of Neptune."

Even no-nonsense veteran seafarers were very much impressed by the *Arctic*. Measuring 284 feet from bow to stern and registered at 3,500 tons, the Collins liner had the distinction of being the second largest vessel in the world. The *Arctic* was also noted for her speed. Although by today's standard the sidewheeler's 13 knots would be considered slow, it was enough to set a record for an eastbound Atlantic crossing in February of 1852 when she arrived in Liverpool just under ten days after departing from New York.

Besides comfort and speed, the *Arctic* offered her passengers safety. She was built of tough oak and planked with durable pine. Iron rods were provided to increase structural strength. In the event of an emergency, the ship's company could rely on the two steam pumps, the powerful bilge injectors, and the four hand pumps. Yet for all of her modern comforts and equipment, the *Arctic*, strangely, was not constructed with watertight bulkheads. Thus, if disaster struck in which a large opening below the waterline resulted, the sea would cascade into the entire vessel, eventually sinking her.

On September 20, 1854, the *Arctic* departed from Liverpool for New York with 282 passengers and a crew of 153. Among the passengers were Mrs. Edward Knight Collins, the wife of the general manager and founder of the Collins Line, and her two children Henry and Mary Ann; a few children of James Brown, the president of the steamship company; diplomat Duc de Gramont; Henry Reed, Professor of Rhetoric and English literature; and a number of renowned individuals all socially and financially fitted for a liner "worthy of Neptune."

Seven days later, on September 27, the crew of the *Arctic* found themselves in the midst of one of the most hazardous conditions in ocean travel: fog. The captain, James Luce, was now confronted with the dilemma many captains before him faced. Should he reduce speed or continue at full steam? To do the latter would be risking the ship and the lives of all aboard, including his young invalid son. However, to slow down would result in a delay and this would hurt the company's reputation for quick passages. So after careful thought, Luce decided to do what most shipmasters do in this predicament: he would continue at full speed with two lookouts posted on the forecastle head. He did not make arrangements for a seaman to blow a tin horn as a warning to all vessels in the vicinity. Luce did not think this step was necessary, for although the weather was not clear, objects were "perceptible at intervals of one-half or three-quarters mile."

Suspecting no danger, Luce returned to his cabin to plot the noon postition. He realized the risk he was running. He also realized the demand for a fast passage. The Collins Line was, after all, competing with the well established Cunard Line. Hence, Luce could scarcely afford to dissatisfy his passengers by arriving in New York late. So he was determined to continue on course at 13 knots despite the poor visibility.

Suddenly at 12:15 in the afternoon, Luce heard the lookout cry, "There's a steamer ahead!" followed by the Officer on Watch ordering, "Hard starboard." Quickly the captain rushed to the bridge.

Steaming out of the fog patches at ten knots, the French steamer *Vesta* struck the starboard side of the *Arctic*. When the two vessels separated, the *Arctic* was on an even keel and appeared to have suffered relatively little damage. The *Vesta*, however, had ten feet of her bow torn off.

Panic quickly broke out on the French ship. Dozens of passengers were seen rushing about on her boat deck. During the confusion, two of her lifeboats were lowered but the men working the davits were not properly co-ordinated and one of the boats capsized. A few of the occupants perished in the cold water.

Captain Luce observed these events in horror. Surely this vessel was in danger of foundering. He took "a hasty glance" at his own command and concluded it was "comparatively uninjured." So the captain followed his "first impulse" and ordered two of his lifeboats to render assistance to the other ship.

Chief Officer Gourlay and six other crew members of the *Arctic* were dispatched in the starboard quarter boat to aid the stricken ship. A second boat with Second Officer Baalham in charge was in the process of being lowered when Luce suddenly realized his own ship was far more damaged than he had previously thought. "Hoist up that boat again, Mr. Baalham," the captain ordered. "I found that our own ship is leaking fearfully."

Baalham climbed down the starboard side of the *Arctic* to inspect the damage inflicted by the collision. To his horror he discovered the wooden hull had no fewer than three holes below the waterline, one at least five feet in length. This was a serious situation for, as was previously mentioned, the *Arctic* was not constructed with watertight compartments. Thus, the water would flow into the uncompartmentalized vessel until she eventually sank.

With this report, Luce ordered emergency procedures. He

instructed his men to drop both of the anchors and the anchor chains overboard to raise the bow. The two steam pumps and the four hand pumps were set in operation. A sail was dropped over the side in order to cut off the inflow of water. Unfortunately, the canvas was unable to fit properly because of pieces of iron deposited by the *Vesta*.

Captain Luce was now faced with another dilemma: should he stay at the scene of collision in order to receive aid from the *Vesta* or should he set course for the nearest land. After a few moments, the captain decided it would be best to run for land. The damaged *Vesta* gave Luce the impression that she would not last long. This being the case, the French ship could not be of any service to the Collins liner. Going forward at full speed would increase the rate of incoming water, but at the same time the bilge injectors would be working at their maximum capacity. Steaming to land therefore seemed like the logical course of action.

So without hesitation, Luce ordered the engines at full speed ahead. He did not have time to rescue any survivors from the *Vesta* or even to pick up his chief officer, but could only hope that both Gourlay and the other vessel would be rescued by a passing ship.

As the *Arctic* sped through the fog patches, the second lifeboat lowered from the *Vesta* suddenly appeared right in its path. Before the steamer could stop or alter course, the doomed lifeboat was caught in the *Arctic*'s iron paddles and was torn to shreds. All of the occupants were battered to death, except for Jassonet Francois who managed to secure a rope thrown to him by passenger Ferdinand Keyn of the *Arctic* and pulled himself aboard the liner.

A few miles away, Alphonse Duchesne, the captain of the *Vesta*, was facing a somewhat less grave situation. Unlike the *Arctic*, the French ship was divided into three watertight compartments. Although a large portion of the bow was torn off, the collision bulkhead was still holding. Duchesne organized his crew to throw the cargo, gear, and other articles overboard to lighten the bow. The foremast was cut down and forced to fall down in the sea. The collision bulkhead was reinforced with mattresses and boards. The crew dropped a sail over the bow to seal off the openings. With this done, Duchesne set course for St. John's, Newfoundland.

Meanwhile, the *Arctic* was steaming at her full 13-knot speed in a race against time. Below, the engineers and firemen were working frantically to keep the fires burning and the pumps going. On the boat deck some of the crew were manning the four hand pumps, while on the bridge the *Arctic*'s officers were eagerly scanning the horizon for land.

Despite the efforts of the crew, the bilge injectors and other pumps could not keep pace with the inflowing water. Less than forty minutes after the collision, the lower fires of the furnaces were flooded out. A half hour later, the upper fires were extinguished. With the fires gone, the steam pressure began to drop and the paddles gradually stopped. Slowly, the rammed liner came to a halt some thirty-five miles from land. The doom of the *Arctic* was now inevitable.

Luce now directed his energies to abandoning the sinking ship. The *Arctic*'s six lifeboats could only accommodate about one half of the ship's company, and, to make matters worse, the starboard quarter boat with the Chief Officer aboard was abandoned when the ship made her futile dash for land. To compensate for the lack of boats, the captain organized some of his men to construct a raft as large as time permitted. In the meantime, Luce wanted the remaining lifeboats to be loaded with women and children and lowered.

There was stiff resistance to the latter order. The stokers disregarded the noble tradition of women and children first and took to the lifeboats themselves. An obedient crewman drew a revolver but was killed by a stoker's shovel.

"Let the passengers go in the boat!" shouted Luce. His threat to enforce his order with a mallet was hopeless. The captain and his loyal, level-headed men were pitifully outnumbered by the hysterical mob.

Portside, a few members of the crew began loading the port guard boat. No sooner were the first few women and children aboard than a group of men rushed the small metallic craft. Efforts to evict the latter failed, and reluctantly the davit men lowered the boat with twenty-eight aboard, only a few of whom were women and children.

Another craft, the port quarter boat, was in the process of being lowered when an uncontrollable mob clambered aboard.

Under the excessive weight, the tackle broke and one end of the boat fell free. All but three of the occupants tumbled into the water.

Quickly, the davit men rightened the boat and made a second attempt to launch it. They filled the boat with women and children and again lowered it to sea. Just as it reached the water, a group of hysterical men leaped into it from the deck. Fortunately, Fourth Officer Graham was able to maneuver the lifeboat away from the ship before it was swamped.

The situation on the starboard side of the doomed vessel was equally chaotic. Second Officer Baalham and a few crewmen were placed aboard the starboard guard boat and lowered away. Baalham proceeded to carry out his orders to row to the stern and pick up women and children who were to be passed down to him by means of a rope, when suddenly a dozen or so men tried to jump aboard from the boat deck. Many of them simply plunged into the frigid water. Baalham disregarded Luce's orders and began to pick up the men struggling in the water. Within minutes the starboard guard boat was too crowded to handle the women and children and her crew began to row away from the sinking liner.

Chief Engineer Rogers and a dozen others under his department seized the forward deck boat and used it to abandon ship. They assured the passengers their purpose for taking the boat was to make repairs on the ship's hull. When these men boarded the boat, however, they carried with them food and other provisions. Once reaching the water, Rogers and his men rowed away from the doomed ship and offered no assistance whatsoever.

With the departure of the forward deck boat, Luce and his obedient crew were left with only the after deck boat. Yet there were more than two hundred fifty men, women, and children still aboard the *Arctic*. To make matters worse, Luce had only one officer, Third Officer Dorain, at his disposal.

The captain wasted no time in reorganizing his remaining crew. He detailed Stuart Holland, an apprentice engineer, to fire the ship's signal gun in hope that a nearby vessel would come to the rescue. He also dispatched the third officer and a few other men in the last boat with instructions to construct a raft. To insure they would not abandon the *Arctic*, Luce saw to it that the oars would be left aboard the ship.

The construction of the raft immediately got underway. The ship's spars were thrown overboard for Dorain and his men to use as the framework. Planks were torn from the vessel and passed down to provide additional wood. The crew and passengers worked frantically for two and one-half hours. If the *Arctic* would only remain buoyant for a few hours more, hopefully a raft large enough to accommodate the two hundred fifty aboard the Collins liner would be completed.

But it was useless. The *Arctic* was sinking too rapidly. It became apparent to those still aboard that the raft could not be finished in time. Soon selfishness and cowardice reappeared.

A group of men made a jump for the after deck boat. Quick-thinking Dorain cut the rope attached to the vessel his men rowed away using axes as paddles. "For God's sake, Captain," cried the third officer, "clear the raft so that we can work. I won't desert the ship while there's timber above water."

By now, Captain Luce saw time rapidly running out. He began dismissing his crew in order that they might save themselves. Some, such as Negro Stewardess Anna Downer, paid no attention. She remained at her pump station to the last.

Stuart Holland, the apprentice engineer operating the signal gun, was also determined. He remained at his post firing the small emergency cannon. "His whole conduct can be accounted for by a simple word duty. . . ." Dorain later wrote. When he fired the last shot, Holland bravely stood by his post with the right side of his face black with powder, waiting for the end.

Others were preoccupied with their safety and that of their families. George Allen, son-in-law of Edward Collins, obtained a life preserver for each member of his family. He also gathered food to carry with them in the eventuality that they'd be in the open sea for an undetermined length of time.

Captain Luce, realizing he could do no more toward saving the passengers, was now prepared to go down with his ship. He refused a life preserver offered to him by his servant, and bade farewell to some of his friends. He took his invalid son, Willie, to the top of the paddle box, and there he waited for the inevitable.

Others were determined to survive. Peter McCabe and the assistant store keeper tied some casks together to construct a raft. Jassonet Francois and a mess boy put one together and departed from the sinking ship. James Smith found escape by use of a small raft the crew had built to make repairs on the *Arctic*. With the crew abandoning ship, Smith felt justified in commandeering the raft.

The end of the *Arctic* came quickly. The stern disappeared first and within minutes the liner was perpendicular to the water. It then began to sink beneath the ocean. Finally at 4:45 on September 27, 1854, the *Arctic*, the ship "worthy of Neptune," plunged to the bottom of the sea.

Over her watery grave, Peter McCabe, who was separated from his raft during the last agonizing minutes, was dragged under by the tremendous suction. He later recalled:

> I retained my consciousness all the time I was under the water, and it was a feeling of intense joy that I found, after about a half a minute, that I was rapidly rising towards the surface. It was all darkness before me, but now I could see a dim light above me, and in a few seconds I was on the top of the water struggling for life. Being a good swimmer, and having, besides, the support of a life preserver, I succeeded in reaching a door, which was floating a few feet from where I rose. I looked around me, but there was no trace of the vessel except a few loose timbers and the rafts which were floating about, some with and others without passengers."

McCabe found that he could not hang onto the door for long, so he swam to the floating barrel, clinging to it for awhile until he eyed the large raft floating nearby. He swam to the wooden structure and joined the seventy-five or so individuals on top of it.

Captain Luce had a similar experience. He too had been thrown into the water along with his son. Pulled under by the *Arctic*'s suction, he managed to surface but was again drawn under. The captain was able to break free a second time and come to the surface but without his son.

Looking around, Luce found that, in his own words, "a most awful and heartrending scene presented itself to my view: two hundred men, women, and children were struggling together amidst pieces of wreck of every kind calling on each other for

help, and imploring God to assist them. Such an appalling scene:
May God preserve me from ever witnessing it again."

Luce caught sight of his son floating by. He attempted to help
the boy when without warning a portion of the paddle box came
up from beneath the waves and fell upon the head of the younger
Luce. Luce pulled his son from under it but it was too late.

The paddle box *saved* other lives, however. A few men, including George Allen, mounted the floating debris. Luce released the
body of his son and joined the men on the paddle box. There
they stood in knee deep 45° water waiting for rescue.

Others did not wish to wait around for a ship to pass by. Second
Officer Baalham assumed command of both the starboard guard
boat and the port quarter boat and began redistributing their
complements to balance the loads. With this accomplished, the
two boats set out for Newfoundland. They lacked a workable
compass but Baalham was able to rely on the stars as guide. To
keep together, the men in the boats occasionally shouted back and
forth.

The after deck boat was unable to undertake such a journey.
This boat, as was pointed out, was deliberately denied oars in fear
that her crew would desert the ship. With the *Arctic* gone, Dorain
and the others began to row over the *Arctic*'s grave with axes and
their hands. They had some thirty individuals aboard and hence
were too crowded to rescue anyone in the water. So Dorain and
his men just drifted.

The situation for others who were forced to remain behind was
grim. The raft Dorain and his men constructed was seriously
overcrowded. The weight of more than seventy occupants forced
it a few feet underwater, leaving those aboard to shiver in knee
deep water. Likewise Captain Luce and his companions found the
water-soaked paddle box they were on to be sinking deeper into
the ocean.

For some, the prolonged exposure without food and water was
too much. Jassonet Francois found himself alone the following
day when the mess boy who shared his raft expired. On the
paddle box, Captain Luce watched helplessly as his companions
died one by one. An even more frightening experience took place
on the raft. As Peter McCabe reported, it was an "awful scene—a
multitude of human beings, in the midst of the ocean, without the

slightest hope of assistance, while every minute one by one was dropping into a watery grave, from sheer exhaustion. Those who had life preservers did not sink but floated with their ghastly faces upwards, reminding those who still remained alive of the fate that awaited them."

"At last morning came, surrounded by dense fog," Luce later reflected, "not a living soul was to be seen but our own party, seven men being left. In the dense fog of the morning, we saw some water casks and other things belonging to our ship, but nothing that we could get to afford us relief."

The first sign of hope appeared on that Thursday, September 28, the day after the disaster, when a sail was sighted by the men in the lifeboat. Dorain and his men waved the boat's sail and handkerchiefs. It was a crude method but it did gain the attention of the crew of the Quebec-bound *Huron*. Within minutes, the *Huron* was alongside of the small boat and began to take the thirty-one survivors aboard.

Before leaving, Dorain rowed back to the raft to pick up any survivors. He found only one, Peter McCabe, alive. With the rescue of the exhausted McCabe, the *Huron* resumed her voyage to Quebec.

The next day, the *Huron* encountered the New York-bound *Lebanon*. In order to reach their original destination, eighteen of the thirty-two survivors chose to transfer to the *Lebanon*. The other fourteen, perhaps weary of taking to the open sea in a lifeboat again, decided to remain aboard the *Huron*.

Meanwhile, ten other survivors were still adrift. All on the water soaked paddle box had expired except for Luce, George Allen and Ferdinand Keyn. The three men, in the captain's words, "began to suffer excruciatingly for want of water." The three were giving up hope when they sighted a bark to the northwest. The weary men tried vainly to attract its attention. In a short time their hopes of rescue disappeared as the bark sailed out of sight.

The survivors had resigned themselves to doom when suddenly another ship was sighted. This time the vessel, the *Cambria*, was steering straight for them, and soon Luce, Allen, Keyn, Jassonet Francois, James Smith, and the five firemen on the two rafts were safely aboard.

Miles away, the two lifeboats under Second Officer Baalham's command finally reached Newfoundland. There, Baalham rented a schooner and returned to the *Arctic*'s last position to search for survivors. Finding none, he returned to Newfoundland.

That same Friday, the crippled *Vesta* limped into St. John's. There, Captain Duchesne and his men were praised for their skill. Newspaper editorials spoke of the captain's great accomplishment in bringing in such a badly damaged ship. Few at the time realized the tragic irony. The *Vesta*'s survival meant that the *Arctic* could have transferred her passengers and crew to the French ship and saved hundreds of lives.

The news of the wreck took some time to reach New York. As late as October 10th, thirteen days after the ship foundered, the seaport still had hopes of seeing the *Arctic* arriving safely. Even the Collins Line manager, Edward Collins, who had several family members aboard, anticipated a safe arrival. He attributed the delay to nothing more than engine trouble.

The next morning, on October 11, 1854, the news finally reached the *Arctic*'s homeport. The *Lebanon* arrived in New York with a group of survivors who recounted the disaster and terrible ordeal. The details were distorted at first but it was finally established that of the 435 who sailed on that fatal voyage, about 350 were lost, including Mrs. Collins, her two children, and five members of the Brown family. No sign was ever found of Chief Officer Gourlay and his men in the starboard quarter boat, of Chief Engineer Rogers and the other men who took the forward deck boat, or of the twenty-eight passengers and crew of the port guard boat.

It was the beginning of the end for the Collins Line, already facing fierce competition from the well established shipping lines of England. Two years after the *Arctic* disaster, another Collins liner, the *Pacific*, was lost* When Congress cut the subsidy rate, the Collins Line was doomed. In February of 1858, the last three ships of the folding company were sold for a ridiculously low price.

---

*The fate of the *Pacific* remains unknown, for there were no survivors. However, there is evidence that she struck an iceberg and sank.

Captain James Luce lived the remaining twenty-six years of his life on land working in the marine insurance business. He had much to ponder regarding the *Arctic* and its fate. Had he only slowed down that day. Had he not sent the lifeboat off to the seaworthy *Vesta*. Had he remained near the *Vesta* instead of making the futile dash for land. Had he maintained better discipline. Luce had to live with Edward Collins' haunting accusation that he had "practically murdered" the Collins family.

2 ■ APRIL 1, 1873

The *Atlantic*
"A Thoroughly Good Ship"

CAPTAIN JAMES AGNEW WILLIAMS of the 3,607-ton White Star *Atlantic* was beset with another problem. This was his second voyage with the White Star liner and he faced disciplinary problems with the fourteen stowaways who were discovered earlier during the voyage. Many of them were not fulfilling their work assignments. Tensions aboard the steamer became high when one of the unwelcome guests attacked a petty officer during a work task.

A more pressing concern Williams had was the rough weather his ship encountered. The winds and waves had reduced the *Atlantic's* top speed of 12 knots to only five at one point. Consumption of coal had increased significantly. In traveling only the last 670 miles, the liner burned at least 192 tons of this fossil fuel.

Now on March 31, 1873, Chief Engineer Foxley was informing the captain that the coal supply was down to 127 tons. Williams knew it would take at least 130 tons to reach Sandy Hook. True, the 435-foot-long steamer was fitted with four masts to convert to sails in case the engines were unable to carry the vessel to her destination. Yet the sails would be slower and less dependable than the 12-knot speed her four two-cylinder engines could produce. The *Atlantic* could scarcely afford to travel slower since the food supply was down to two days.

After weighing the situation carefully, Williams decided it would be best to replenish his fuel at Halifax, Nova Scotia, the nearest port. Unfortunately the lane to Halifax was dangerous, and to complicate matters, Williams had never docked in that port before. It would be a blemish on the White Star Line's record, for none of the company's ships up to this time had been forced to divert to resupply. The *Atlantic* in particular had a good reputation, "a thoroughly good ship" as one government surveyor described her. On the other hand the ship might run out of coal before the journey was completed and the 931 people aboard the liner would be out in the open sea with little food. The falling barometer signaled another phase of bad weather. At Halifax, Williams could purchase coal at a reasonable price and thus be able to complete the voyage to New York.

So Halifax it was. He put the vessel at 12 knots on a course to this port. At 11:50 PM the captain saw a red light. He surmised it was Sambro Light, which was about nine miles eastward of Sambro Island. Williams made this assumption without consulting his charts.

"Keep a lookout for loose ice and keep the same course until six bells (3:00 AM), then call me," Williams instructed the officer on watch, Cornelius Brady. With that said the tired captain retired to his cabin, leaving the navigation through this dangerous area in the hands of the third officer.

What both Williams and Brady were unaware of was that the light at Sambro was white and not red. The red light they saw was actually Peggy's Point. Instead of nine miles east of Sambro Island they were in dangerous water nineteen miles farther east.

At midnight, the third officer was relieved by Chief Officer John Firth and Fourth Officer John Brown. He passed on his instructions to awaken the captain at six bells to Firth and then went to his cabin to catch some sleep. The *Atlantic* meanwhile continued on her dangerous course at 12 knots.

One warning of oncoming danger was passed to the officers standing watch. Quartermaster Dunn came to the bridge and told Second Officer Henry Metcalfe, who was now on watch, "I believe the ship has run its distance to make the Sambro Light. Take care and don't run aground."

Dunn was only a quartermaster and was duly ignored. "You're

not the captain of this ship nor the mate," he was told. With this rebuke, Dunn stalked out of the bridge and the officers resumed their duties as the *Atlantic* continued on her dangerous course with no one in authority to prevent it. (On the other hand the officers of the *Atlantic* insisted that Dunn never gave such a warning.)

At 2:40 AM, a cabin boy with hot cocoa for the captain was about to rap on the master's door but Fourth Officer Brown told him to let the captain sleep. So the cabin boy left the captain and returned to his quarters. Meanwhile, the *Atlantic* proceeded on her disastrous course with her master sound asleep.

At 3:00 AM, six bells, the captain was still sleeping in his cabin. Neither Metcalfe nor Brown made any attempts to awaken him. Instead they remained on the bridge guiding the White Star liner on her perilous course. No one aboard the *Atlantic* bothered to consult the charts. No precaution was taken to make certain the vessel was not heading towards the dangerous rocks at Mars Head.

April 1, 1873, fifteen minutes after six bells, Captain Williams was awakened not by a knock on the door by an officer or a cabin boy but by Able Seaman Joseph Carroll shouting, "Breakers ahead! Breakers ahead!" Williams sprang to his feet and rushed to the bridge.

Down below, a steerage passenger felt the ship vibrate slightly. "There goes the anchor," he remarked. Then the second more violent jolt ended all thoughts of anchor laying. "Good God, she's ashore," he suddenly realized.

Nearby, Joseph Kelly also thought it was the "anchor being let go." The bumping that followed ended this illusion. "Boys, jump up." he shouted to his companions, "the ship is sinking!"

The half naked man led his shipboard friends up the steerage gangway, but the group encountered a locked door. Kelly threw his weight against it and cleared the path of this obstacle.

Once on the boat deck, Kelly discovered he was separated from the rest. He quickly got hold of himself and sought safety.

Kelly was one of the fortunate ones to escape. The *Atlantic* with her disproportional length to her beam of almost 11 to 1 ratio was hurled back and forth on the reef by the waves. The angle iron plates were unable to resist the pressure and gave way. Tons of water cascaded through the openings in the side and bottom. An estimated 300 individuals were drowned within minutes after the ship struck the reef.

In the boiler room, Fourth Engineer Paterson felt the ship touch bottom. He immediately ran to the engine room where he saw the telegraph at Full Astern. Instinctively, he rushed below to shut the service sea cocks.

At once, Williams realized his command was doomed. Immediately he ordered emergency measures to be taken. Meanwhile, Quartermaster Raylance, on his own initiative, began to fire the ship's distress rockets. The rockets soared up in the cold air and exploded in a brilliant burst of color.

While Raylance was firing the rockets, other crewmen were attempting to lower the lifeboats. The portside boats were unable to be launched for they were all submerged when the liner developed a list to the port. Fortunately, the *Atlantic*'s crew still had the starboard boats at their disposal.

Third Officer Brady cleared his lifeboat on the starboard side and began to place women in it. No sooner had he put two women in it than a rush for the boat was made. "Women first," the third officer cried. Despite his efforts, about a dozen men forced their way aboard. Seeing he could not evict them, Brady gave the order to lower away, and the lifeboat descended down the ship's side. When it reached the water level the liner suddenly gave a violent shudder and heeled over on her beam ends. The lifeboat was overturned and the occupants drowned in the turbulent water.

First Officer John Firth also had trouble in lowering the boats. With an ax, he cleared two of them on the starboard side. He was about to fill them with passengers when without warning a wave swept the two boats overboard, and Firth saved himself by clinging to the rigging.

Quartermaster Raylance, who by now had given up hope of attracting attention with the distress rockets, directed his efforts to launching lifeboat 5. He loaded the boat with women and children and began cutting through the tackle with an ax. Nearby, Captain Williams observed Raylance and began considering any detail the quartermaster may have overlooked.

"Are the plugs in?" the captain asked.

Suddenly, Raylance realized the plugs were not in. He quickly informed the captain of the predicament. Before the quartermaster could tend to the problem, the list increased and the boat rolled overboard.

Captain Williams took two women to a lifeboat in hope of saving them, but seeing it could not be lowered, he carried them to the main rigging. He left them there certain they were safe and went forward to see if he could find means of escape there.

Just then a boiler exploded. The liner rolled over and dumped dozens, including Second Officer Metcalfe, into the water. Williams staggered to the main rigging only to discover the women he had left there had also fallen overboard.

The *Atlantic*, by this time, was in a desperate situation. Down below, hundreds of trapped passengers were drowning. On the boat deck, dozens were sliding off the slippery deck as the ship listed 50° to the port. The lifeboats either could not be lowered or were lowered only to be capsized.

In the mizzen rigging, Third Officer Brady surveyed the situation. The passengers and crew of the *Atlantic* were doomed unless they could safely abandon ship. Yet at the present moment there was no foreseeable rescue. Escape by lifeboat was out of the question for the list and turbulent sea made launching too hazardous. If Brady was to save any of the passengers and crew aboard the *Atlantic*, he would quickly have to come up with a feasible solution.

Accompanied by Quartermaster Speakman and Quartermaster Owens, the third officer slowly made his way forward. When the three men reached the forerigging, they began to search for land. Brady spotted a large rock he judged to be about ninety feet away. If the passengers could make it to this rock, he thought, they would have a fighting chance to survive. Yet how could this be done?

Then came an idea. "Get me a hundred feet of line," he instructed the two quartermasters. What the officer had in mind was for someone to swim to the rock with the rope. Then the passengers could be sent across the water on this line.

"I will go, sir, if you clear the way," Owens offered, "I'm a good swimmer."

With one end of the rope tied to his waist, Quartermaster

Owens leaped into the water and swam as best as he could for the nearby rock. He reached it but was unable to climb to the top. After numerous futile attempts, the quartermaster grew tired and could no longer hold on to the rock. Quickly, Brady and Speakman pulled the exhausted Owens back to the ship.

Next to try was Brady. The officer had better luck than Owens. He was able to reach the rock and ascend to its top. He secured the rope and, with the aid of the two quartermasters, hooked up four more lines from the ship to the rock. With this done, the three rigged a sling and pulley and began to transport the passengers from the stricken ship.

One by one, the passengers and crew crossed to the rock by use of the line. Brady swam back and forth pushing them along. He finally became exhausted after transporting a dozen or so men and had to be relieved.

Back on the *Atlantic*, Captain Williams and Fourth Officer Brown were doing their best to keep the remaining passengers and crew alive. They walked back and forth on the rigging poking those who began to fall asleep. "Don't go to sleep!" the captain shouted. "Keep awake!" To lift their sagging spirits, Williams passed the word that rescue would soon arrive.

When his strength returned, Cornelius Brady began to consider the problem the survivors faced. The rock was becoming crowded with some 200 people on it. To make matters worse, the waves began to wash over the rock. After careful thought, the officer decided the logical solution would be to swim ashore to Mars Island, set up a network of lines, and transport the people from the rock to the island.

So Brady again plunged into the cold, choppy water and struggled toward the island. With superhuman effort, he managed to reach the shore and stagger inland. After setting up the line between the rock and shore, Brady set out to seek help and was able to secure the aid of the island's only occupants, a fisherman named Clancey and his daughter. With their help, a sailor was given a horse and sent to Halifax.

At 5:00 AM, nearly two hours after the *Atlantic* struck the reef, a few fishing boats came to the rescue. They could not have come at a better time. Many of the people aboard the ship were freezing in their wet clothes. The sight of the fishing boats lifted the spirits of the passengers and crew of the *Atlantic* immensely, and for the first time since disaster struck, there seemed to be hope.

The fishermen quickly went to work. One group came upon two men who were thankful to see the small boats but unable to agree on who should be rescued first.

Twelve-year-old John Henley was saved from the doomed liner in a very uncomfortable manner. He was by a porthole when another passenger pulled him out by the hair. He was then taken to shore.

Chief Officer Firth was by the mizzen rigging holding on to a woman. He was near exhaustion when, as he later explained, "At one o'clock in the afternoon, after we had been in the rigging for ten hours, Reverend Mr. Ancient, a Church of England clergyman, whose noble conduct I can never forget while I live, got a crew of four men to row him out to the wreck. . . ."

Suddenly, a wave swept both Firth and the woman overboard. Firth was pulled in by Ancient. The woman was hurriedly hauled aboard the boat but for her it was too late. She was a lifeless corpse with, according to the first officer, "her eyes protruding, her mouth foaming."

Soon the *Atlantic* began to sink. There was a violent explosion as the cold water engulfed the boilers. Within minutes, the White Star liner was gone. Her grave was marked with tables, chairs, broken pieces of wood and bodies.

Some of the stronger passengers and crew who remained aboard were to be picked up by the fishing boats. The majority of them, however, succumbed to the rough freezing water.

Shortly after the survivors were brought ashore, another fleet of rowboats appeared on the scene. They were not attempting rescue but were on scavenging purposes. Bodies were searched for valuables, thrown back into the sea, and then the men moved on to the next ones. The contents of the few trunks and suitcases recovered were also taken and sold.

At 7:00 AM, on April 2, 1873, the White Star Offices in Liverpool received a coded message which read, "Brady Third Officer Arrived Halifax *Atlantic* Illegitimate Cape Prospect About Cheshire Chain Boulogne People Including Captain Saved Intended

Imprecation Have Despatched Pennel Naval." Decoded, the message disclosed the *Atlantic* was totally wrecked with a large number of lives lost.

The public became outraged when this news of the captain's navigational blunder broke. Some people referred to it as "the crime of the century." Of the 931 individuals who were aboard the *Atlantic* during her final voyage, 481 perished. Not one single woman survived and only one child, John Henley, lived to tell of the ordeal.

At the investigation hearings held by the Dominion Government of Canada, Williams testified on his decisions he made while commanding the White Star liner. He stated in part:

> . . . the ship increased her speed after I bore up for Halifax because we were not then so anxious to economize coal. The speed at twelve o'clock was about 12 knots. I reckoned then that we were forty-eight miles off Sambro Ledges. I had never before brought ships into Halifax, or been on the coast: the third officer had been in the harbor twice: none of the other officers had ever been here. I did not use the lead at all in coming to Halifax: I knew we were within soundings north of La Have; I did not sound because the night was clear and Sambro Light should be seen twenty-one miles in clear weather, and in moderate weather fifteen miles: the bridge was thrity-six feet above the level of the sea. I knew I was approaching the shore: the cleanness of the night and the certainty of seeing the light were my only reasons for not sounding. . . . If I had been sounding regularly between twelve and three o'clock, I would have been on deck, and the ship would not have gone ashore.

The testimony of Captain Williams was self-incriminating. The White Star Line had little hope of clearing the master of negligence. However, the company was determined to exonerate itself of the charge of providing its vessels with insufficient coal. In a statement released to the public, the White Star Line claimed:

> We are in a position to prove that the quantity put on board this vessel before leaving Liverpool was 967 tons, and that her consumption for the outboard passage to New York, when an average taken from 18 voyages which she had successfully accomplished, was only 744 tons, while the largest quantity ever

consumed in the worst inter passage, say in December and January, never exceeded 896 tons.

The company demanded an investigation into the issue of the *Atlantic*'s coal supply. The request was granted and a board was set up to look into the matter. Once again the facts of the case were heard. The findings of the hearing pleased the White Star Line. It concluded that the *Atlantic* had ample coal on board her last voyage.

The question of the *Atlantic*'s coal supply is one of the most controversial issues in the history of maritime disaster. Some writers severely criticized the White Star Line for not providing a sufficient amount of coal while others insist the owners did load the vessel with an ample supply. C.H. Milson, author of *The Coal Was There for Burning*, claims that Engineer Foxley underestimated the coal supply during the early stages of the voyage and, on the 31st of March, gave the estimate of 127 tons in order to square with his earlier reports. Milson insists the *Atlantic* had 160 tons left, enough to reach Sandy Hook.

In either event, this writer feels that blaming the White Star Line is unfair. The most coal consumed by the *Atlantic* in the past was 870 tons, and she had about that much on her last voyage. The company should not therefore be accused of not putting enough coal on her last voyage. In this connection, it is worth noting that no other ship of the White Star Line was forced to divert to Halifax.

The question whether or not the White Star Line had provided sufficient coal for the *Atlantic* notwithstanding, there could be no doubt of the captain's negligence. As the presiding judge correctly stated, Williams's "management of the ship during the twelve or fourteen hours preceeding the disaster was so gravely at variance with what ought to have been the conduct of a man placed in his responsible position, as to call for severe censure." Despite this unfavorable judgment, Williams's license was revoked for only two years. The main charge against the captain was his failure to take soundings.

That was by no means his only blunder. Williams had taken his command into dangerous waters without consulting his charts. This led to his mistaking the red light he saw for Sambro Light. A second serious mistake was retiring to his cabin, leaving the ship to a subordinate. Yet despite these grave errors of judgment, the court allowed James Williams to return to a ship's bridge in two years.

The license of Fourth Officer Brown was suspended for three months for his failure to awaken the captain at six bells. But Brown may not have known his orders. It was the fault of Second Officer Metcalfe who was lost. Suspending Brown's license, in this author's view, appears to have been an attempt to penalize Metcalfe in absentia.

Many were of the opinion that Williams's penalty was too light. The court probably had taken into account the captain's brave conduct after the disaster struck. In either case, the authorities could not have imposed a stiffer penalty on the captain than his own conscience. "To think," he said, "that while hundreds of men were saved, every women should have perished. It's horrible. If I'd been able to save just one I could bear the disaster, but to lose every women aboard, it's too terrible."

3 ■ NOVEMBER 18, 1874

The *Cospatrick*
"The Best of Her Type on the Register"

B Y THE SECOND HALF of the 19th century, the old sailing ships were steadily being replaced by the new iron steamers. The old fashioned sail ships simply weren't as fast, dependable, or safe as the new iron hulled steamers. In face of this superior competition, the wind powered vessels began to fade from the maritime picture.

One exception was the teak-hulled *Cospatrick*. Launched in 1856 by the Naulmein shipyard of Burma, this frigate, which was considered "the best of her type on the register," had sailed as a passenger ship for many years for the Blackwell firm. While she flew the Blackwell flag, the *Cospatrick* had helped lay the submarine cable in the Persian Gulf in 1863. Some years later the 1,200-ton 190-foot ship was bought by the Shaw Savill Line and converted into an emigrant carrier.

On September 11, 1874, the *Cospatrick* departed from Gravesend the Thames, England, for Auckland, New Zealand, with 429 emigrants. Although it was the *Cospatrick*'s second voyage under the Shaw and Savill Line, the vessel was no stranger to its captain, Alexander Elmslie; he had commanded the ship when it was under the Blackwell firm. He was so confident that the *Cospatrick* would make a safe passage that he brought along his wife and four-year-old son on the voyage.

Elmslie had good reason to feel safe. His ship was run in accordance with safety rules, especially in fire prevention. Smoking below decks was strictly prohibited. Each hatchway was lighted by a locked battle lantern to prevent someone from smoking undetected. To enforce these rules, a few "constables" were to patrol the living space area to watch for breaches of fire regulations. To further insure the safety of the vessel from the hazards of fire, a stationary water pump was kept in the fo'c'sle. This pump was capable of producing enough pressure to extinguish even a large blaze if by chance a fire should break out.

The pump was not the only item stored in this area. Rope, paint, varnish, kerosene, coal and several tons of alcoholic beverages were also stored there. The fo'c'sle of the *Cospatrick*, in short, was a tinder box.

Halfway through the voyage, the vessel encountered a problem which has plagued man since the earliest days of seafaring: mal de mer. This trip in particular was rough on those aboard since it was taking place during the cold months. By the second month out of England the problem of seasickness became widespread aboard the ship. Even the captain's wife and son were among those ill. Cadle, the ship's doctor, tried to help the best he could.

By November 18, the *Cospatrick* was rounding the southern tip of Africa. She was some 300 miles south of Cape Aguhas, halfway to her Pacific destination. Making 200 miles a day, the Shaw Savill vessel would take another three months or so to cross the Indian and Pacific Oceans.

Second Mate Henry MacDonald retired to his cabin early that morning. He had just turned over his watch to another officer and was now preparing to sleep. It was 12:30.

Suddenly, MacDonald became aware of cries of "Fire!" He quickly sprang to his feet and raced outside his cabin to see what the commotion was about.

There, the second officer was in company of screaming, panic stricken passengers. His attention was drawn to smoke from the forepeak. A fire was raging in the fo'c'sle.

Immediately, Captain Elmslie took action. He ordered the helmsman to "haul her about!" The helmsman turned the wheel only to find the *Cospatrick* was slow to respond to the light breeze, but it finally did turn until it was behind the wind. Now the wind could not blow the flames through the entire ship. Thus the fire would be confined in the forepeak long enough for the crew to put it out.

Other problems persisted, though. Some of the crew were unable to get to their post because the terrified passengers were blocking their way. Those who managed to get by found that the chief firefighting apparatus, the water pump, was in the very center of the fire.

With the hose gone, the crew organized bucket brigades to combat the fire. This was a slow process. Buckets had to be dropped to the sea, pulled up to the ship, passed to the head of the line, and the water thrown on the flames. Yet as it was carried out, there appeared the possibility that the fire might be brought under control.

Then things quickly deteriorated. The *Cospatrick* suddenly swung directly into the wind. Quite possibly the captain made an error in issuing an order or perhaps the helmsman misinterpreted one given to him. In any case, the wind began to fan the flames until the fire was out of control.

The passengers made a mad rush to the boats, several of which were already aflame. Other boats were undamaged but could not be lowered because they were overcrowded. An attempt was made on the starboard side to lower a lifeboat made for forty with over eighty aboard. The weight proved too much for the davits. The rope broke under the excessive strain and the boat tumbled down into the water, crushing or drowning all aboard.

Chief Mate Charles Romaine tried to maintain some degree of order. Standing by a portside lifeboat, Romaine shouted, "No one touches her, unless myself or the Captain." The Chief Mate meant to enforce his order with force if necessary. Turning to MacDonald he said, "Shoot anyone who tries. Smash 'em."

The situation grew steadily worse. The flames set the three huge masts on fire. One by one, the charred masts toppled down on the deck, crushing scores of passengers and crew.

By now, Captain Elmslie had given up all hope for his ship. He threw his wife in the water and then jumped in after her. Dr. Cradle took the master's son and leaped overboard. None of the four was ever seen again.

Meanwhile, MacDonald and Romaine managed to lower away at least two of the lifeboats in spite of the chaos. One with thirty-nine was commanded by the chief mate. The second was filled with forty-one and lowered away with the second mate in charge. The remaining lifeboats were left on the burning deck as were hundreds of individuals.

They didn't last very long. The fire soon spread from bow to stern. A violent explosion blew out the *Cospatrick*'s stern. Within minutes, the vessel sank.

The two boats were now alone. There were neither mast nor sails in either boat. These items must not have been provided or were disregarded during the confusion on board. MacDonald at least was able to improvise by attaching a girl's petticoat to an oar.

The second officer wasn't able to overcome the lack of food and water. "Thirst," he later stated, "soon began to tell severely on all of us." The man assigned to the tiller grew weak and fell overboard. Three other men that day went mad and died. Their bodies were thrown overboard.

On November 21, 1874, three days after the *Cospatrick* sank, the lifeboats were caught in a storm. Romaine's boat was never seen again. All hands were lost.

MacDonald and his men managed to pull through, but again the survivors were without food and water. The boat drifted for three days with the few survivors in the boat dying off one by one. On the 24th, the situation was so desperate that those still alive were driven to cannibalism.

By the next day, one week after the disaster, the original forty-one complement was reduced to eight. The lack of water drove these men beyond the edge of sanity. Everyone, including Second Officer MacDonald, drank sea water. There seemed little chance of rescue.

The hopes of the men in the boat were lifted when a ship was spotted. MacDonald and the others hailed her but the ship sailed out of sight. The second officer, his mind under considerable strain, thought the ship did see them but continued on anyway.

Two days later, November 27, the number of survivors was down to five, MacDonald and three seamen plus a surviving passenger. There seemed to be little hope of rescue. Some ships did pass by but they were too far away. In any event, the five were too feeble to call out for help.

Then a ship, the *British Sceptre*, spotted the group. Her captain quickly set course for the boat. When the five men were taken aboard, the passenger and one of the seamen had expired. In the end, of a crew of forty-four, only Second Officer Henry Mac-Donald, Quartermaster Thomas Lewis, and Seaman Edward Cotter lived to tell the horrible tale. None of the 429 passengers survived the terrible ordeal.

In the years that followed, there have been fires at sea. However, few will ever equal the disaster that befell the 429 emigrants seeking new prospects in New Zealand.

4 ■ FEBRUARY 15, 1898

The *Maine*
"The First Battleship of Importance"

CAPTAIN CHARLES SIGSBEE, commander of the 6,682-ton battleship *Maine*, was enjoying a late evening cigar. It was warm in Havana Harbor this night, February 15, 1898. The sky, he noticed, contained a few stars. A short distance away the beautiful lights of the city were glowing.

The *Maine* had been moored here since the 25th of January. The American battleship had been sent to Havana to protect American lives in wake of recent riots that had broken out there. So far there had been no disorder but Sigsbee and his men were ordered on alert for a situation which might alter without warning.

There was indeed a great deal of uncertainty in this part of the world. So much so that when the *Maine* entered Havana twenty-two days earlier, she was inconspicuously prepared for battle. As events proved, the only shots fired between the American battleship and the Spanish warships were salutes. Nevertheless the possibility of hostilities remained.

It was ironic that the *Maine* was sent to a Cuban port, for this very island was the root cause of the squabbles between the United States and Spain. The "pearl of the Caribbean" was a controversial issue in 1898. Spain was determined to keep her few remaining colonies including Cuba regardless of America's sympathy for the Cuban insurgents.

Some of this bitterness can be seen in the De Lome letter. In January 1898, Señor Depuy de Lome, Madrid's envoy to the United States, wrote a letter to his superiors in which he characterized President William McKinley as "weak and a bidder for the admiration of the crowd, besides being a would-be politician who tries to leave a door open behind himself while keeping on good terms with the jingoes of his party." The letter also expressed the opinion that "nothing will be accomplished in Cuba." Unfortunately for Spain, this letter was intercepted by the Cuban insurgents and made public. Not only did it insult the honor of the United States, it also convinced many Americans that Spain was not conducting the negotiations on Cuba in good faith.

Nor was William Randolph Hearst, the newspaper tycoon, helping matters. His papers and other sources were constantly bombarding the public with stories of atrocities committed against the helpless Cubans. One headline bannered "500 Women Butchered." The "yellow journalism" went so far as to publish a story of Spanish officials conducting a strip search of a woman suspect, and even contained a drawing of a nude woman standing in front of the lustful officials.

The American public was outraged. The readers of course were not told that the woman in fact was searched by a female inspector. There appeared to be no real story, or at least that was what one of Hearst's men cabled to his editor. However, Hearst replied, "You furnish the story. I'll furnish the war."

Other matters were seriously complicating Spanish-American relations. The United States was a rising naval power and needed coaling stations and bases. For this reason, many Americans were eyeing some of Spain's overseas possessions which could serve such purposes.

There was little sign of friction this night. Captain Sigsbee had seen the exact opposite during his twenty-one day visit. He later stated, "My relations with the officials were outwardly cordial, and I have no ground for assuming that they were not really cordial. . . . My visit was pleasantly received and promptly returned."

Every act by the officials at least pointed that way. When Sigsbee decided to attend a bullfight, General Parrado, the temporary governor-general of Cuba, gave the American captain tickets. Later, Parrado sent a case of fine sherry to the *Maine*. A pioneer in underwater exploration, Sigsbee kindly returned the favor by sending the Governor a copy of his own work, *Deep-Sea Sounding and Dredging*.

Not *all* welcomed the presence of the American man-of-war. Departing from a luncheon held at the Havana Yacht Club, Sigsbee was handed a circular which read:

SPANIARDS
Long Live Spain With Honor!

What are you doing that you allow yourselves to be insulted in this way? Do you not see what they have done to us in withdrawing our brave and beloved [Governor of Cuba] Weyler, who at this very time would have finished with this unworthy, rebellious rabble who are trampling on our flag and on our honor?

Autonomy is imposed on us to cast us aside and give places of honor and authority to those who initiated this rebellion, these low-bred autonomists, ungrateful sons of our beloved country!

And finally, these Yankee pigs who meddle in our affairs, humiliating us to the last degree, and, for a still greater taunt order to us a man-of-war of their rotten squadron, after insulting us in their newspapers with articles sent from our own home!

Spaniards: the moment of actions has arrived. Do not go to sleep! Let us teach these vile traitors that we have not yet lost our pride, and that we know how to protect with the energy befitting a nation worthy and strong, as our Spain is and always will be!

Death to the Americans!   Death to Autonomy!
Long live Spain!   Long Live Weyler!

Later, as a ferry boat passed the moored *Maine*, a number of insults were hurled at the Americans. Sigsbee heard these remarks but concluded they were coming from only a handful of people aboard the boat.

Though he considered these incidents as only isolated episodes and felt the reception was generally cordial, Sigsbee still adopted extra precautions to insure the safety of his command. Armed sentries were posted on the forecastle and poop. Steam was kept up in two boilers instead of the usual procedure of only one. Shells for the second battery were kept nearby in case of an emergency. All non-personnel coming aboard were to be carefully watched. Sigsbee instructed the officer of the deck to inform him of all events no matter how trivial they appeared.

If a battle were to occur, the 324-foot-long *Maine* could give a good account of herself. Though reclassified as an armored cruiser, this warship was, as one writer stated, America's "first battleship of importance" She was armed with four 10-inch guns, six 6-inch breach loading rifles, six 6-pounders, eight 1-pounders, and two gatling guns. She was also armed with torpedoes. Double screw, the battleship could make 18 knots. Although the appearance of the Dreadnaught eight years later would render such a vessel obsolete, the *Maine* was, in 1898, a valuable ship in the United States Navy.

The *Maine* also had an important asset in its commanding officer. A graduate of the United States Naval Academy at Annapolis, Charles Sigsbee had an impressive record during his thirty-nine year career. He displayed bravery during the assault on Mobile in 1864. For four years, he competently managed the hydrographic office.

Sigsbee was also noted for making split-second decisions. He displayed this ability seven months earlier when the *Maine* was in New York. The battleship was passing Hell Gate when the excursion boat *Isabel* moved in her path. Sigsbee quickly changed course and rammed a pier instead. The *Maine* suffered relatively light damage but the *Isabel* escaped harm. For taking this quick action which may have saved hundreds of lives, the captain received a letter of praise from his superiors. Thus there could be no doubt of his abilities to function competently during emergencies.

Yet it did not seem like anything out of the ordinary would occur on this night, February 15, 1898. To Sigsbee, there was no sign of danger as he threw his cigar overboard. All was well as far as he could see, so he retired to his cabin and began writing a letter to his family. It was 9:40.

Sigsbee suddenly was startled by "a bursting, rending, and crashing sound or roar of immense volume." So powerful was the explosion that windows in Havana were shattered. The *Maine*'s power plant was destroyed and darkness set in.

Lt. George Holman was with three other officers in the wardroom mess when the ship shook violently. He then heard a second deafening explosion, which to Holman resembled a submarine explosion he had heard, only on a larger scale.

Lt. Commander Richard Wainwright was in his office when he felt a very heavy shock followed by objects falling on deck. Immediately the executive officer assumed the ship was under attack. He quickly rushed outside to confirm his suspicion.

On the quarter-deck, Lt. Blandin was casually chatting with Lt. Hood. Hood jokingly asked Blandin if he was asleep. "No, I am on watch," he said. In the next instant, Blandin heard "a dull, sullen roar." The startled officer was struck on the head by a piece of cement.

On the poop deck, Apprentice Ambrose Ham was startled by a "flame, which seemed to envelop the whole ship." Before the young apprentice could react, he was struck in the face by a piece of debris. A split second later, Ham heard a second explosion that sounded like a roar.

John Chidwick, the *Maine*'s chaplain, was in his room when he was shocked by a loud explosion. When the lights in his cabin suddenly went out, the chaplain rushed to the door, and as he did so, he noticed the vessel was listing to port.

In the forward room of the steerage, Naval Cadet Amon Bronson, Jr., was interrupted in his reading by a violent explosion followed by a loud crash. When he overcame the shock, the cadet also felt the ship was developing a list to port.

Instinctively, Captain Sigsbee hurried to the starboard cabin ports. Upon looking out, it occurred to him it would be better to feel his way along the dark passage leading to the superstructure.

Nearing the outer entrance, the captain bumped into his orderly, William Anthony, who apologized and informed him that a terrible explosion had taken place down below.

Hearing this, Sigsbee headed to the quarter-deck to survey the situation. It was then he heard what he made out to be shouts of cheers coming from the shore. The captain immediately assumed his command was under attack and ordered additional sentries posted around the ship.

Inside the officer's mess, Lt. Holman recovered from the shock of the explosion and called to the other officers in the room to "get up on deck." Holman, followed by Lt. Jungen, Chief Engineer Howell, and Lt. Jenkins, stumbled in the darkness until they came across the wardroom ladder. Holman, Jungen and Howell ascended the ladder and soon emerged on the main deck.

Jenkins, however, lost his way in the darkness and was separated from the rest. The young officer stumbled around until he came upon Mess Attendant John Turpin.

"Which way?" Jenkins asked as he seized Turpin's arm.

"I don't know which way," the frightened mess attendant answered.

"Which way?" Jenkins persisted.

"I don't know, sir, which way."

"Which way?"

"I don't know, sir."

"Then the whole compartment lit right up," according to Turpin. "I saw Mr. Jenkins throw up both hands and fall, right by the steerage pantry."

Turpin wasted no time. He left the mess room and quickly sought the wardroom ladder. He was unable to locate the ladder but came across a suspended rope. He pulled himself up and emerged on the main deck.

Lt. Holman, still believing the ship was under attack, sent Turpin in search of the cutlasses, and once again he found himself below stumbling about in the darkness.

In the forward room of the steerage, Cadet Amon Bronson listened in horror to the cries from the nearby compartment. His attention was then drawn to the sound of running water coming from the passageway. Alarmed, Bronson climbed out of his bunk and began to make for the main deck.

Moving in the darkness, he bumped into a fellow cadet, W.T. Cluverius.

"Come on," Bronson said, "We'll make it."

Together, the two cadets waded through the ankle deep water to the junior officer's hatch. Seeing this avenue was sealed off by wreckage, Bronson and Cluverius made for the wardroom, and within a few minutes they were safely on the main deck.

On the quarter-deck, Captain Sigsbee conferred with his executive officer and decided to flood the magazine before it exploded. Wainwright and a few others proceeded to follow the captain's orders when they discovered water was already coming up from the magazine. The gravity of the situation was now clear.

Sigsbee by this time was faced with the fact that a fire was raging out of control in the mess amidship. Wainwright called for volunteers to help combat the conflagration. Lt. Hood, cadet D.F. Boyd, Jr., and other able bodied men joined the executive officer in his futile efforts to extinguish the blaze.

Meanwhile, Sigsbee's attention was drawn to the water. His eyes, now accustomed to the darkness, made out the white forms floating by to be his men. Immediately he ordered the lifeboats to be lowered and sent to rescue them. It was then he learned that 12 of the 15 boats were too badly damaged to be lowered. This left him with only the barge, the captain's gig, and the whale-boat.

The crew of the *Maine* was forced to make do with what it had. Under the supervision of Lt. Blow, Apprentice Ambrose Ham and a few other crewmen began to lower the gig. The list to the port presented some problems but the men working the davits finally managed to successfully launch the boat. Ham and other members of the crew jumped in and began to fish their mates out of the water.

Lt. Jungen and five crewmen directed their efforts to launching the barge. They too had problems owing to the list but were finally able to get the boat waterborne. The barge with Chaplain Chidwich, Lt. Jungen and five others began plucking the wounded men from the water.

They were soon joined by lifeboats from nearby vessels. The Spanish cruiser *Alfonso XII* quickly lowered away several of her boats to help their American visitors. The master of the Ward Line *City of Washington* overcame his shock of having iron objects and other fragments falling on his ship's pantry and sent assistance to the *Maine*.

Meanwhile, some of the *Maine*'s crew were abandoning ship. Mess Attendant John Turpin abandoned his search for the cutlasses and returned to the main deck, then dove overboard and swam rapidly away from the burning battleship. He later was picked up by one of the boats.

By now it became apparent the *Maine* was beyond hope. After all that was possible had been done to save the wounded, Sigsbee decided it was time to abandon ship. It was a "hard blow," he later recalled, for him and his men to leave their ship. Yet it was pointless to remain aboard. It was only a matter of time before the

Maine would founder. The forward 10-inch magazine was in flames and was liable to explode at any minute.

So after the others had left, and with a sense of deep regret, Captain Sigsbee and his officers began to abandon the *Maine* themselves. Wainwright and Lt. Holman both offered a hand but their commander declined. He told them to get into the boat themselves and then he would follow. After all, it was the "proper" procedure for the master to be the last to leave his ship.

Shortly afterwards, the abandoned battleship began to sink deeper in the harbor. Numerous explosions occurred as the fire consumed the ammunition. The *Maine* finally settled to the bottom with part of the poop deck protruding from the water.

A muster of the surviving crew revealed 258 enlisted men and two officers were lost. (Lt. John Blandin died a few months later, increasing the number to three officers lost.) Of the ninety-four saved, fifty-four were injured. Up to this time it was the worst disaster in the history of the United States Navy.

At once, Sigsbee relayed to his superiors in Washington, D.C., "I can not yet determine the cause but competent investigation will decide whether the explosion was produced from an interior or exterior cause. I can not say anything until after such an investigation has been made. I will not and can not conscientiously anticipate the decision, nor do I wish to make any unjust estimate of the reason for the disaster."

At first, most naval officials theorized the cause of the calamity was nothing more than an accident. Secretary of the Navy John Long issued his opinion that, "the indications are, however, that there was an accident—that the magazine exploded. How that came about I do not know."

Other naval officers offered their own theories. One admiral suggested that chemical action caused the magazine to explode. Another officer believed a fire in the bunkers near a magazine was the cause of the disaster. Yet some naval officers were skeptical of this explanation. "Had the magazine exploded," one of them stated, "the ship would have been blown to flinders."

Certain government officials of Spain also offered their theories on the cause of the disaster. Captain General Blanco of Havana reported to Madrid that the *Maine* blew up by an "undoubtedly chance accident believed to result from an explosion of the boiler or the dynamo." The Spanish *chargé d'affaires* explained, "Of course I look upon the horror as due in every respect and solely and simply to an accident . . . all the evidence thus far available goes to sustain it."

Not everyone readily assumed the *Maine* was destroyed because of an accident. Senator George Perkins, himself a one-time navigator, insisted, "I can not conceive that such an explosion as that which is reported to have wrecked the *Maine* could have resulted from an accident. The chances, it seems to me, are 999 in 1,000 that the calamity did not result from an accident."

Congressman Amos Cummings also found it hard to believe the destruction of the battleship was caused by an accident. Never, he stated, had such an accident happened before. Therefore, Cummings reasoned, the Spanish must have had a hand in it. Evidently the good Senator did not recall the *Missouri* disaster in 1885 which closely resembled the one that befell the *Maine*.

Another Senator was more blunt. "I am too mad to talk about it. I can't see how the explosion could have been the result of an accident and I think the time is rapidly approaching when this country must do something."

There was one person in particular who wanted to do something—specifically, wage war. Assistant Secretary of the Navy Theodore Roosevelt believed this nation needed a war and "Spain will do fine." When President McKinley resisted the cries "Remember the *Maine*!" Roosevelt was said to have characterized his superior as having the "backbone of a chocolate éclair."

McKinley at this point was simply not sure which course of action to take. Instead of acting hastily without all of the facts, the President waited for the naval board of inquiry to issue its findings.

The court was not caught in the war fever. Neither did it attempt to whitewash the actions of Sigsbee and others in the Navy as some have claimed. The questions put to the witnesses were carefully framed. The witnesses did not experience any pressure to answer in any predetermined way but instead were allowed to express themselves freely.

The court of inquiry opened its hearings aboard the U.S.S. *Mangrove* anchored at Havana harbor. Captain Sigsbee was the first to testify. Although a witness himself, Sigsbee was allowed to question other witnesses. Some people have correctly pointed out that this was a dangerous procedure, for his presence may have intimidated his own men while they gave their evidence. This was possible; although there is no indication Sigsbee had any such effect on the investigation.

In its report, the court found no fault with Sigsbee or any of his men. It instead blamed the disaster on a submarine mine which caused the partial explosion in two or more forward magazines. The basis of this assumption is the testimony of the divers who found plates and the keel to be forced inward. The court fell short of naming the perpetrators.

The issue was now settled though. Little by little relations between Spain and the United States worsened. On April 25, 1898, sixty-nine days after the *Maine* was destroyed, members of Congress declared war on Spain. The Spanish-American War began.

It was a brief one and victorious for the United States. When the peace treaty was signed in December of that year, Spain formally relinquished to the United States several of her possessions- Cuba, Guam, the Philippines, Puerto Rico, and American Samoa. The deaths on the American side mounted to only 2,466. Moreover, 2,061 of this number succumbed to malaria, yellow fever, and other non-combatant deaths.

In retrospect, we can safely conclude the attack on the U.S.S. *Maine*, if one took place, was not the deliberate work of the Spanish government. It most likely was the work of overzealous Spaniards acting without Madrid's knowledge or rebel Cubans hoping to embroil the United States. Yet while there may be little doubt the government of Spain did not set out to destroy the American warship, there are many maritime historians, including an admiral of the United States Navy, who still wonder whether the *Maine* was a victim of a mine at all.

These skeptics question the official finding which holds that the *Maine* was rocked by two explosions. They cite the testimony of Captain Sigsbee and a few other officers who reported hearing only one. However it is important to remember that two explosions occurring a split second apart could be mistaken for one. Most of the crew, including Lt. Holman, who was an expert on explosives, testified they clearly heard two explosions. Moreover, others who were aboard nearby vessels at the time claimed to have also heard a second explosion.

Other points raised by this school of thought is the small amount of water thrown up and the absence of dead fish that usually accompany a mine explosion. It is possible a mine was positioned directly under the vessel or at a depth sufficient enough to minimize the quantity of water blown into the air. An absence of dead marine life need not rule out a mine, for it may be that the fish were merely stunned and swam away after recovering, or that there were only a few fish in the area at the time of the explosion.

Perhaps the best evidence for the internal explosion theory is the time factor. The official news of the *Maine*'s dispatch to Havana did not reach the Spanish officials until January 24, a day before the battleship arrived in the harbor. Hence it seems to be insufficient time for anyone to rig up a mine.

What is often overlooked is that even before January 24 there had been rumors circulating in Havana of an American warship being sent to Cuba. There were, after all, riots in Havana and many Americans were concerned for the safety of their fellow citizens who were in the city. Even without these rumors, practically anyone could have guessed an American vessel would be dispatched to Havana. In the late 19th century, it was not uncommon for a naval power to send a warship to a troubled port and the United States would have been eager to display this strength.

Various alternative theories have been advanced to account for the disaster: the grounding of the electric plant, an exploding boiler, an accident in the magazine, and a fire in the coal bunker. Yet each theory has a flaw. The grounding of the electric plant, for instance, seems unlikely, for members of the surviving crew were in agreement that the ship's lights were in perfect order and did not flicker off until after the explosion. A bursting boiler may also be ruled out, for the two active ones on the night of the disaster were situated a good distance from the magazines. Furthermore, they were designed to work at pressure of 120 lbs. per square inch, and at the time of the explosion, it was only 100 lbs. per square inch. An accident in the magazine seems doubtful, for it was clearly established the crew was careful in handling the ammunition. It is unlikely a fire took place in the coal bunkers, for neither the fire alarms nor the engineers working in this area detected any smoke or flames. Furthermore, some coal had been recovered by divers and, upon examination, showed no signs of being in a fire.

By far the most important evidence concerning the cause of the disaster is the condition of the battleship itself. As was previously mentioned, the divers found (and their observations were later confirmed when the vessel was salvaged) that the plates and keel were bent inward indicating an external explosion. (The *Maine* was raised in 1911 and reexamined. It was concluded that the court was correct in its conclusions. The ship was then sunk in deep water in 1912.) Some have theorized that the keel and plates buckled inward by pressure exerted as the bow sank and the stern remained afloat. Yet the author finds it difficult to accept this as being sufficient pressure to force the keel inward by 34 feet. The *Maine*, being a warship, was built proportionally strong for her size and it seems doubtful that her plates and keel would bend to this pressure.

After careful consideration, this maritime historian comes to the conclusion the court of inquiry was correct. Nevertheless, this answer is a qualified one; until more evidence emerges any conclusion as to what caused the destruction of the U.S.S. *Maine* should be qualified.

Another issue involving the *Maine* is the effect, if any, its destruction had on the diplomatic relations between Spain and the United States. It can safely be said that this event did not alone cause the brief war. Tensions between the United States and Spain were high even before the *Maine* arrived in Havana. The reason for sending the ship to Cuba and her preparedness for battle as she entered port is evidence of the strained relations. Other factors therefore must have contributed to the Spanish-American War.

Still, the *Maine* was an important cause of the 1898 war. That it had an impact on the negotiations with Spain can be clearly seen in John Long's journal. On February 28, 1898, before the release of the court's findings, the Secretary of Navy confidently wrote, "I believe war will be averted." Then on April 2, after the report was released, Long gloomily observed, "It looks very much as if war might be precipitated."

The destruction of the U.S.S. *Maine* had a tremendous influence on three segments of American society. One of these, of course, was the business sector. From 1897 to early 1898, businessmen favored non-intervention. One economic journal, *Banker's Magazine*, summed up this sentiment in one of its editorials. War, it stated, is "never beneficial from a material standpoint." Other financial periodicals such as the *Wall Street Journal* made similar statements.

Then in late March and early April of 1898, the opinion of the business community took a 180° turn. John Jacob Astor, William Rockefeller and Thomas Ryan were "feeling militant." In late March, Senator Henry Cabot Lodge informed President McKinley that he had "talked with bankers, brokers, businessmen, editors, clergymen and others in Boston . . . everyone wanted the Cuban question solved."

What apparently had happened was businessmen at first feared the effects a war would have on the stock market. It was believed that a conflict with Spain would disrupt trading on Wall Street. Then, from late March to April, there arose serious doubts that the United States would remain at peace. This uncertainty interfered with investments in the stock market, for many were not sure whether to invest in the production of war goods or peacetime commodities. As the March 20 issue of the *Wall Street Journal* reported, "The market was extremely irregular. . . ." This uncertainty was not created by yellow journalism, the De Lome letter, or the "taste of empire," for these factors existed before March of 1898.

The cause of the uncertainty must have been the *Maine*. News leaks on the condition of the keel and the release of the report coincided with the market fluctuation, and doubts if peace could be maintained began to surface. This led many industrialists to demand the country go to war to "solve" the Cuban issue once and for all. Thus, the destruction of the *Maine* had a tremendous influence on the thinking of a powerful segment of American society that could not be ignored by an administration committed to catering to needs of the business sector.

The second group on which the *Maine* had an impact was the political leaders of the United States. Many members of Congress such as Senators Perkins and Cummings expressed the view that the destruction of the American warship constituted an act of war. After the release of the board's findings, even those who believed the Spanish government was not directly involved in the disaster came to the conclusion that the *Maine* incident still provided justification for intervention. The report of a congressional committee investigating the situation in Cuba stated in its report, "If there be no prohibition, the ports of a friendly nation are considered as open to the public ships of all powers with whom it is at peace . . . they are under the protection of the government of the place."

Finally, the destruction of the U.S.S. *Maine* had an enormous influence on public opinion. When McKinley chose to wait for the board to investigate the disaster, many Americans showed approval of his cautious approach. Letters to the White House praised the administration's course of action. Even organizations such as the Daughters of 1812 supported the President.

However, when McKinley continued to pursue a peaceful course of action after the release of the court's findings, the public poured its wrath on him. One letter to the President stated, "I regret your decision." There were also public demonstrations against both the President and Spain. In at least one major city, McKinley was burned in effigy, and in a bar in New York a man stood up and said, "Gentlemen, remember the *Maine*." The cry "Remember the *Maine*" was broadened to "Remember the *Maine*, To Hell with Spain!"

A further indicator of the bitterness of the American people was a letter to the president by Henry Cabot Lodge, a sharp observor of public sentiment. In late March, he wrote to McKinley, "If the war in Cuba drags on through the summer with nothing done, we should go down in the greatest defeat ever known before the cry, 'why have you not settled the Cuban question.'" The voters, according to Lodge, "think the destruction of the *Maine* is justification" for intervention.

Hence, the destruction of the U.S.S. *Maine* actually was an important event in American History. It was not, as has been wrongly averred by some historians, merely an incident with little influence on the outbreak of the Spanish-American War.

5 ■ NOVEMBER 26, 1898

The *City of Portland*
"A Mystery From Start to Finish"

AMERICANS HAD good reason to feel confident in 1898. Their country had just emerged victorious in the war with Spain. Their industries were second to none. The American people were experiencing such prosperity as they had never known before.

Late in that year, on November 26, the nation was not in such a festive mood, though. The northeastern portion of the country went through a terrible storm. It was New England's worst since the Lighthouse gale of 1851. In New York alone, the snowfall was recorded as 7½ inches. To complicate matters, a strong northeast wind swept this area, keeping the temperature just above freezing.

The damage caused by the storm was immense. Telephone lines across New England were felled. Destruction to buildings and homes added up roughly to $10 million. This figure did not include the loss of business. Transportation in particular suffered. Underground trolley cars were rendered inoperable. Streetcars were unable to move an inch. At least one line on Broadway in New York City was stopped completely.

Transportation by sea fared little better. The windblown snow obstructed visibility like fog. Many Sound boats were forced to go through the East River; ferries were delayed, others were cancelled. The New Haven boat *Richard Peck*, for instance, was to depart at 5:00 PM but remained at her pier well beyond 8:00. The 39th Street Ferry discontinued service at 8:00. Even large ships such as the Cunard Line *Lucania* and the Atlantic Transport liner *Mantitol* were forced to remain in quarantine.

Many ships traveling through this area were caught in the storm and wrecked. Yet out of the seventy or so sinkings, one shipwreck in particular, the *City of Portland* of the Boston and Portland Steam Packet Company, gained national attention. The storm in fact has been referred to as the *Portland* gale. For eight years, this 2,300-ton 281-foot-long sidewheeler had provided comfortable service for travelers between Maine and Massachusetts. Her 1,200-horsepower engine could drive the vessel at a speed of more than 10 knots. The *Portland*, along with her sistership, the *Bay State*, offered her passengers telephone service, electric lights, hot and cold water, and many other modern conveniences.

It is of no wonder that some of those returning home from the annual Merchant Fair in Boston decided to take passage on this steamer. It was, after all, much more comfortable than steam trains, and seemed like an ideal way of ending the Thanksgiving vacation.

The ship's master, Captain Hollis Henry Blanchard, was determined not to disappoint his passengers, bad weather or no bad weather. He himself had an appointment at a family reunion in Yarmouth. The captain did receive a message from Captain Alexander Dennison of the *Bay State* that the wind was "blowing like sixty down here." Still, Blanchard insisted that he would sail. He explained to Dennison that the storm probably would not reach Portland before he docked there.

One passenger, Captain C.J. Leighton, realized that there was grave danger to the *Portland* if it sailed. "By George," he told his friend, the captain, "I don't think this is a fit night to leave port." He gathered his baggage and left the ship. The effect of this must have had a greater impact on the captain than the previous warning. He called to the watchman standing by: "I might come back!" Nevertheless, the *City of Portland* cast off from Boston and set sail with 200 passengers and a crew of 100 in one of the most terrible storms to hit the Atlantic coast. (The exact figure on how many sailed is unknown for the purser did not keep an accurate count.)

The storm grew steadily worse as the day became grayer. At around 7:20, the weather in the *Portland*'s path deteriorated at an alarming rate. By 9:30, a critical situation developed. The wind velocity reached sixty miles per hour and later reached a terrible peak of ninety. Visibility was severely restricted. Violent waves pitched and rolled the ships caught in the storm's path.

Several ships were sunk or badly damaged that night. A two-masted vessel was wrecked on the rocks off Martha's Vineyard island; the steam ship *Ohio*, bound for Boston, went aground on Spectacle Island; the *William Blakely* and the *Ellen T. King*, both two-masted schooners, were also lost that night. Several other ships were reported to be in distress near Race Point.

No one knows exactly what happened to the *Portland*. After casting off, the steamer was seen passing Deer Island by the crews of both the steamer *Kennebec* and a tug. The captain of the schooner *Maude S* and the *William Thomas* and the lightkeeper at Thatcher's Island reported seeing the *Portland* passing Gloucester around 9:00 PM. The rough weather must have impeded the progress of the sidewheeler, for two hours later, some fishing vessels spotted the boat being tossed and turned by the waves. One fisherman tried to warn the night boat of the danger it was in by firing a flare. He then waited for a response that never came.

At 11:45 PM, Captain Pellier of the schooner *Edgar Bandall* turned just in time to avoid a collision with what was probably the *Portland* some fourteen miles off Eastern Point Light. He noticed the superstructure of the other vessel was damaged.

On Sunday morning, November 27, 1898, at 7:00, Captain Michael Hogan of the *Ruth M. Martin* caught a glimpse of a large sidewheeler through dense clouds. Hogan tried to reach the ship in the hope he could help its crew. But the other ship was under steam and the *Martin* had lost her sails. Fortunately for Hogan, his ship was washed safely ashore.

At 7:45, Samuel Fisher of Race Point Life Saving Station heard four blasts of a whistle. Its volume indicated that it was from a large steamer. Fisher fired flares and rang a bell. He looked but could not see or hear the vessel.

The fate of the *Portland* was soon learned after the storm. While walking along the beach near his summer house at Wellfleet, Dr. Maurice Richardson came across three piano keys, a piano cage, items of furniture upholstered in red plush, and the bodies of a man and a stout woman. Both bodies had life preservers from the *Portland* around their waists.

Other bodies and debris were later found. One body was that of a girl about twenty in a life preserver, with the initials I.G.E. inscribed in her ring and a gold watch with the hands stopped at 9:17. No survivors were ever found.

Thus the last hours of the *City of Portland* will never be known. From what was seen and heard from those on other ships and nearby land, it is safe to say the vessel was on her course until midnight on the 26th, though her progress may have been impeded. The storm then must have pushed the sidewheeler southwards. The sighting of wreckage coming ashore at 7:30 on the evening of the 27th indicates the ship was intact until approximately 6:00, for had the end come sooner, wreckage would have washed up on Cape Cod. The discovery of bodies with life preservers suggests that the people aboard were aware of the critical situation at least a few minutes before the ship foundered.

It is not certain how the *City of Portland* met her doom. The discovery of the debris from the *King Phillip* near the area where items from the *Portland* were found indicated the possibility of a collision. Some, however, say she was smashed against breakers. Others believe she may have capsized. Still there were some who expressed the opinion that the waves battered the upper fillings until the water poured into the ship. Perhaps water broke through the hull and made contact with the boilers, causing an explosion.

One persistent question remains the responsibility of Captain Blanchard. Some seafarers stated flatly that they would not have sailed that day. This, however, was said with the gift of hindsight. Indeed most master mariners who testified at the investigation hearings expressed the view that the weather at the time of embarkment wasn't severe enough to cancel the voyage. They may very well be correct, but when the weather did deteriorate, Blanchard should have sought shelter. Why he did not when he had the chance will never be known.

Many questions trouble the people of New England, and the fate of the *City of Portland* to this day remains a mystery. As one man put it, "Take my advice. Don't try to understand it, for that would be impossible. It is just a mystery and it always will be. There is so much that can't be explained, so many things happened that just couldn't happen, that we are all mystified by the whole affair. What happened to the *Portland* will always stay a mystery from start to finish. Mark me well."

6 ∎ JUNE 28, 1904

The *Norge*
"...More Appalling Consequences"

THE DEFENDENT, Captain Gundle, waited for the verdict to come in. It was Christmas Eve, 1904, and he was at the Maritime and Commercial Court in Copenhagen. He was uncertain if the court would hold him responsible for the loss of his late command, the *Norge*.

The tragic story began on June 27, 1904. The *Norge* left Copenhagen for a voyage to New York. By the 28th, she was off the coast of Scotland. Captain Gundle was on the bridge with Chief Officer Corphtler.

The *Norge* was an important ship of the United Steamship Company. She was 340 feet in length and 3,318 in gross tonnage. Her single screw was driven by compound engines giving her a speed of 13 knots.

The ship had seen much of the sea. Built in 1881 by Alexander Stephens & Sons, Ltd, the *Pieter de Coninck*, as she was then called, served the Thingnalen Line for many years. In 1898, the iron-hulled liner was bought by the United Steamship Company and renamed the *Norge*.

Now on June 28, 1904, the *Norge* was carrying 703 passengers and a crew of 71. As the Russo-Japanese War was in progress at this time, some of the passengers were from Russia probably trying to evade military service. Others were returning to the United States after a visit to their old homes.

47

Most of these passengers were unaware that they were traveling in a dangerous area. The Rockall rock, which lies near Hebrides, is well known to mariners. It is 75 feet high and projects five miles into the sea. Sailors treat it with respect and usually give it a wide berth.

At around 7:30 in the morning, the *Norge* shook suddenly. The liner had struck the Rockall reef. Perhaps the currents had carried the vessel off course. In any event, the forward hull plates buckled and water cascaded into the ship.

The passengers immediately realized something was wrong. Several of them were awakened by the vibrations. Those already out of bed were thrown against the wall or onto the floor.

One passenger was lying in his bunk waiting for breakfast. He suddenly heard a "slight bump followed by another bump." He rushed on deck, then, realizing the ship might sink, returned to his cabin to retrieve his valuables.

Katerina Sillander was awakened by the crash. Quickly she dressed her baby and ran to the boat deck.

On the bridge, Captain Gundle barked a series of commands. He called out, "All hands on deck!" He ordered soundings to be taken in the forward hold, and then ordered the pumps to be employed. Gundle also passed the word that all passengers were to put on their life jackets and report to the boat deck.

The soundings revealed there was already five feet of water in the forward hold. The sea was pouring in at an alarming rate. The pumps were not keeping pace with the inflow of water.

Numerous passengers by now appeared on deck. Some of them were wearing life jackets; others wandered about without them. Panic soon broke out. Some of the crew rushed to the lifeboats, pushing the woman and children aside. As one passenger remarked, "We had no time in that fierce fight for life to think of anything but getting of seats in the boats."

Other members of the crew behaved splendidly. One of the engineers, Jans Peters Jansen, rushed to the cabin where his relatives slept. He informed them that the liner was seriously damaged and urged them to go to the boat deck. Jansen then went below and remained at his post to the end.

Seaman Karl Mathieson assisted the third mate with the boats. There were only seven on the vessel. He noticed that some of the boat stations lacked men to work the davits. "Had men been set to work at each boat, more would have been saved," he later lamented.

A rush was made for one of the boats. The third mate threatened to kill anyone who entered the boat without authorization. This seemed to work, for the crew settled down.

Unfortunately, there were other problems in lowering the lifeboats. At one station, a tackle broke and one end of the boat fell, dumping several of the passengers into the water. A wave smashed the boat against the ship's hull, reducing it to splinters.

Efforts were made to launch a second boat. Filled with woman and children, it was soon lowered. Then a wave struck, smashing the boat and killing some of the occupants.

Other boats were successfully lowered. Karl Mathieson assisted the third mate with one of them, and as it descended to the water the two of them jumped in.

Soon other boats became waterborne. The crew discovered a hole in one, but quick repairs were effected and it was lowered. But in all, only a few lifeboats pulled safely away.

Numerous passengers did not wait for a boat. Several jumped overboard and into the turbulent water below. Some of the life jackets were rotten and could not keep the wearers buoyant. As one survivor later related, "Dozens of people who jumped into the sea with lifebelts were drowned before our eyes." Others remained aboard, among them Captain Gundle. Gundle had been at sea for many years and was determined to go down with his ship.

The *Norge* soon began to sink lower in the water. The bow dipped under the sea. Water washed over the boat deck, carrying dozens of people over. Then at around 7:50, some twenty minutes after striking the reef, the *Norge* disappeared beneath the sea.

In the turbulent water, hundreds of people struggled for survival. Many of the ineffective life jackets came off and passengers drowned. Others were washed against the rocks.

In one of the successfully launched lifeboats, a mate considered the situation carefully. The boat was seriously overcrowded so he decided to leave it and swim for another. As he began swimming, however, he discovered the water was too rough, and he drowned before he could reach a boat.

Others in the water were more fortunate. Captain Gundle went down with his command. His right leg was caught between two stanchions, but he managed to break free and surfaced. He swam for several minutes until coming across Second Engineer Brunn. They agreed to swim in company and spied lifeboat No. 1 under the command of Able Seaman Peter Olsen. They struck out for it and were taken aboard.

For days the lifeboats drifted. There were no sails in any of them so lifejackets were tied to oars and were used instead. The provisions were rationed. In one boat, there was no water and only two biscuits per person per day. Some survivors suffered from salt water in cuts on arms and legs.

On Saturday morning, four days after the disaster, the people in Gundle's boat noticed a large schooner-rigged steamer about four miles away. Quickly a blanket was put on an oar but the steamer passed on without noticing. The following day, a bark passed by but, according to Gundle, with "the same result."

On Sunday, the *Silvia* appeared on scene. She was off course, which proved fortunate. Henry Glover, the second engineer, was on deck when he spotted something off in the distance.

"Is that a buoy out of place?" he asked.

"You don't see no buoy," said the ship's cook.

Glover got binoculars on it and saw it was a lifeboat with a jacket in the air. He quickly informed the captain who in turn set course for the lifeboat, the one under the command of the third mate. When all were aboard the *Silvia*, it was discovered that twenty-six were saved.

At about noon on Sunday, July 3, boat No. 1 came within sight of St. Kilda. "The drooping spirits of all were revived," according to Gundle. Then the *Energie* was sighted. This time the ship arrived and rescued Gundle and the others.

On July 5th, the steam trawler *Largo Bay* rescued the people in a third boat. Seventeen survivors were accounted for in this lifeboat.

Once ashore, the survivors of the *Norge* were rushed to a hospital. There, two children died. Fortunately, most of the injured pulled through.

The news of the disaster shocked the world. Of the 774 aboard the liner 701 perished. *The New York Times* stated, "No tragedy of the sea has had more appalling consequences and none has occurred in a shorter time."

One of the relatives of a woman aboard the doomed ship lamented, "Oh, don't tell me that; she was all I had in the world." Another relative was found dead by a railroad track, an apparent suicide.

At once, the question arose whether the *Norge* was overcrowded. A.E. Johnson, an agent for the line, went on record as saying:

> I do not know what the certificate given the *Norge* on the other side allowed, but I am sure she did not carry more than the number of passengers allowed by law. No steamship would dare to do that. I believe she had two certificates, one from this side and one from the authorities in Europe. I have frequently known her to come here with from 600 to 900 passengers so that she must have been allowed to carry that number on her certificate from the other side. She never took anything like that number of passengers away with her however.
>
> I do not know anything about her lifeboat and life preserver equipment. I am expecting some information on that score by cable.

But this was in the past. On December 24, 1904, the court rendered its verdict. Captain Gundle was declared "not guilty" of negligence. The directors of the line were also absolved of blame. The ordeal of the *Norge* was over.

7 ■ JANUARY 24, 1909

The *Republic*
"A Handsome Ship"

Fog BANKS are a common sight off the coast of Nantucket Island. Many vessels have cruised through dense fog and have paid a heavy price. On July 4, 1898, for instance, the French liner *La Bourgogne* was rammed by the iron-hulled schooner *Cromartyshire* in such fog patches. It was one of the worst sea disasters ever to take place. When the *La Bourgogne* sank, more than 500 passengers and crew were lost.

Yet in the eleven years that followed, the shipping world continued to depend on this route for voyages to and from New York and Boston. Even in the worst visibility conditions, cargo ships and even passenger liners have ventured into this region at high speeds in order to meet deadlines. The captains of these ships were in a sense taking a calculated risk.

One such shipmaster was Captain William Sealby of the White Star Line *Republic*. He was well aware of the possibility and consequences of collision as his 570-foot-long steamer encountered fog on January 23, 1909. His command was one of the most important vessels of the White Star Line since the day she was bought from the Dominican Line in 1907.* This 15,400-ton liner was the flagship of the Boston to Europe passage and had set speed records for voyages between Boston and Queenstown. She was "a

*The ship was named the *Columbus* when she was under this line.

handsome ship," as *The New York Times* later described her. And of course there was the safety of the 440 passengers to be considered.

On the other hand, the *Republic* had a schedule to meet. Her passengers as well as her cargo of food supplies for the American battleship fleet were due in the Mediterranean. Besides, the *Republic* offered all the safety of 20th century shipbuilding. She was built with a double bottom and a double layer of steel throughout her hull.

So with all risk considered, Captain Sealby decided to continue on course with his speed only slightly checked. As a further precaution, he had the ship's whistle blown at intervals to alert all nearby vessels of his position. He then took his place on the bridge to oversee the navigation of his ship.

Some miles east of the White Star Liner, the Lloyd Italiano Line *Florida* was westbound for New York with 900 Italian immigrants. Her captain, 29-year-old Angelo Ruspini, had also taken steps to insure the safety of his steamer, with the speed reduced and the lookouts doubled. The fog sirens, like the whistle of the *Republic*, were activated at intervals to alert all ships in her path. Then Ruspini, like Sealby, stood on the bridge to supervise the navigation of his command through the fog.

At 5:47 AM on January 23, 1909, the officers on the *Republic*'s bridge heard the *Florida*'s whistle about three or four points on the port bow. Immediately, the engines were stopped and then reversed. The helm was put hard-a-port and the fog horn was given two blasts to designate her left turn in hope the oncoming vessel would do likewise.

Ruspini on the nearby *Florida* heard the blast of the whistle but for some reason the helm was put in hard-a-starboard instead of hard-a-port. It was later suggested that the helmsman had made the error and the captain angrily struck him, but this version of the story was later denied by the crew of the Italian ship. In any case, the *Florida* was put on a collision course with the *Republic*.

A short distance away, the officers on the *Republic*'s bridge saw the mast light of the *Florida* coming straight towards them. Quickly, the engines were rung Full Speed Ahead to clear their way of the *Florida*.

It was too late. The Italian ship's bow struck the White Star Liner amidship. It appeared as if she was going to break the *Republic* in two but fortunately the *Florida*'s weak bow crumbled up.

Aboard the *Florida*, first class passenger Filomena Cayliofera, returning from a visit to her relatives in northern Italy, was strolling on deck. She was unable to rest this night for the ship's whistle had "driven sleep from me." Cayliofera heard another ship's whistle from somewhere out in the fog. Suddenly, this other vessel appeared in the *Florida*'s path.

Mrs. Cayliofera quickly grasped a tight hold on the ship's railing. The *Florida* began to vibrate. To her it appeared as if the Italian ship "rebounded a bit from the *Republic* and then the two vessels came together again."

Below, Domini Roberto was chatting with another first class passenger. "I think I hear another whistle," Roberto said. In the next instant, he was hurled to the floor. Scrambling to his feet, he rushed on deck where he saw "the big hull of the *Republic*, a faint blur in the darkness."

On the *Republic*, Brayton Ives, the president of the Metropolitan Trust Company, was awakened by a loud noise. Running to the hallway, he saw several half-clad passengers wandering about. He was met by a steward who told him to put on his life jacket and report to the boat deck.

The loud crash also woke S.H. Smallman and his wife. At first Smallman thought it was nothing serious, and he tried to turn on the cabin lights but discovered the power was out. He now realized the situation was more grave than he had believed.

In another cabin, Mrs. Herbert L. Griggs was interrupted in her sleep by the crash. The lights flickered out. Getting over the shock, she found the ceiling had collapsed on her. She began banging on the walls in a frantic plea for help.

James Connolly heard "a grinding, tearing sound" and quickly went topside. There he noticed "a few of the ship's people . . . running about."

"Jack" Binns, the ship's wireless operator, was awakened by a grinding noise. His first impression was that the *Republic* had run aground, but then he glanced around his cabin and saw that a wall and half of the roof was missing.

In the engine room a state of confusion reigned. The stokers fled their posts as the sea poured in at an alarming rate. Fourth Engineer Legg kept his head. Before leaving, he sensibly turned on the injector valves which admitted cold water gradually and lowered the boiler pressure. This action undoubtedly prevented a disastrous explosion when the cold sea water made contact with the boilers.

Nevertheless, the damage inflicted by the *Florida* was severe. The engine room was flooded within minutes of the collision. Two staterooms were demolished (an anchor from the *Florida* was deposited in one of them). Almost immediately the White Star liner developed a frightening list to the portside.

"Jack" Binns immediately went to work. He unsuccessfully attempted to telephone the bridge to inquire as to what had happened, so he reported to the bridge in person and was told by the captain to transmit a signal of distress. Binns hurried back to the wireless cabin and proceeded to carry out his order.

With his conventional power gone, Binns set up emergency batteries and began to transmit "CQD [the call of distress British ships used at that time] stand by for captain's message." At once, he received in reply from the radio station at Siasconet, Nantucket, "All right, old man. Where are you?" A few minutes later, Binns tapped out the master's message, "*Republic* rammed by unknown steamship. Twenty-six miles southwest of Nantucket. Badly in need of assistance." Minutes later, radioman A.H. Ginman of Nantucket rebroadcast the MKC (the *Republic*'s call letters) distress message.

The *Republic* was in luck. Ginman was able to make contact with several nearby ships. Captain Ransom of the White Star Line *Baltic* acknowledged the call and immediately set course for the stricken liner. Soon the French ship *La Touraine*, the Cunard Line *Lucania*, and several government vessels joined in what was to be one of the largest rescue attempts in maritime history.

The passengers by now had been assembled on deck. The stewards began distributing coffee and blankets. Word was passed that everything was under control.

To Miss Agnes Shachilford, this was no new experience. She had been shipwrecked twice before. Once she was aboard a vessel that caught fire and on another occasion she was on one that ran aground. She noticed that in this case everyone seemed to act calmly. There were no signs of panic.

A few members of the crew were busy helping passengers who were trapped in the wreckage. Mrs. W.J. Mooney was pulled from her cabin by two seamen and taken on deck. In the next cabin, Mrs. Griggs was carried out through a hole cut in the wall and on to the salon.

Meanwhile, the *Florida* was facing difficulties of her own. Four of her seamen had been killed instantly in the collision. The ship's bow was crumpled up for thirty feet. The passengers soon appeared on the deck in bewilderment.

Captain Ruspini acted quickly. He sent some of his officers to assure everyone that the ship would remain afloat. He ordered a sail dropped over the bow to plug up any leaks. Then Ruspini set course for the scene of the collision.

Guided by the fog horns, the *Florida* safely managed to approach the *Republic*. Within shouting distance, Ruspini offered to take aboard all of the passengers of the stricken White Star liner. Captain Sealby accepted.

"Passengers of the *Republic*," Sealby calmly stated, "I want to advise you that the steamer has been injured in a collision. We are in no immediate danger but I want to ask you to standby and act with calmness and judgment. There is, I repeat, no danger, but to be on the safe side it is necessary for you to be transferred to the *Florida* as soon as possible. It will take time, and I expect that you will be cool and not excited. Take your time getting into the lifeboats. Remember, the women and children go first, and the first cabin next, and then the others. The crew will be the last to leave this vessel."

The passengers were reassured. H.J. Hoover gave considerable credit to the "coolness of the officers." Practically everyone remained calm and later paid tribute to the crew's efficiency. The only complaint came from J.B. Connolly, who was upset because the crew were unable to save the passengers' luggage.

The moving operation proved a long and difficult task even with the cooperation from the passengers. There were hundreds to be transferred and only ten lifeboats in use, and the choppy sea made matters more complicated. Nevertheless the transfer was accomplished and by 12:30, all were evacuated except for a handful of crew members who remained at their posts.

One of them, Marconi-man Binns, was persistent. He stayed at his wireless set for fourteen straight hours. Along with Ginman, he had contacted no fewer than seven ships. He finally decided to take a break at 8:00 at night in order to satisfy his appetite. He climbed down the companionway and swam to the galley in search of food. Most of it was ruined, but Binns was able to salvage a few crackers and almonds. He then returned to the wireless shack and resumed his work.

By daylight, Binns spotted, outside near the wireless cabin, the mangled bodies of a man and a woman. They were later identified as W.J. Mooney and Mrs. Eugene Lynch. The sight was disturbingly chilling to Binns. To his relief the ship's doctor came by and covered them with a blanket.

Binns remained undaunted. When the *La Touraine*'s wireless man asked him how things were, Binns relayed, "I'm on the job. Ship's sinking, but will stick to the end." Overhearing this, the *Baltic* wired encouragement, "Don't worry, old man, we are bursting our boilers to get to you."

That was by no means an idle boast. The liner *Baltic* was making a swift run to reach the stricken ship. She finally arrived at the vicinity around noon on January 24. However, she could find neither the *Republic* nor the *Florida* in the thick fog banks. For twelve hours the two White Star Line steamers drifted a few miles apart firing rockets, blowing horns and detonating bombs. Finally, the *Baltic* set off her last bomb and waited. In a moment, Binns tapped triumphantly to the *Baltic*, "You are right on course."

When the vessels were in voice range, the three captains discussed the pressing situation. With the *Republic* sinking and the *Florida* damaged and dangerously overcrowded, the captains agreed that the best course of action would be to transfer the passengers to the seaworthy *Baltic*. Captain Ransom did not mind this. His ship was not nearly filled to capacity and could easily accommodate the additional 1,600 or so from the two liners.

So there was a second transfer at sea. Again there was the traditional rule of women and children first, then the first class, followed by the remaining passengers. However, this time there was no voluntary agreement. The doubtless panicky Italian immigrants felt that class distinction should not extend to the lifeboats. A passenger mutiny almost broke out over the longstanding maritime procedure but according to one officer, "the privilege of class was upheld." There was no great loss of life in any particular group because of this but three years later there would be.

The second transfer was made easier with the lifting of the fog. The sight of the *Baltic* was a relief to the victims of the collision. Binns in particular was grateful to see the first sign of hope in the "nightmare." "I never expected to see New York again," he later reflected. Now, with the sight of the *Baltic*, things were different. He realized a rescue ship was the most beautiful sight in the world.

With the safety of the passengers now secure, Captain Sealby began to prepare for his men to abandon ship. He arranged for himself and an officer to remain alongside in a lifeboat while the remaining crew would row to the *Baltic*.

By the next morning, the *Republic* was still buoyant. Determined to salvage her, Sealby and the officer reboarded the ship. The captain requested volunteers among his crew to return with him. Thirty-six, including Binns, offered to join him. The *Republic* was taken in tow with the *Gresham*, a revenue cutter (then the term for a Coast Guard cutter), and the Navy destroyer *Senca* pulling and the Anchor Line *Furnessia* at her stern to act as a rudder. The idea was to beach the White Star Liner in the nearest shallow water, but as the ships approached the area the *Republic* began to rapidly sink deeper into the ocean. Beaching her was now out of the question.

Sealby now saw no need to keep the others aboard. He ordered them all to leave while he would stay, but they demanded that he allow them to remain aboard. The captain agreed to have just one stay with him, and chose Second Officer Williams because he was competent with the signaling lamp and was unmarried.

The nearby ships watched the *Republic* in suspense. It was only a matter of time before she would sink. The crew of the rescue ships were waiting for Sealby to fire a blue flare, the signal to cut the cables attached to the sinking liner.

By 6:00, Second Officer Williams had no doubt that the *Republic* would soon founder, and he decided to have one final meal before the ship sank. He descended the dark slanting passageway to the ship's pantry where he was able to find some cake. He returned to Sealby and together they feasted on it.

Sometime around 8:00 PM, the *Republic* began her plunge to the bottom. The sea closed over the stern. "Well, old man," Sealby asked, "what do you think about it?"

"I have an idea it won't be a long race now and when you are ready, I am," Williams replied.

"Burn the blue light," Sealby ordered.

The two attempted to light the blue flares to signal the rescue ships to cut the cables but the flares were too wet to be ignited. Sealby fired five shots from his revolver in the air instead.

"Take to the forerigging; get as high as possible," Sealby told Williams.

The two fled the bridge deck as the water began pouring over it and ran to the salon deck. Sealby and Williams began climbing up the rigging. Williams lost his balance and fell to the railing. He observed the captain ascend the mast with "the agility of a monkey," and then lost sight of Sealby as he climbed out of range of the searchlights.

By now, Williams thought, the stern was resting on the bottom, for the *Republic* was 570 feet in length and the depth of the water was only 270 feet. There was, in his words, a "violent roar and a jar." Williams released his grip and fell into the water.

Sealby meanwhile was continuing his climb up the rigging. He covered a distance of almost 100 feet. He tried a second time to activate the blue light. Once again he found the flare was too wet. Giving up, he fired the last round in his revolver.

Slowly, the *Republic* began to sink beneath the water. Williams observed, "When the water closed over the vessel there seemed to be a great hole in the water, and there was a roar like thunder." It was at 8:40 PM, on January 24, 1909, many hours after her collision with the *Florida*, when the White Star Line *Republic* plunged forty-five fathoms to the bottom of the ocean.

In the water, Second Officer Williams struggled to get as far away from the sinking liner as he could. He was fearful of being carried under by the suction, but to his surprise it was weaker than he anticipated. He was able to swim from the *Republic*'s grave with relatively little difficulty.

Williams came upon a three-by-five-foot grating hatch and tried to get on top of it, but each time it capsized and he was dunked into the water. He gave up and simply clung to it. Later, he came across another hatch and used the two to support his body above the water.

Captain Sealby had a similar experience. As the liner plunged to the bottom, he found himself caught in a whirlpool. Fortunately the air under the greatcoat he was wearing kept him buoyant. After he was pulled under a few times, however, the coat became soaked and was a liability rather than an asset and he tried unsuccessfully to peel it off. He managed to swim to a nearby floating table and to cling tightly to it.

Not far away, Second Officer Williams was waiting for help to arrive. He knew from the way the searchlights were plying over the water that the *Gresham* and *Senca* were looking for him and the captain. To his relief, he saw one of the lifeboats coming straight towards him, and he was soon hauled aboard.

Captain Sealby was still holding onto the table, but growing weak and numb from the cold. He managed to reload his revolver and fired a shot in the air and was surprised that it still worked after being in the water. After a few minutes, he fired a second shot.

Shortly thereafter the lifeboat containing Williams appeared. Sealby picked up a towel floating nearby and waved it frantically. The boat's crew spotted him and quickly came to his rescue.

"Game to the last," Sealby told Williams as he came aboard the boat. "She went down with her colors flying."

Shortly after the disaster, a controversy surfaced. First class passenger James Connolly, while aboard the *Baltic*, let it be known that he was angered by the crew's failure to save any of the baggage. He was also critical of Captain Ransom and the ship's purser for not allowing him to send a message by wireless.

While Connolly was chatting with a few friends, the *Republic*'s barber, G.F. Fletcher, appeared and gave maritime writer Connolly a piece of his mind. "You have little to do to talk of cowards. You were the coward. You tried to force your way into the boats ahead of the women and children."

A fight nearly erupted but Connolly's friends separated the two. Later, though, a steward wrote an affidavit which stated:

Dr. J.J. Marsh pushed Connally back when he tried to get ahead of the women and children who were being transferred from the *Florida* to the *Baltic*. I stood at the top of the gangway for twelve hours without moving, and I saw this happen."

Fletcher and one of the *Republic*'s chefs signed as witnesses.

Connolly emphatically denied this. He charged the *Baltic* with "looking after her company's property." He claimed the men in charge of the boats "didn't even know how to pull an oar." He blamed the *Republic* for steaming too fast in the fog and concluded "the fog-speed law is a farce."

Despite this controversy, the atmosphere in New York was one of excitement. When the *Florida* arrived in port, the Italian Consul General greeted Captain Ruspini with a kiss and told him, "Your conduct has been noble and I have come here expressly to tell you so." Both Sealby and Binns were greeted at the pier by cheering crowds. "Hail the Conquering Hero" was played especially in their honor. The name "Jack" Binns became a household word both in America and Great Britain.

Three years later, another White Star Liner was to founder. When the rescue ship arrived with the survivors, there were no cheering crowds or songs to greet them. There was only an atmosphere of grief.

8 ■ APRIL 15, 1912

The *Titanic*
The Ship "God Himself Could Not Sink"

DURING THE early part of the 20th century, the seafarers of the world experienced an increasing confidence they never had known before. To many mariners, the sea seemed less dangerous and formidable than it had in the previous centuries. The modern ship with a steel hull and watertight compartments was much safer than the old wooden craft of the past.

By 1912, the greatest achievement of the shipping world was the new R.M.S. (Royal Mail Steamer) *Titanic*. Launched on May 31, 1911, the White Star Liner was by far the largest vessel afloat. She was 46,328 gross tons and had 66,000 tons displacement, which made the ship half again the size of either of her Cunard line rivals, the *Lusitania* and the *Mauretania*.

Her dimensions were equally immense. She was 175 feet from keel to the top of her four funnels (higher than the Statue of Liberty less her pedestal), 92.5 feet in width (about half the height of the Leaning Tower of Pisa), and 882.5 feet in length. The *Titanic* was so huge that if placed vertically by the base of the Metropolitan Tower, then one of the largest edifices in New York, she would surpass it by 182½ feet.

Another amazing feature of this vessel was the modern luxurious accommodations. Competing with the Cunard Liners, the White Star Line installed a Turkish bath, a modern gymnasium equipped with an electrical horse and camel, a swimming pool, a squash court, a French "sidewalk cafe" and other items of comfort that the early 20th century could offer. The *Titanic* even had elevators, a convenience not common on most passenger liners at this time.

In addition to her comforts and size, the *Titanic* also offered speed. Triple screw, the ship had two sets of four cylinder reciprocating engines each driving a 38-ton wing propeller and a set of low pressure turbine engines powering a 22-ton center screw. Together, these engines could produce well over 50,000 horsepower and at full speed the ship could make between 24–25 knots, which exceeded the top speed of most liners in 1912.

The most notable feature of this engineering marvel was its safety design. It was constructed with a cellular double bottom and was divided into sixteen watertight compartments. The bulkheads separating the compartments were fitted with watertight doors which could be closed by an electrical switch in the bridge making the *Titanic*—in the words of her builders—"virtually unsinkable." This description, unfortunately, was sensationalized by the press which publicized the *Titanic* as "unsinkable."

In actuality, the *Titanic* had a fatal flaw in her design. The bulkheads did not extend to the top deck of the ship. In some of the middle compartments, the bulkheads ran only as high as E deck. This meant if the first five compartments were flooded, the ship would list and the water would overflow into the remaining compartments. Yet an occurance of this situation seemed impossible, leading one member of her crew to say, "God Himself could not sink this ship."

With the ship prepared for her maiden voyage, the White Star Line began to muster a crew worthy of this vessel. The company installed the Commodore of the Line, Edward J. Smith, as captain. A tall, well-built man of sixty-two, Captain Smith, or "E.J" as he was called, had been at sea for over thirty years and was one of the most respected captains on the North Atlantic. He had commanded no fewer than seventeen vessels for the White Star Line including the *Titanic*'s sistership, the *Olympic*. This stern but good natured man was to command the *Titanic* on her maiden voyage and then retire.

Once aboard his new command, "E.J." decided to replace his chief officer, William M. Murdock. He chose Henry Wilde to be the new chief officer and reassigned Murdock to first officer. The old first officer, Charles Lightoller, became second officer replacing David Blair, who was transferred.

During this shuffle of posts, the binoculars for the crow's nest were misplaced, a seemingly minor but ultimately fateful matter. What apparently happened was that Blair who was in charge of the glasses had them locked in his quarters before leaving. When Lightoller took his place, he was unable to locate them, but he assured the lookouts that he would provide them with the binoculars, although in the rush of events, nothing of the sort was done. Hence the six lookouts were deprived of binoculars on this voyage.

In addition to the shakeup of senior officers, the crew encountered many other problems before sailing day. Many of them were strangers to both the ship and each other. Some of the crew members had spent hours just finding one particular room on the large liner. It took Second Officer Lightoller, for instance, two full weeks before he could move from one area of the ship to another by the shortest route.

On sailing day, April 10, 1912, there were difficulties maneuvering out of Southampton. As the mammoth liner edged out of the harbor, the suction caused by her huge propellers drew the moored American Liner *New York* from her dock in her direction. The cables attached to the *New York* snapped like string and the vessel drifted out of control towards the *Titanic*. Collision seemed certain until Captain Smith ordered the engines be stopped. The tugboats *Vulcan* and *Neptune* quickly towed the *New York* back to her pier. It would appear that both the captain and the pilot had underestimated the power of such a huge liner.*

After the *New York* was safely returned to her dock, the *Titanic* sailed out of Southampton for Queenstown via Cherbourg. The next day, with all passengers and cargo aboard, the new liner resumed her maiden voyage to New York City. Among the First Class passengers were business tycoon John Jacob Astor, smelting and mining king Benjamin Guggenheim, Macy's store partner Isador Straus, railroad giants Charles Hays and John B. Thayer,

*Some time earlier, the *Olympic* collided with the cruiser *Hawke* under similar conditions. It wasn't until the near collision with the *New York* that the suction theory was taken seriously.

the *Titanic*'s builder Thomas Andrews, who was aboard to iron out any bugs, White Star Line managing director Bruce Ismay, and many other figures of wealth and status, collectively worth over $250,000,000. Included in its cargo was a new English automobile, expensive chinaware, and a jewel-encrusted copy of the *Rubaiyat* of Omar Khayyam.

The *Titanic* was well on its way to New York on April 14, 1912, when the captain received an iceberg warning from the S.S. *Caronia* at 9:00 AM that day, reporting that she encountered ice at 42° north latitude, 49° to 50° west longitude. The *Titanic*'s master formally acknowledged the message. It was the first ice warning the "floating palace" was to receive that fateful day.

At 1:42 PM, another message, this one from the *Baltic*, pointed to the presence of ice in the same general vicinity of the *Caronia*. Three minutes later, the *Baltic*'s warning was followed by a wireless message from 41° north latitude, 50° west longitude by the *Amerika*. Again the *Titanic* relayed her thanks and continued on her course.

To her master, Captain Smith, this was of little danger for shipbuilding had come a long way since the days of the *Arctic*. Ships of this century are much more sturdier than the wooden vessels of the past. Smith himself reflected on this security five years earlier when in command of the *Adriatic*. When once asked if he thought the modern ship could remain afloat long enough for the company to abandon ship, he replied, "I will go a bit further. I will say I can not imagine any condition which would cause a ship to founder. I can not conceive of any vital disaster happening to this vessel [*Adriatic*]. Modern shipbuilding has put an end to that."

Moreover the weather was clear, which meant the icebergs should be seen in time. Nevertheless he did not completely ignore these warnings. He informed his employer, Bruce Ismay, of the *Baltic*'s warning and consulted his officers on the subject. If visibility were to be in the least bit hazy, they were to slow down. Otherwise he would remain in his quarters and the ship would continue at the speed of 22½ knots.*

---

*Some of the *Titanic*'s boilers were not in service at this time. Hence her top speed was not to be reached.

The venerable seaman may not have been aware of two important factors. First, visibility might seem clear from the bridge but higher above in the crow's nest it could be hampered by mist. The second point was the lookouts lacked binoculars.

By 7:30 PM, one of the *Titanic*'s wireless operators overheard a message from the Leyland Line *Californian* to the S.S. *Antillian*: "To the Captain, *Antillian* 6:30 PM apparent ship's time: lat. 42° 3/ n., long. 40°9/ w. Three large bergs five miles to the southward of us." The message was dispatched to the bridge but the ship continued on her maiden voyage at the previously set speed.

As the *Titanic* steamed closer to the ice field, the sea temperature began to drop. At 7:30 that Sunday night, it was 39°. By 9:00, the temperature was down to 33°. Concerned, Second Officer Lightoller alerted the engine room to watch the fresh water supply for it could freeze up. He also instructed Sixth Officer Moody to warn the lookouts in the crow's nest to be on the alert for icebergs and growlers. For caution's sake, he had the junior officer repeat the message as Moody had forgotten to mention growlers the first time he phoned it in.

It would seem that the second officer did not act with undue concern. At 9:40, a message came in from the *Mesaba* stating "much heavy pack ice and a great number of large icebergs. Also field ice." The position reported was latitude 42° to 41° north, longitude 49° to 50° 30/ west, which was right in the *Titanic*'s path. The White Star liner's senior wireless operator, Jack Phillips, replied, "R. Tks" (Received Thanks). However, some maritime historians believe he did not send this vital message to the bridge but instead lost it in a stack of Marconigrams.

Soon it was four bells (10:00). The first officer relieved Lightoller as Officer on Watch. After a brief conversation about speed, position, weather and the ice reports, the second officer left the bridge, leaving Murdock in charge of the ship. Murdock was aware, as Captain Smith was, of the ice problem but he made no arrangements for extra lookouts. Nor was speed reduced by a fraction of a knot.

At the same time Murdock came on duty, lookouts Fredrick Fleet and Reginald Lee reported to duty in the crow's nest. After being briefed on the situation by the men they were relieving, the two lookouts began their watch over the cold calm Atlantic. In addition to a lack of moonlight, vision was handicapped by the absence of waves that would reveal any obstacles by washing against them and by a slight degree of haze. Lee remembered his partner remarking, although Fleet denied saying it, "Well, if we can see through that, we'll be lucky."

Other parts of the ship were more lively. A few of the passengers were having a small dinner in honor of their captain. The company included streetcar magnate George Widener and his son Harry; Clarence Moor; President Taft's military aide, Archie Butt; and of course "E.J." Nearby, Spencer S. Silverthorne was seated comfortably in an armchair reading the best seller *The Virginian*, while Lucien P. Smith was engaged in a game of bridge with three Frenchmen. Elsewhere, passengers were involved with card games while two acquaintances, Hugh Woolner and Lieutenant Hokan Bjornstrom, were enjoying warm drinks.

Down in the galley, Chief Night Baker Walter Belford was baking rolls for the following day. On the after bridge, Quartermaster George Rowe was standing watch. In the wheel house, Robert Hitchens, another quartermaster, was acting helmsman.

At 11:00 PM, Senior Operator Jack Phillips was still on duty. For him it was a long hard day. The Marconi set had been repaired recently and the delayed messages were piling up. He attempted to reach Cape Race for passenger telegrams when the Leyland Line *Californian* intervened, "Say, Old Man, We Are Surrounded By Ice And Stopped." The *Californian's* operator forgot to use the MSG (Master's Service Gram) and consequently Phillips did not realize its importance. Angrily, he relayed back, "Shut Up, Shut Up! I Am Busy. I Am Working Cape Race!" It was a vital warning but it did not reach the bridge.

By 11:40, activity on the ship began to quiet down. The crew were due to rotate in twenty minutes. Up in the crow's nest, Fredrick Fleet and his co-lookout Reginald Lee stood their uneventful watch. Occasionally the two would talk about the cold but mostly it was silence.

Then Fleet saw it. It was a dark object straight in the path of the ship. There was no mistaking its identity—an iceberg. Quickly, Fleet rang the crow's nest bell three times. He lifted the phone and called down to the bridge.

"What did you see?" asked Sixth Officer Moody.

"Iceberg right ahead," answered Fleet.

"Thank you," Moody courteously replied.

With the warning passed to him by Moody, the first officer acted quickly. He pulled the engine telegraph to Full Speed Astern, closed the watertight doors, and ordered Quartermaster Hitchens to put the helm "a hard-a-starboard."

High above, Fleet and Lee stood by and watched the iceberg draw nearer and nearer. Finally, thirty-seven seconds after phoning the warning, the ship turned at what seemed to be the last possible instant and the berg swept across the starboard side. It had appeared to Fleet that the sea had granted the *Titanic* a reprieve.

Then unexpectedly, there was a jolt throughout the entire ship. Quartermaster Rowe on the after bridge noticed a break in the rhythm of the engines. He turned and saw an iceberg, he judged, about 100 feet above the water.

Miss Edwina Troutt was awakened and noticed that the vibration of the engines had stopped. Putting on her coat and shoes, she went into the passage way to inquire what happened, and was reassured by a steward that it was nothing serious.

Seventeen-year-old Jack Thayer was preparing for bed when he felt a jar so slight that if he had a bowl of water, he thought, not one drop would spill to the floor.

Sixty-one years later, Margaret Delaney would recall being in her room with two friends when she felt the ship "shudder." She then noticed that the engines stopped.

In C-51, Colonel Archabel Gracie, a military historian and author of *The Truth About Chickamauga*, was awakened by a sudden shock and noise from somewhere forward on the starboard side of the ship. At first, Gracie thought the *Titanic* had collided with another vessel.

He jumped out of bed and made his way to the door. A quick look in the corridor revealed nothing. He wasn't able to hear the ship's engines vibrating; only the sound of escaping steam was audible.

Gracie dressed and wrapped himself warmly in a Norfolk coat and went topside to investigate. He looked out over the portside to see what they had struck.

Seeing nothing, the Colonel climbed over the iron gate and fence that separated the first class from the second. Although thankful no officer was around to remind him of the "not allowed" sign posted by the fence, he did not think that this breach of rules would hurt anyone under these circumstances.

Three decks below in the second class quarters, London schoolmaster Lawrence Beesley felt "an extra heave of the engines and a more than usual obvious dancing motion of the mattress." He too noticed that the engines had stopped. Beesley was under the impression that a propeller blade was lost.

He rushed into the hall near the salon, came across a steward and asked why they had stopped.

"I don't know, sir," the steward replied, "but I don't suppose it is anything wrong."

Below the jolt was more terrifying. As First Officer Murdock closed the watertight doors, Fireman Fred Barrett and Engineer James Hesketh quickly escaped from No. 6 boiler room to No. 5 boiler room just as the watertight door separating the two compartments closed. Other crew members were not as fast and were forced to climb ladders and leave through escape hatches.

Some 10–15 miles away, Charles Victor Groves, the third officer of the *Californian*, noticed a steamer approaching from the east. From the blaze of light there was no doubt it was a large passenger liner. Groves tried to contact the vessel by the Morse lamp and inform her that the *Californian* was stopped by ice but he received no response. At around 11:40, the other ship stopped and most of her lights seemed to go out.

Back on the *Titanic*, First Officer Murdock pulled the engine telegraph levers to "Stop." The officer clearly knew he had failed to avoid the iceberg. No sooner had he put the engines at "Stop" than Captain Smith appeared on the bridge.

"Mr. Murdock, what was that?"

"An iceberg, sir. I hard-a-starboard and reversed engines, and I was going to hard-a-port round it but she was too close."

"Close the emergency doors."

"The doors are already closed."

With that, Smith, Murdock, and Fourth Officer Boxhall rushed out on the port wing. Murdock extended his arm and pointed to a large dark object. After it disappeared, the captain sent the fourth officer below on a fast inspection tour. Boxhall reported a few minutes later that he had been as far forward in the steerage as he could go and found no damage.

Not satisfied, the ship's commander ordered the officer to find the carpenter and get him to "sound the ship." Boxhall climbed down the bridge ladder when he bumped into Carpenter Hutchinson, who muttered, "She's making water fast!" as he dashed to the bridge.

Not far behind him, mail clerk Iago Smith pushed on toward the bridge past Boxhall, shouting, "The mail hold is filling rapidly!"

Upon hearing the reports from Hutchinson and Smith, "E.J." took a look at the commutator to check the ship's stability. "Oh my God," he said to himself, for the needle revealed the ship was already listing by 5° to starboard.

At this time, Chief Officer Wilde appeared on the bridge and inquired of the captain about the seriousness of the damage. "Certainly," he answered, "I'm afraid it's more than serious."

Next to arrive was Bruce Ismay, White Star Line president. He asked about the meaning of the jolt. Captain Smith told him the news of the iceberg. Persistent, Ismay asked if the *Titanic*'s damage was serious. After a pause, Smith answered, "I'm afraid she is."

Indeed she was seriously damaged. Below, the "black gang" was busily closing the dampers and drawing the fires. Within ten minutes of the collision, water had poured in at such a rate that escaping air forced up the No. 1 hatch cover and hissed out of the fore deck tanks. Water was also seen swirling around the foot of spiral stairs in the cargo area. In the mail hold, the clerks gave up the losing battle to salvage the letters and packages.

With these reports piling in, the captain decided to inspect the damage himself. First, he ordered the wireless operators, Phillips and Harold Bride, to stand by to relay a distress call. Then he called for Thomas Andrews, the ship's builder, to join him on his inspection tour.

Of all aboard, only Andrews could study the ship's damage and evaluate it correctly. He knew every detail of the ship from the simple ice-making machine to the low-pressure turbine engine.

Andrews also seemed to know the passengers and crew of the ship as well as he knew the vessel itself.

Now he was called on to perform an important task. To inspect the damage first hand, he and the captain took the crew's stairway below to attract less attention. The two men then applied their knowledge of the ship and concluded the *Titanic* had a 300-foot-long gash with the first five compartments flooded.

Andrews carefully explained to the captain what was to be expected. The bulkheads separating the compartments did not extend to the top deck. If all of the first four compartments were flooded instead of five, the ship would not list enough for the water to fall into the twelve behind them. But with the first five exposed to the sea, the list would be enough to overflow into the remaining eleven until all of the compartments would be flooded. The conclusion therefore was simple if gloomy: the *Titanic* was going to sink.

The situation was indeed dire. Both Andrews and Smith knew that the *Titanic* carried only sixteen conventional lifeboats and four Englehardt collapsibles. Altogether the boat capacity was 1,178 people or 52 percent of the 2,207 aboard. This left about 1,029 at the mercy of the sea which was a frigid 28°.

As the Captain returned to the bridge, he realized there was some hope. The *Titanic's* Marconi set might be able to summon help from the nearby vessels. Possibly one or more of them might arrive in time to rescue all aboard. This seemed promising since by now the lights of a ship could be seen.

A few minutes after midnight, on April 15, Captain Smith began dispensing orders to his assembled officers. He instructed Chief Officer Wilde to uncover the lifeboats, First Officer Murdock to gather the passengers, Sixth Officer Moody to get the list of boat assignments, and Fourth Officer Boxhall to wake up Second Officer Lightoller and Third Officer Pitman. Smith then made his way to the wireless shack and ordered Phillips and Bride to "send the call for assistance."

Phillips took the headphones from the junior operator and began to send out the emergency call. With the *Titanic's* position as worked out by the fourth officer, the senior operator began tapping, "CQD," the standard call of distress, followed by "MGY" (the *Titanic's* call letters) and the position with a few words to describe the general situation. Again and again, Phillips relayed the message across the Atlantic.

Some 10–15 miles away, Wireless Operator Cyril F. Evans of the Leyland Line *Californian* (call letters MWL) was in his bunk reading a magazine. He closed down his set at 11:30 shortly after giving the *Titanic* an ice warning which was sharply cut off. With no one to relieve him, there was no one to keep watch. He made no attempt to talk with his usual night company, Third Officer Groves.

"What ships have you got, Sparks?" Groves asked as he entered the cabin.

"Only the *Titanic*," Evans responded.

Interested, Groves placed the headphones over his ears and tried to tune in on the White Star Liner. He listened carefully but was unable to hear anything. Groves had forgotten to wind up the magnetic detector, and consequently he heard nothing.

Meanwhile, on the *Titanic*, Fourth Officer Boxhall had little difficulty in awakening Second Officer Lightoller. "You know we have struck an iceberg?" he said as he barged into the cabin.

"I know we have struck something," Lightoller replied, dressing for duty.

In a few minutes, the evacuation process had begun. Chief Officer Wilde had some of the men uncover the lifeboats. Charles Joughin, the baker, had his staff prepare food for the boats. In other areas of the ship, Doctor O'Laughlin, the chief surgeon, purser McElroy and some stewards were calming the passengers. The situation was thus far harmonious.

The crew, however, soon faced numerous difficulties. In addition to the problem of insufficient lifeboats, there were many passengers who actually refused to leave the sinking vessel. Many, such as Isador Straus and Ben Guggenheim, balked at boarding a lifeboat before others. Some women, such as Mrs. Isador Straus, wanted to remain with their husbands. Still others could not believe a modern liner such as the *Titanic* could sink. After all, she *was* "unsinkable."

Many of the crew members dealt with this problem with outright force. Mrs. Emil Taussig was clinging to her husband when two seamen tore them apart and dropped her into lifeboat No. 8.

Two others did the same to Mrs. Charlotte Collyer, who had refused to leave her family. Joughin, the baker, used similar methods for some women he found on the promenade deck.

Miss Edwina Troutt was returning to her room when she encountered an officer who told her to put on a life jacket and proceed to the boat deck. Troutt quickly went back to her cabin and aroused her roommate. The two donned their life jackets and went topside.

Nine-year-old Frank Goldsmith awakened to find his mother dressing him. Then, with his parents and sixteen-year-old Alfred Rush, who was traveling with the Goldsmiths, he went topside.

Some of the passengers stood on the deck and listened to the soft music the *Titanic*'s band was playing. Bandmaster Wallace Henry Hartley and his musicians stood in the First Class lounge playing ragtime. Later they moved near the grand staircase and continued their music. This pleased the crowd who did not suspect the danger they were in.

Finally, after much confusion, a few lifeboats were filled. First Officer Murdock gave the order to lower the first lifeboat, No. 7. Soon other boats followed.

On the after bridge, Quartermaster Rowe became suspicious. He already had felt the jolt and saw an iceberg. Now he was seeing lifeboats floating off by the side. He phoned the bridge and asked for an explanation. Realizing he had forgotten him, "E.J." ordered Rowe to gather the distress rockets and report to the bridge.

There, Rowe and Boxhall were ordered by Captain Smith to "fire one and fire one every five minutes."

About ten miles away, Apprentice James Gibson of the *Californian* noticed a brilliant light in the sky. It came, he saw, from the strange ship that had stopped an hour or so ago. Within minutes, more rockets were exploding over the mysterious ship.

The O.O.W., Second Officer Herbert Stone, also spotted the bright light. It was a white colored rocket he observed. It seemed strange to him that a ship out in the middle of the Atlantic would stop and fire rockets. By use of the speaking tube, Stone informed Captain Stanley Lord of the white rockets. Lord ordered the second officer to hail the other ship with the Morse lamp. Oddly, the captain did not bother to come out on deck and see for himself, or did he make an effort to awaken "Sparks" to find the meaning of the affair.

Inside the *Titanic*'s wireless cabin, Senior Operator Phillips was making better progress. By 12:30, he had made contact with the Cunard Liner *Carpathia*. Her wireless operator, Harold Cottam, had reached the *Titanic* with some private messages. Phillips immediately brushed them aside and tapped back, "Come At Once. We Have Struck A Berg. . . . Position 41°46/ North 50° 14/ West."

A few minutes later, MPA (The *Carpathia*'s call letters) informed the *Titanic* that she was 58 miles away and was "coming hard."

Captain Smith welcomed the news of the *Carpathia*. He then asked what code of emergency they were using. "CQD," replied Phillips. This gave the junior operator an idea. Why not, asked Harold Bride, use the new code, S.O.S. It may be, he said, their "last chance to send it!" A brief laugh followed that remark but Phillips took Bride's advice. So at 12:45 AM, on Monday, April 15, 1912, the *Titanic* dispatched S.O.S. The *Titanic*, it should be noted, contrary to legend was not the first to dispatch an S.O.S.

Meanwhile, more lifeboats were lowered. With Third Officer Pitman in charge, Lifeboat No. 5 was launched. Fifth Officer Lowe, while working No. 5's davits, was annoyed by a man trying to be helpful to the point of distracting him. With one hand on the davit and the other waving in the air, the man shouted, "Lower away! Lower away! Lower away! Lower away!"

"If you'll get the hell out of the way," Lowe said angerly, "I'll be able to do something! You want me to lower away quickly? You'll have me drown the whole lot of them!"

Without uttering a word, the man walked to Lifeboat No. 3. Lowe was to later discover that he was talking to his employer, Bruce Ismay.

Thomas Andrews was aiding in a more useful manner. He strongly advised the women to wear their life jackets and to enter the boats as quickly as they can. "You cannot pick and choose your boat. Don't hesitate," he urged, "Get in, get in!" Despite these warnings many women refused to depart in a boat.

Some 58 miles away, the 13,500-ton *Carpathia* was steaming as fast as she could to reach the *Titanic*. Her master, Captain Arthur Rostron, ordered his chief engineer to put all available stokers to work. To generate more energy, he had the heat cut down and piled every ounce of steam in the engines.

Rostron made other preparations. He had First Officer Dean and Second Officer Bisset ready the lifeboats for rescue work and prepare to drop nets and ladders along the side to haul up people, and he placed extra lookouts to be on the alert for ice and wreckage. He also alerted the ship's chief surgeon, Dr. McGhee, to expect the possibility of required medical help for a large number of individuals.

With these measures taken and a new course set, the *Carpathia* began to cruise, not at her usual speed of 14 knots, but at an amazing 17½! Everyone, including Rostron, did not expect such speed, yet the little Cunard liner was doing it.

Within a few hours, the lookouts thought they spotted the *Titanic* or at least a large object with a light. A closer look revealed that it was not the doomed ship but a star reflected off an iceberg.

The *Carpathia* swerved around it and continued on her course. It was getting late and they still had a long way to go. Regardless, Rostron was determined to steam onwards in the race against the clock.

Back on the *Titanic*, time was running out. Some of the crew were trying to help matters with the ship's pumps. In No. 5 boiler room, Fireman Barrett and Engineers Harvey and Shepherd, along with a few others, began to set up the pumps. One of them, Shepherd, broke his leg in the process. By 1:00, the pumps were working and spirits began to lift slightly.

Suddenly, the water came pouring in. The pumps could not keep pace. The bulkhead between the two rooms finally collapsed under the excessive pressure, rendering the pumps ineffective.

As the doom of the *Titanic* became evident, more passengers entered the lifeboats on a voluntary basis. Seven-year-old Eva Hart and her mother were placed aboard a lifeboat by her father, Benjamin. He told Eva to "look after Mummy." As the boat dropped down to the sea, Eva Hart saw her father leaning over the deck rail and knew it would be the last she would ever see of him.

The Goldsmith family encountered a gate on its way to the deck. The crew stationed there allowed only women and children. Mr. Goldsmith said to his son, "So long Frankee, I'll see you later." A member of the crew offered his arm to Alfred Rush, but the boy said, "No. I'm going to stay here with the men."

On the starboard side, Lifeboat No. 13 was in the process of being lowered when a crew member aboard called back, "Any ladies on your deck?"

Lawrence Beesley who was standing nearby replied, "No."

"Then you had better jump," came the reply and with that Beesley climbed aboard the boat.

On the other side of the ship, Lightoller ordered Lifeboat No. 6 to be lowered away. It was half way down the side when he noted that the craft had only one crewman aboard. Lightoller called for a seaman but there was none around. First class passenger Arthur Peuchen offered his services since he was a yachtsman, and Lightoller allowed him to pass if he could climb down the side of the vessel. With no difficulty at all Peuchen slid down the rope and into the boat. With no further delays, Lifeboat No. 6 rowed away from the stricken liner.

While the first and second class passengers were experiencing little difficulty in gaining access to the boats, the bulk, those in steerage, were facing problems. Many of them could not speak English or understand the orders to put on their life jackets. Interpreter Mullen found it nearly impossible to explain to a group of Finns and Swedes to abandon ship, and wasn't even successful in getting them to don their life jackets. Besides the obvious language barrier, Mullen failed because he was alerting them to the danger they were in while at the same time trying to reassure the immigrants by telling them there was nothing to be concerned about.

In another area of the ship, the efforts were reversed. Kathy Gilnagh, Kate Mullins and Kate Murphy were barred from the boat deck by a seaman. Another Irish passenger by the name of Jim Farrell, however, demanded, "Great God, man! Open the gate and let the girls through!"

Near the bow, Daniel Buckley and a few other third class passengers also encountered a closed gate. When the men tried to pass through, the seaman on duty locked it. One of the third class passengers threw his weight against the gate and smashed it. The seaman fled and Buckley and his group raced on deck.

A similar situation developed in the after well deck. Olaus Abelseth and other steerage passengers waited for a long while for the gates to be opened. Finally an officer appeared and called for the women and children. It wasn't until the last boat pulled away that the men were allowed up.

Margaret Delaney recalled seventy-one years later that she and her two friends were on their way topside when one grew ill and could not go any further. She left her friends to seek help, reached the boat deck, and decided to board a lifeboat.

By 1:30, one hour and fifty minutes after the mishap, signs of panic began to appear. A mob made a rush on lifeboat No. 14. Fifth Officer Lowe, who was in charge of the boat, and his men cleared most of them out. One of the panicky passengers, Daniel Buckley, managed to get a woman's shawl over his head and was able to stay aboard.

The davit men began to lower the boat once more when another group of men rushed the boat. Seaman Scarrott held them back with the boat's tiller. "If any one else tries that," Lowe called back, "this is what he'll get!" With that he fired three shots from his revolver. Lowe found no further trouble and Boat No. 14 dropped down to the sea.

Boat No. 15 had similar problems. A wave of men made an attempt to board it. This time, they had to deal with the first officer. "Stand back! Stand Back!" he shouted, "It's women first!"

At the forward end of the ship, a rush was made on a collapsible. C. Purser McElroy fired twice in the air. "Get out of this!" Murdock told them, "Clear out of this!"

This time some of the men balked and it took force to evict them. With the help of passenger Hugh Woolner and his friend Lt. Steffanson, Murdock and the purser cleared the boat. With its problems behind it, Collapsible C was lowered away with Quartermaster Rowe in charge. Along with the woman and children, the boat contained Bruce Ismay, who had been working the davits of some of the boats for the last hour or so. Now, at the last moment, he climbed aboard the boat. It was, as young Jack Thayer explained, ". . . every man for himself."

On the portside, Lightoller faced the same problem. A group of men dropped into one of the boats. The second officer produced a handgun and forced them out. It was entirely bluff for the gun was empty.

At 1:40, the eighth and last rocket was fired. Again there was no response. Giving up, Boxhall took charge of Boat No. 2. A few minutes later No. 4, the last of the conventional lifeboats, was lowered to the sea. The drop wasn't much, only fifteen feet. Time was running out.

There was only one boat left on the boat deck, Collapsible D. Lightoller took no more chances. He ordered a few crewmen to lock arms around the Englehardt and allow only women and children through. During the loading, two babies were presented by a "Mr. Hoffman." He was in reality a Mr. Navratil and the children had been kidnapped from his estranged wife.

While women and children were boarding, two women, Miss Edith Evans and Mrs. John Brow, approached the boat. As they neared the boat, Evans turned to her companion and told her, "You go first. You have children waiting at home."

Mrs. Brown entered. The collapsible was then lowered away without Edith Evans. The boat safely reached the water and cast off. As it pulled away, Seaman Lucas called back to Miss Evans, "There's going to be another boat put down for you." But Edith Evans was left standing on the sinking ship.

With the last boat lowered, Captain Smith began to relieve his men. At 2:05, the old mariner entered the radio shack for the last time. He gave the wireless operators their last order. "Men, you have done your full duty. You can do no more. Abandon your cabin. Now it's every man for himself." Bride and Phillips heard their commander but continued with their work. "Look out for yourselves," Smith said, "I release you." It was useless, for the two remained at their post.

Others took the captain's advice and quickly abandoned ship. Night Baker Walter Belford leaped overboard and swam for a lifeboat. Likewise, Greaser Fred Scott and Steward Cunningham dived into the icy water and swam for Lifeboat No. 4. Passenger

Fredrick Hoyt jumped from the ship and made his way for his wife in Collapsible D. After being pulled in, Hoyt took the job of rowing to keep himself warm.

Others elected to remain aboard the ship. Lightoller noticed Lamp Trimmer Samuel Hemming still on the *Titanic*. Hemming, he knew, should have gone with Lifeboat No. 6 some time earlier. The second officer approached him about this but Hemming only replied, "Oh, plenty of time yet, sir."

Some had no intentions of leaving at all. In the first class smoking room, Thomas Andrews stood alone with his arms folded. His life jacket was lying on a nearby table. A steward asked him, "Aren't you going to have a try for it, Mr. Andrews?" The *Titanic*'s builder did not answer. He just stood there and waited for the end.

Captain Smith also refused to leave his ship. For him, this night was indeed stunning. Only three hours earlier, he was enjoying a cigar after a meal in his honor. Everything was secure. Now, in a few minutes, his command would founder.

In the wireless shack, Jack Phillips began to tap out the last message before the *Titanic* was to fall silent. Harold Bride meanwhile was gathering some possessions. As he returned, he discovered a stoker "gently relieving Mr. Phillips of his life jacket."

Bride sprang at the intruder. Phillips joined in. After a brief scuffle, Bride held the stoker while Phillips swung his fist until they subdued him.

By now the water could be heard entering the bridge. Phillips and Bride dropped the stoker and raced out of the radio cabin.

Outside, Bride noticed a few crew members trying to free Collapsibles A and B. It was a difficult task owing to the list of the ship, and only after numerous attempts did they succeed in releasing them. The list, though, made lowering them impossible.

Bride was distracted by the music from the band. The tune was familiar to him. It was an Episcopal hymn entitled "Autumn." He paid no further attention to this for his life was in jeopardy.

Jack Thayer and his friend Milton Long were standing by the starboard rail preparing to abandon ship. They shook hands and wished each other good luck. Thayer told Long, "Go ahead, I'll be right with you." Long slid down the rope facing the ship. Thayer dove overboard and swam from the doomed liner.

Colonel Gracie and his shipboard companion, Clinch Smith, both tried to jump to the officer's roof but the weight of their life preservers prevented them from reaching the top. Gracie crouched down and leaped as a wave rolled in. The crest carried the Colonel to the top of the roof. Gracie turned but could not see Smith.

Some of the men were still trying to lower the collapsibles when a wave swept Bride, Lightoller and others from the ship. Behind them, the forward funnel broke off and crushed several people. At the same time, the falling funnel created a wave that pushed the group by the two collapsibles, further from the *Titanic*.

Slowly the ship dipped under the water. Within a few minutes, she was perpendicular to the Atlantic. From the lifeboats the sound of breaking glass and falling furniture could be heard. The lights blinked out as the water flooded the generator room.

Slowly the ship began to slide down into the water. She began to pick up speed as she sank deeper. Finally, at 2:20 AM, on April 15, 1912, the *Titanic*, the ship "God Himself could not sink," plunged to the bottom of the Atlantic Ocean.

Aboard the *Californian*, Second Officer Stone observed the neighboring ship disappearing. He sent Apprentice Gibson to the chart room to inform Captain Lord that the nearby ship had fired a total of eight rockets and was steaming away. At 2:20, Stone was certain the ship was gone and decided to relay the news to the captain himself via the speaking tube.

Lord took the news with no doubt that everything was fine. He made it a point to ask the second officer if the rockets were by chance company rockets. The answer was the same: they were all white light rockets. Neither the captain nor anyone else bothered to wake up Wireless Operator Evans to request an explanation from the other ship during this entire time. Nor did any of the officers bother to record the rocket firings in the ship's log. It was as if it were perfectly normal for a ship on the high seas to fire rockets in the middle of the night.

While Stone resumed his watch, the occupants in the lifeboats listened horrified to the cries of the hundreds of people in the water. One seaman in Lifeboat No. 13 advised Miss Celia Troutt and the other women to drown out the cries by screaming.

In the icy water, Colonel Gracie swam as far away from the

Titanic's grave as he could. He feared being scalded to death as had happened to some of the crew of the *Victoria* (a British battleship that sank after colliding with another warship). The suction dragged him under but he was able to make his way to the surface.

While hundreds of people struggled in the water, the lifeboats stood by and did nothing. Several were near enough to help at least some of the poor souls drifting in the water. Even so they just stood off and made no attempt to help those who were drowning or freezing to death.

Nor could all of the lifeboats claim to be overcrowded. True, some of the boats were dangerously filled, yet there were some not so nearly loaded to capacity. Lifeboat No. 1, for instance, held only twelve occupants but was made for forty. Symons, one of the lookouts who was in charge, wanted to return to the scene but the passengers aboard feared the suction and the possibility of being swamped. Third Officer Pitman met similar protest when he suggested returning to help. He gave in despite the fact that there was room in his boat for at least 25 more. In Boat No. 2, Fourth Officer Boxhall conceded to the fears of his passengers and allowed the lifeboat to drift although it could hold dozens more.

Only Lifeboat No. 14 offered any help. The bold fifth officer began to organize his boat for rescue work. He transferred the women on board to other boats. This task took considerably more time than he anticipated. At one point, he shouted to a woman, "Jump, God damn you, jump!" He noticed another "woman" in a shawl moving too quickly for her age. Lowe removed the shawl and revealed a man. Angrily, Lowe threw the man into the boat.

After forty minutes of organizing, Lowe returned to the scene and began to pluck some of the people from the sea. In all, he picked up Steward John Stewart, a passenger named W.F. Hoyt, a Japanese man floating on a door, and one other. It was a near impossibility to pick a man out of the water this night before he froze to death in the 28° temperature. Of the four Lowe rescued, one of them, Hoyt, died an hour later.

Some of the swimmers were fortunate enough to get out of the water. Eight people managed to reach Boat No. 4. Others made it to the two capsized collapsibles. Third class passenger Olaus Ableseth and about a dozen others climbed aboard Collapsible A while Second Officer Lightoller, Harold Bride, Jack Thayer, Colonel Gracie and a few others swam to Collapsible B.

For some time, the lifeboats drifted in the calm sea, although the cold weather brought discomfort to many of the survivors. Four-year-old Louise Kink found some comfort from the blanket wrapped around her.

The situation was worst for the people who stood on the two capsized Collapsibles. Some of them succumbed to the frigid water and one by one fell overboard. Second Officer Lightoller did the best he could to keep the boat buoyant but the collapsible sank deeper into the water.

At 3:30, one hour and ten minutes after the *Titanic* foundered, the Cunard Line *Carpathia* finally arrived. From the bridge, Captain Rostron discovered that he was clearly too late. He had arrived at the position the *Titanic*'s operator gave him yet there were neither lights nor any other sign of the White Star Line. Instead, Rostron discovered numerous lifeboats scattered around the vicinity. He stopped the *Carpathia* and began to retrieve the survivors.

To be certain of the *Titanic*'s fate, Captain Rostron called for the doomed ship's fourth officer and asked, "The *Titanic* has gone down?" It was more of a statement than a question. Boxhall's answer came as no surprise, "Yes, she went down at 2:30."

Once all aboard, a count was taken of the survivors. With Second Officer Lightoller, Third Officer Pitman, Fourth Officer Boxhall, Fifth Officer Lowe, Harold Bride, Olaus Abelseth, Colonel Gracie, Trimmer Hemming, Jack Thayer, and others, a total of 705 or 32 percent of the 2,207 on the maiden voyage of the *Titanic* survived. This count also revealed a total of 1,502 perished that night including Captain Smith, First Officer Murdock, Jack Phillips, the entire band, every one of the engineers, plus Thomas Andrews, John Jacob Astor, Benjamin Guggenhiem, Isidor Straus, and many others of the social elite.

By this time, the *Californian* learned of the *Titanic*'s predicament. Her chief officer, George Stewart, advised Captain Lord to awaken the wireless operator and have him make contact with the strange ship that was firing rockets. Instead, Evans reached the *Mount Temple* which informed him of the sinking.

Captain Lord wasted no time. He set course at full speed for the *Titanic*'s last position. The *Californian* arrived hours too late. Lord offered to help with the rescue but Rostron told him to search the area for bodies.

With all survivors aboard his ship, Rostron ordered a new course for New York. He also called the survivors, along with some of the *Carpathia*'s crew and passengers, to the main lounge and held services. They gave their thanks for the living and prayed for the dead.

Seventy-three years later, Dr. Robert Ballard of the Woods Hole Oceanographic Institution led an expedition to locate the *Titanic*. On September 1, 1985, his efforts were rewarded. The hulk was found by Argo, a sonar and video platform. The lost liner was broken in two with the stern 600 yards from the bow section. Between the two lay debris such as coal, safes, boilers and even a copper kettle.

The following year, Ballard returned to the site and examined the *Titanic* in more detail. Ballard concluded that the great liner split in two at about 1,000 feet below the surface as a result of water pressure. He also discovered that the vessel did not suffer a 300-foot gash as was long believed but rather that her hull plates buckled as the liner struck ice and water was able to seep into the cracks and flood the compartments.

Another recent development is the story of an alleged suicide of one of the *Titanic*'s officers. From the letters of two surviving passengers, the story emerged that a few minutes before the ship sank, an officer declared, "Gentlemen, each man for himself. Goodbye," and then shot himself. It may be true but it is the belief of this author that the incident did not take place.

Many factors contributed to the doom of the *Titanic*. The main cause was the abnormal ice conditions. Ice had been seen in the area before but it is a rare occurance for it to appear that far south. A large floe broke away and drifted towards the shipping lanes. This ice condition proved to be fatal to the *Titanic*.

Another major cause for this disaster lay with the faulty conduct of the wireless operators. At 9:40, the *Mesaba* message which reported ice right in the path of the ship was received but it may not have been relayed to the bridge. Likewise the *Californian*'s warning was cut off by a sharp reply to "shut up." Evans of the *Californian* was partly to blame for this. He interrupted Phillips without a proper signal, such as a Master's Service Gram (MSG).

Still another cause of the calamity was the visibility conditions. The night of April 14 was calm with no moon. Had there been a moon or waves to wash against the base of the berg, it might have been seen earlier. Also there was a slight amount of haze in the icefield. Thus with these conditions and without binoculars, neither Fleet nor Lee was able to spot the iceberg in sufficient time. Perhaps it would have been better if the lookouts had been posted at the bow instead of high in the crow's nest where visibility may have been hampered by mist. It is interesting that the lookouts posted lower on the *Carpathia* spotted the icebergs first.

Captain Smith shares some of the blame for the loss of his command. Despite having received numerous ice warnings, he continued on course without placing extra lookouts on duty or even slowing down so much as a fraction of a knot. On his behalf, he may not have been aware of the *Mesaba* warning and of the haze. Even so, he should have taken more prudent measures to guarantee the safety of his ship.

In this connection, it may be worth mentioning that Geoffrey Marcus, the author of *Maiden Voyage*, claims that the *Rappahannock* had notified the *Titanic* by Morse lamp on the night of April 14 of an immense icefield in her path. Marcus' source is Captain A.E. Smith, the master of the *Rappahannock*. However, as Walter Lord, the author of *A Night to Remember*, pointed out, none of the lookouts or the officers on duty recalled the event. Smith was remembering an event in the distant past and he may have been suffering from faulty memory. Walter Lord has found some evidence that the *Rappahannock* informed the *Titanic* on the night of April 13 and not the 14th.

The *Titanic* herself had some faults. Although the liner was one of the safest vessels to travel the ocean, it, like everything else created by man, was not perfect. The bulkheads separating the watertight compartments did not extend to the top. If the bulkheads had extended to the top or even one deck higher, the ship might have remained afloat and not a single life would have been lost.

It is interesting to note that had Murdock kept the *Titanic* on course, she would have collided with the iceberg head-on and only two of her compartments would have been gone.* While this is true, the author believes the first officer should not be blamed for the disaster. He did what would seem to be the logical course of action. Any criticism of his conduct would be unfair.

It would not be unfair, however, to blame Captain Stanley Lord of the *Californian* for his action or rather inaction on that fateful night. Despite hearing reports of eight rockets, he remained in the chartroom and did nothing other than to order Stone to continue Morse-ing. Lord did not have the wireless operator make contact with the nearby steamer, nor did he even come to the bridge to see the rockets for himself. It was for this reason that Lord Mersey, who conducted the formal hearings into the disaster, censured the master of the *Californian*.

Yet, in recent years, the Mercantile Marine Service Association and others have attempted to clear Captain Lord of the heavy charges against him. According to the "Lordites," there were two other ships in the icefield that night. One of these was seen by those aboard the *Titanic* while the other was the one Second Officer Stone and Apprentice Gibson observed. It was the rockets from the latter ship and not the *Titanic* that Stone and Gibson saw. Thus the "Lordites" concluded Captain Lord was unjustly accused of not rendering assistance to the *Titanic*.

Unfortunately no other ship was discovered firing rockets in the area on that night. The official inquiry made a serious attempt to find such a vessel but, as Lord Mersey reported, "no other ship to fit this theory has ever been heard of." Nor has anyone since 1912 been able to prove another steamer sent up eight white rockets at about the same time the *Titanic* fired hers.

Part of the pro-Lord theory holds the position of the *Titanic* was incorrect. Her fourth officer was, after all, calculating the position in a hurry and may have made an error. The "Lordites" believe the *Californian* was not ten miles but 25 to 30 miles from the White Star Liner.

Yet, the hydrographer of the United States Navy carefully

*Two years later, the captain of the *Royal Edward* rammed his ship directly into ice and thus minimized the damage.

studied the matter and concluded the position Boxhall worked out was correct. Furthermore, the *Carpathia*, using the position supplied by the stricken liner's wireless, was able to rush to the scene and locate the survivors without encountering any problems. Finally, Dr. Ballard, after studying the position where he found the *Titanic*, concluded that the liner was about five miles northeast of her position which puts her closer to the *Californian*.

Another point the defenders of Captain Lord raise is that both Second Officer Stone and the captain were of the opinion that the neighboring vessel was a small tramp steamer. They saw no blaze of light they would have seen if she were the White Star liner. Therefore the mysterious steamer must have been some other vessel rather than the *Titanic*.

What is overlooked is that sometime earlier when the ship appeared on scene, Third Officer Groves noticed a large amount of light. "I could see her deck lights and that made me pass the remark that she was evidently a passenger steamer," he later testified. The reason Lord and Stone failed to see a blaze of light was due to the fact that the vessel had turned two points to port.

The "Lordites" also point out that both ships, the *Titanic* and the *Californian*, were signaling with their Morse lamps but the officers of neither vessel saw a reply. Surely, the supporters of Captain Lord reason, if the *Titanic* and the *Californian* were in sight of each other, the signal lamps would have been seen.

What is not taken into account is the two steamers may have been just beyond the range of the Morse lamps. Hence they could have been Morse-ing but would not have seen each other's signals.

The defenders of Captain Lord additionally insist that some of the survivors of the *Titanic* saw the neighboring steamer move. Since the *Californian* was stationary, the ship seen from the *Titanic* could not have been the *Californian*. However, other witnesses were positive that the mysterious steamer was stationary. The people in Boat No. 8, for instance, rowed toward her until the *Carpathia* arrived. Furthermore, as Craig Wade, author of *The "Titanic": The End of a Dream*, emphasized, the *Californian* did turn in a circle while drifting which may have caused some of the *Titanic*'s survivors to conclude she was moving.

The American battleship *Maine* on its side after the mysterious explosion that sank her. (AP/Wide World Photos)

Captain A. B. Randall of the S.S. *Republic*, with his 2nd officer, Fred A. Dear, just before the disastrous sailing. (UPI/Bettmann News Photos)

The S.S. *Republic* steaming out of New York Harbor, flying the banner of the Cortelyou Club. Their members were en route to a tour of England and the Continent. (UPI/Bettmann News Photos)

The White Star liner S.S. *Titanic.* It sank on its maiden voyage with a loss of 1,517 lives among the 2,000 passengers. (AP/Wide World Photos)

The dead being unloaded from the *Empress of Ireland* disaster.
(UPI/Bettmann News Photos)

The S.S. *Lusitania*, which was torpedoed by a U-boat of the Imperial German Navy. (AP/Wide World Photos)

Banner headline of *The New York Times* of May 8, 1915. (AP/Wide World Photos)

The Lost Cunard Steamship Lusitania
X Where the First Torpedo Struck. XX Where the Second Torpedo Struck.

The S.S. *Britannic*, which was reportedly sunk by a U-boat fleet while on hospital duty in the Aegean Sea. (UPI/Bettman News Photo)

Full view of the ill-fated S.S. *Vestris* under full stem. (UPI/Bettmann News Photos)

The Italian liner *Andrea Doria* sinks to a watery grave after colliding with the Swedish liner *Stockholm*. (AP/Wide World Photos)

The Greek cruise liner *Lakonia* after the blaze which forced 900 passengers and crew to abandon ship. Scores of people died. (AP/Wide world Photos)

The capsized British ferry *Herald of Free Enterprise*, which sank in the English Channel in 1987. (UPI/Bettmann News Photos)

Without question, the evidence overwhelmingly supports the findings of the official inquiries. The *Californian* saw a steamer stop at 11:40 PM about the same time the *Titanic* collided with an iceberg. Between 12:45 and 1:45, the second officer saw eight white rockets. It was at this time the *Titanic* fired rockets. The *Titanic* sank at 2:20, which was about the same time Stone observed the nearby ship disappear. It would be an extraordinary coincidence that another vessel entered the same icefield, stopped, sent up eight rockets and sailed on or sank at the approximate time as the *Titanic*. As was mentioned before, "no other ship to fit this theory has ever been heard of."

Even if such a vessel were to be discovered, it would not excuse Captain Lord of his inaction. Had another ship shot rockets, then Lord is at fault for not coming to that vessel's rescue. In short, Captain Lord did not respond to the rockets in a seaman-like manner.

Some have argued that even if the ship the *Californian* observed was the *Titanic* and Captain Lord had rushed to her side, the Leyland liner could not have arrived in time to offer any help. When Captain Lord did learn of the *Titanic*'s predicament, it took him a few hours to reach the radioed position. Thus, the *Californian* could not have saved a single life if she had set course for the mysterious steamer immediately after the first rocket.

This may be true. Yet does this exonerate Captain Lord of his inaction? The author believes it does not. Although nothing may have changed, the master of the *Californian* could have at least attempted a rescue. Captain Rostron, it is to be remembered, also failed to arrive in time but there is a great difference between the *Carpathia*'s captain who made the attempt and Stanley Lord who made no move to help. It was his duty to try and his failure to do so should not be excused on the grounds the attempt would have been futile.

Some time after the disaster, an international convention was called to adopt measures for protection of life at sea. The route the ill-fated *Titanic* took was changed for a more southerly one. This and the formation of the International Ice Patrol were important measures against the dangers of icebergs.

Another significant reform was the new requirement dealing

with lifeboats for ships. Before the *Titanic*'s loss, any vessel exceeding 10,000 tons had to carry sixteen lifeboats to hold a total of 962 passengers and/or crew. The White Star Line did more than that. They installed enough for 1,178. This still provided boats for only 30 percent of the *Titanic*'s capacity and 52 percent of those aboard on her maiden voyage. Today, the rules demand enough lifeboats to hold every single person aboard.

In addition to having more lifeboats, rules were passed in handling of them. Boat drills were made mandatory. Also, there would be no discrimination in filling them. Lord Mersey concluded, "I am satisfied that the explanation of the excessive proportion of Third Class passengers lost is not to be found in suggestion that the Third Class passengers were in any way unfairly treated." The evidence goes against this. There have been many instances where steerage passengers were barred from going to the boat deck for the first hour or so of the sinking. Today, all passengers are allowed equal access to the lifeboats.

Along with new lifeboat laws, requirements regulating the use of radio at sea were adopted. All ships had to carry more than one operator in order to have a 24-hour radio watch. S.O.S. was formally to be used as the international distress call.

Perhaps the most important reform was not in rules but in practice. No longer would seamen believe their ships to be immune from danger. The sea is still a dangerous adversary. This is the most important lesson of the *Titanic*. Many mariners heed it well as they avoid the area near 41°43/ north latitude, 49°56/ west longitude where the ship "God Himself could not sink" rests at the bottom of the sea.

9 ■ MAY 29, 1914

The *Empress of Ireland*
"One of the Finest Steamers"

T WO YEARS after the *Titanic* horror, the shipping world was to suffer another terrible maritime disaster. This one, the loss of the *Empress of Ireland*, was one of the most appalling shipping tragedies to ever take place not just on the St. Lawrence River but, for that matter, anywhere. When the vessel plunged to the bottom of the river, more than a thousand lives were lost.

There were no indications of forecoming disaster as she rested in her Quebec City dock on May 28, 1914. To her master, Henry George Kendall, everything seemed to be in order. It appeared nothing could go wrong on his second voyage as captain of the *Empress of Ireland*.

To become captain of such an important vessel was quite an accomplishment, and was in large part due to Kendall's impressive record. He first went off to sea at fifteen aboard a training ship in Liverpool. He had been serving the Canadian Pacific Line capably for the last eleven years. In 1912, he won praise when, in command of the *Lake Champlain*, he came to the rescue of the *Corsican* after the latter had struck an iceberg. Two years later, he was entrusted with the command of the *Empress of Ireland* which was considered "one of the finest steamers engaged in the North Atlantic trade."

The *Empress of Ireland* was indeed a fine steamer. She was 548 feet in length and weighed 14,191 gross tons. Driven by quadruple expansion engines, the liner had an impressive speed of 20 knots. Although she was dwarfed by the new ships of the White Star Line and was slower than the record breakers of the Cunard Line, the *Empress of Ireland* was one of the best liners in the world.

There were few passengers as wealthy or glamorous as those who patronized the mammoth British liners. Of the 1,000 or so who embarked on the *Empress*, only Lawrence Irving, son of the famous Shakespearean actor Henry Irving and an accomplished actor in his own right, his actress wife Mable Hackney, and big game hunter Sir Henry Seton-Karr were celebrities. The remaining passengers were composed mostly of immigrants returning to their homes in the old world and 171 delegates attending the Salvation Army international conference in London.

At 4:30 that Thursday, the double screw ship slowly edged out of her pier. Bandmaster Edward Hanagan and his Salvation Army band appropriately struck up "God Be With You Till We Meet Again." They were off on their oceanic voyage to Liverpool.

By 1:20 on the morning of May 29, 1914, the *Empress of Ireland* made her routine St. Lawrence stop at Father Point. This brought back memories to Captain Kendall, for it was here that he performed his most notable deed at sea. It was neither a navigational feat nor a rescue mission, but good detective work.

Like most others on July 20, 1910, Kendall had read the account of mysterious "Dr." Crippen and his mistress Ethel Le-Neve. Both were wanted by Scotland Yard for the murder of Mrs. Crippen and were believed to be fleeing England. Henry Kendall at that time was in command of the *Montrose* and was on a voyage from Europe to Canada. He like other captains at the time, was on the lookout for the fugitives.

However, Kendall had better luck than the others. While conducting a routine inspection, he observed the behavior of two male passengers, one Mr. Robinson and his son, on the boat deck. The manner in which they were holding hands, Kendall thought, showed signs of romantic love rather than a father and son relationship.

On the scent, Kendall surreptitiously examined the Robinsons' hats as the two were dining. He found little of suspicion with the older man's hat but he found wrapped tissue paper in the rim of the "boy's" hat, evidently to make it fit a smaller head. More determined, the captain began a conversation with the two in hope his jokes would cause the older man to laugh and possibly betray dentures was which was one of the features noted about Crippen. Sure enough, when his guest chuckled, Kendall spotted what he was looking for. Later, on the boat deck, he suddenly called out "Mr. Robinson." As he expected, the older man did not respond until his "son" nudged him. He explained that he could not hear the captain on account of the weather. Kendall pretended to accept this explanation but he knew perfectly well it was because the man was not used to being addressed as Mr. Robinson.

On the ship's wireless, Kendall relayed his suspicion to Scotland Yard, and Inspector Walter Dew, who was working on the case, was immediately dispatched. Dew took passage on the faster White Star liner *Laurentic* and beat the *Montrose* to Father Point by two days.

When the *Montrose* reached Father Point, Dew spotted and apprehended Crippen and his mistress. The "Dr." was brought to trial, convicted and hanged. LeNeve was acquitted. Kendall became an instant hero.

All of this was behind him now. He courteously bade farewell to pilot Adelard Bernier as he climbed down the tug *Eureka*. Several bags of mail were exchanged between the tug *Lady Evelyn* and the *Empress of Ireland*. With all business completed, the captain put the engines at Full Speed Ahead and the *Empress* resumed her voyage.

At 2:00 AM on this fateful day, the *Empress of Ireland* passed the Cock Point gas buoy. It was then that Kendall and the officers on the bridge noticed the lights of an oncoming steamer, some ten miles away and rapidly closing in on the liner.

A few seconds later, fog descended on the St. Lawrence. This came as no surprise to the captain. The cold Atlantic winds mixed at this point with the warmer inland currents often produced fog banks. This situation would seriously complicate navigation, however.

The Norwegian collier *Storstad* was steaming upstream to her rendezvous with the pilot at Father Point. At around 2:00, her chief officer, Alfred Toftenes, who was standing watch, and others on the bridge spotted two white mastheads some distance downstream. The other ship's red light was showing, indicating she was approaching on the portside. A few seconds later, she was swallowed up by fog.

Kendall meanwhile was keeping his ship on a parallel course with the stranger at 15 knots. He saw the other ship, which he judged to be about two miles away, but suddenly it was obscured by a fog patch. Alarmed, Kendall put the engines at Full Speed Astern and gave his horn three long blasts to designate he was reversing engines.

Two miles away, the chief officer of the *Storstad* heard the three horn blast. He began to ponder the possibility of collision. The other ship appeared to be approaching on the port side, so a turn to starboard would increase the margin of passing.

Still worried, Toftenes alerted his captain, Thomas Andersen, of the predicament. Andersen came to the bridge but not in time to see the lights or hear the horn. To be on the safe side, he ordered Full Speed Astern and sounded the horn.

A short distance away, Captain Kendall heard three blasts of a horn. He peered through the fog but could not see the other vessel. When his ship came to a complete stop, he ordered the horn to be sounded to inform the stranger that he had stopped. Then he waited.

Suddenly, Kendall saw a haze of light. To his horror, two white masthead lights appeared, which meant the *Storstad* was coming straight for the *Empress*! He ran to the bridge wing and several times shouted through his megaphone, "Go Full Speed Astern."

Captain Andersen by now also realized what was happening. He quickly put the engines at Full Speed Astern. He ordered Third Officer Saxe to give the horn three blasts.

It was too late. The 3,561 ton *Storstad*, loaded with 10,000 tons of coal, struck the *Empress of Ireland* between her twin funnels. The sharp bow of the Norwegian collier, designed to pierce ice, easily cut through the liner's hull plates.

On the *Empress*, Dr. Grant, the ship's doctor, was rolled out of his bed. Just as he leaped to his feet, the cabin lights flickered off. He struggled in the darkness until he reached the door.

In another part of the ship, Alfred Keith was awakened by what he thought to be "the boat which was removing the pilot from the liner . . . bumping the side of the *Empress*." When he heard shouting, he knew it was something more serious than that. He jumped out of his bed and saw water pouring into the passageway porthole. Keith immediately woke his three roommates and told them to evacuate the cabin.

Mr. and Mrs. Atwell thought the ship had struck a rock. They quickly got up and fled their cabin to investigate.

Some, with the memory of the *Titanic* still fresh, believed they had struck an iceberg. Ensign (his real first name) Pugmire heard "a grazing sound as if we were touching a berg," and he quickly went topside to see what had happened.

The Reverend Wallett was also under the impression the ship had struck ice. He had been lying in his bed listening to the *Storstad*'s horn. Just as the last blast died he heard a crashing sound. Quickly he got out of bed and rushed to the promenade deck.

Traveling businessman J. Furgus Duncan knew exactly what had happened. Minutes earlier he heard the sounding of the horns. After the ship vibrated, he climbed up to the boat deck and saw the Norwegian collier disappear in the fog. Thinking nothing of it, he returned to his cabin but then decided it would be safer topside.

Overcoming the shock, Captain Kendall called to the other ship through his megaphone to "keep going ahead on your engines." He hoped the *Storstad* would act as a plug in the hole she had created. Andersen tried to keep his ship in the side of the liner but the two vessels separated and drifted away.

Immediately, Kendall ordered the watertight doors closed. However, the bulkhead doors were not controlled by an electrical switch in the bridge as in the case of modern liners but were instead operated by members of the crew who were to report to the deck above the doors and crank them shut. The inflowing water prevented many of the crew from even reaching their stations. A few were able to begin closing the doors but their panic forced them to flee their posts before effectively sealing the bulkheads. Hence, the water cascaded throughout the ship.

With the water pouring into the hole at an alarming rate, Kendall decided to beach his ship on the nearby shore. He notified the engine room to give him full power. Chief Engineer Sampson grimly reported there was no steam. There was now no chance of beaching the vessel in the shallow water which lay mockingly a few miles away.

In the wireless cabin, Senior Operator Ferguson took over the key and quickly relayed out, "Stand by for distress call. We have hit something." He dispatched Edward Bamford, the junior operator, to the bridge for instructions. He returned with authorization to transmit a distress signal. Without delay, Ferguson tapped out, "S.O.S., we have hit something, sinking fast, send help."

The signal was immediately picked up by the junior operator at Father Point. He quickly called it to the attention of the senior operator, John McWilliams, who took over the key and advised the tug *Eureka* and the launch *Lady Evelyn* of the *Empress*'s dire predicament. The two boats quickly set course for the liner's last position.

Meanwhile, Captain Andersen was tending to his own ship. He ordered the chief officer to sound the forward holds. Toftenes' report was encouraging. The ship, though badly damaged, was apparently still seaworthy. Andersen ordered the lifeboats to be uncovered and set course back to the scene of the collision.

Time was running out, however, for the *Empress of Ireland*. Many of her passengers were trapped below deck. The "fan" companionways, the ominous list, and the blackout made gaining access to the boat deck nearly impossible for hundreds of men, women and children. Thus during the first five minutes after the collision, several passengers were drowned.

In the bridge, Captain Kendall grimly surveyed the situation. Kendall by now knew his command was doomed. His major concern, of course, was for the safety of the passengers. He ordered his officers to "prepare to abandon ship."

Under the supervision of First Officer Jones, the crew began to uncover and launch the starboard lifeboats. They were able to lower three of them successfully but owing to the list they could not get a fourth boat waterborne. Jones slipped and fell into the river. After being pulled aboard one of the boats he had launched, Jones began organizing the flotilla for rescue work.

The men working lifeboat L's davits were encountering great difficulty. The boat came loose and plunged into the St. Lawrence carrying half a dozen men with it. The boat was righted and the crew began to take passengers aboard.

The crew on the portside were even less successful. A group of seamen worked vainly to lower boat No. 12. The list made getting the boat over the side impossible. After wasting valuable time, the davit men gave up and directed their energies to the starboard boats.

The men at No. 8 station also met disastrous results. While they were trying to lower the metallic craft, the tackle broke and the boat crushed to death one of the ship's company. It was evident the list was far too great to safely lower any more boats.

Numerous passengers meanwhile were milling about on the deck. Most were too busy asking questions to panic. "I never heard people speak with such tenderness to each other in that time of great distress and danger," commented one survivor. Most were overwhelmed with bewilderment rather than fear despite the fact the ship was listing to starboard.

Commissioner David Rees, the leader of the Salvation Army delegates, was too overcome with illness to tend to himself. A fellow salvationist found him and took him up the staircase leading to the boat deck. The list caused the other man to slip and fall down the stairway. When he emerged on deck, he could not locate Rees.

Lawrence Irving and his wife came across Fred Abbott, a first class passenger, in the passageway near their cabin. Irving asked, "Is the boat going down?" Abbott expressed the opinion that it was. Irving told his wife, "There's no time to lose" whereupon she began to cry. Irving reassured her that all will be safe as he gathered the life jackets.

"Can I help you?" Abbott asked.

"Look after yourself, old man," Irving replied, "God bless you, all the same."

Abbott left the two and made his way topside. The Irvings followed him up the slanting stairway and emerged on deck. There they meet Clayton Burt, who told them, "Save yourselves, for God's sake. We're sinking."

Elsewhere, Seton-Karr, the big game hunter, was wandering through the passageway trying to find his way to the deck. He bumped into Merton Darling who was also on his way topside. Noticing that Darling was not wearing his life jacket, Seton-Karr offered his help to fasten it on.

Other passengers were busy looking for their loved ones. Mrs. Thomas Greenaway was searching in vain for the husband she had married only the week before. She asked a few of her shipboard friends but they could not help her. Down below in the Greenaway cabin, Mr. Greenaway was gathering warm clothing for his wife and himself. He dutifully closed the portholes so no water would flow in the cabin. He quickly returned to the boat deck but was unable to find his wife.

J. Fowler, a member of the Salvation Army band, did his best to save his fellow passengers. Below deck, he tried to calm everyone in order to prevent a panic. He helped fasten life jackets on children. He then led a group of passengers up to temporary safety on the boat deck.

Seeing the lifeboats as a dangerous venture, several of the passengers dove in the water and swam clear of the sinking ship. Alfred Keith, an excellent swimmer, jumped from the portside and swam as far away from the doomed liner as he could, but he swam so carelessly that he banged his head on a floating log. Nearly unconscious, Keith held on to the log and waited for rescue.

Ten-year-old Helen O'Hara went overboard in the arms of her father. He sank to the bottom but Helen managed to break free from his grasp and swim clear. "I was very glad that I have taken swimming lessons where I go to school," she later explained. Her only difficulty was that the St. Lawrence was "awful cold."

Slowly the *Empress of Ireland* rolled over on her side. Those who remained aboard held onto the railing until the ship was portside up. To Dr. Grant, who observed the scene from a porthole, the people looked "as though they were walking down a sandy beach into the water to bathe."

J. Furgus Duncan lost his grip and tumbled into the river. He surfaced and found himself surrounded by a group of people, who, panicking, seized him and began to drag him under. Duncan broke free and swam away from them and the ship.

Captain Kendall was also thrown overboard. When he surfaced he discovered a piece of wreckage floating nearby and clung to it until one of the ship's lifeboats picked him up. He took command of the boat and set out to help others in the water.

Newlywed Thomas Greenaway had resigned himself to the fact that his bride was dead. He could not, he thought, live without her. So he took firm hold of the rail and waited for the ship to drag him under.

He didn't have to wait long. Finally, fourteen minutes after her collision with the *Storstad*, the *Empress of Ireland* rolled over. To Captain McIntyre of the Salvation Army it appeared "as if she turned turtle." An explosion rocked the liner, throwing many aboard her into the water. Seconds later the ship was at the bottom of the river.

In the open water, Greenaway was clinging to a floating table. The explosion had thrown him clear of the sinking ship. He no longer entertained thoughts of suicide although he still believed his wife had perished. He decided instead to hang on to the table and wait for one of the boats to pick him up.

Unknown to Greenaway, his wife was also thrown from the ship by the explosion. She landed on a floating deck chair with only superficial burns and cuts. Ultimately, a lifeboat came and fished her out.

Mr. and Mrs. Atwell were thrown overboard together when the liner plunged to the bottom. The Atwells were dragged under three times before they broke completely free from the suction and then swam to a nearby lifeboat.

The Reverend Wallett spotted a piece of wood drifting a few feet away. He started to swim to it when suddenly he was seized by a rather large man. Unable to shake him off, Wallett persuaded the man to remain still and swim together. The other man agreed and the two were able to reach the plank safely and cling to it until they were plucked from the St. Lawrence.

By now, the damaged *Storstad* had returned to the scene. On her bridge, Captain Andersen was peering through the fog looking for the vessel his ship had rammed a few minutes earlier. He could not see the liner or hear her whistle but numerous cries were plainly audible. Andersen did not know then that the other ship had sunk some five minutes before.

Informed by Chief Officer Toftenes from the bow that they were dangerously close to the survivors, Andersen stopped the engines and ordered the *Storstad*'s four lifeboats to be lowered.

Third Officer Saxe took command of one of the boats and set out toward the source of the screams. He filled his boat with as many women and children as possible and took them to the *Storstad*. After transfering them to the collier, Saxe and his men returned to the *Empress*'s grave.

Second Officer Reinertz took charge of another boat and began searching for survivors. He was able to save some fifty people; he took them to the *Storstad*, and resumed looking.

Andersen and his men meanwhile were making the survivors comfortable. Some members of the crew donated articles of clothing to the half-naked group. The captain distributed the ship's alcoholic beverages to the survivors. It was a relief to the captain to see the arrival of the *Lady Evelyn* and the *Eureka*. Their help was welcomed by the Norwegian collier which had limited accommodations.

When the rescue was completed, some 467 survivors were picked up, including Dr. Grant, Mr. and Mrs. Greenaway, Helen O'Hara, Alfred Keith, Ensign Pugmire, Furgus Duncan, the Atwells, Chief Engineer Sampson, and Captain Kendall. An estimated 1,012 passengers and crew were lost. Among them were Lawrence Irving, Mabel Hackney, Sir Henry Seton-Karr, and Commissioner Rees of the Salvation Army. Of the number lost, 840 were passengers, the greatest number lost on the North Atlantic trade in peacetime.

Immediately there was an outcry. The *Storstad* was held entirely accountable for the collision. Lord Mersey, the very man who presided over the investigation of the *Titanic* disaster, concluded at the inquiry in the sinking of the *Empress of Ireland* that the *Storstad* was totally at fault. Chief Officer Toftenes was stripped of his license for two years. Interestingly, a Norwegian court later found both the *Storstad* and Toftenes blameless in the matter.

In retrospect, it is difficult to affix blame for this terrible tragedy. During the inquiry, Deputy Minister of Justice Newcombe stated an "excess of caution" on the part of the *Empress of Ireland* by stopping and "the improper use of port helm by the *Storstad*" led to the disaster. He may very well have been right, though many have differed with him then and now.

As can be expected, the officers of both ships placed the blame on the other side. The *Storstad*'s crew insisted the *Empress* made a turn to the port which put her on a direct course to the collier. Kendall and his officers maintained their ship did not make such a turn and hence the *Storstad*'s evasive turn to the starboard resulted in the collision. There is no evidence to suggest either side was purposely untruthful.

One possible cause may have been that the stearing gear on the *Empress of Ireland* was faulty. During the inquiry, one of the liner's quartermasters testified that the rudder did not respond properly to the wheel. According to this witness, the liner nearly collided with a schooner in Traverse Channel. He claimed to have mentioned this problem to the second officer and Pilot Bernier but was shrugged off. Later, Bernier denied ever hearing the quartermaster mentioning any such difficulty. The quartermaster's version of the near collision with the schooner was also discredited by other witnesses. The issue was not pursued further.

One interesting theory has been advanced by James Croall, author of *Fourteen Minutes*, who holds that the helmsman of the *Empress* had briefly allowed the ship to swing too far to the starboard. It was at this moment when Toftenes and the others on the bridge saw the liner's red light and assumed the ship was going to cross the *Storstad* port to port. The helmsman corrected this deviation but not before the ship disappeared in a fog patch. Thus Toftenes, attempting to avoid an accident, put the helm to the starboard. Unknowingly he put the *Storstad* on a collision course with the *Empress of Ireland*. There is no proof for this theory but this writer believes it is the most likely explanation.

This disaster produced heroes as well as controversy. The radiomen of the *Empress* were praised for remaining at their post. Captain Kendall was cited for his bravery. It was glory reminiscent of the earlier Crippen case, only this time the honoree refused to take the bow. He reflected bitterly, "I wish I had gone down with her." The captain's luck ran out a second time. His command, the *Calgarian*, was sunk in 1918. Kendall remained on land until his death in 1965.

10 ■ MAY 7, 1915

The *Lusitania*
"Greyhound of the Sea"

THE PEACEFUL WORLD of the early 20th century gave way to the nightmare of the First World War. It was difficult for the simple people of the world to understand how an assassination of an Austrian-Hungarian Prince in Sarajevo could result in war since they could not fathom the political and diplomatic complexities that proved to be the underlying causes. But total war was the result. It was nearly impossible to evade its cruel reality.

The once plentiful consumer goods, for instance, rapidly began to disappear with the curtailment of consumer production and the rechanneling of industry towards war goods. By 1915, practically all resources were mustered for the war effort, leaving the population to endure the burden of heavier taxes to finance the military.

Nor was there a large number of young males readily available. Conscription laws were passed. This drain of many young men had a terrible impact on their families. The war was claiming hundreds of thousands in Flanders Field, the Argonne and other areas of Europe.

Even the civilian population suffered casualties. Millions died from disease and starvation. Nor was civilian death confined to continental Europe.

Only the luxury liners seemed to be immune from the war.

These "floating palaces" still offered comfort during these times of cruel hardships. Yet by 1915 even they were being threatened by war. The German Navy had developed a modern version of an old warship: the submarine. Far less time-consuming and expensive to build than the battleship or cruiser, the U-boat was equipped with deadly torpedoes and could strike without warning.

This revolutionary tactic was against the old "cruiser" rules which required a warship to give full warning before attacking an unarmed merchant ship. Yet the submarines with their slow speed, light surface armament and thin hull plates were too vulnerable to surface. Besides being vulnerable to ramming, the submarines ran the risk of facing concealed guns on supposedly civilian ships.

This apparently did not hinder Atlantic passenger traffic. Many Americans on May 1, 1915, did not take this threat seriously even though the German Embassy had an ad printed in the shipping page of American newspapers that stated:

NOTICE:
TRAVELERS intending to
embark on an Atlantic voyage
are reminded that a state of
war exists between Germany
and her allies and Great Britain
and her allies; that the zone of
war includes the water adjacent
to the British Isles; that in
accordance with formal notice given
by the Imperial German Government,
vessels flying the flag of Great
Britain, or of any of her allies,
are liable to destruction in these
waters and that travelers sailing
in the war zone on ships of Great Britain
or her allies do so at their own risk.
IMPERIAL GERMAN EMBASSY
Washington D.C., April 22, 1915.

Few, seemingly, showed any interest in that notice. Many who were to embark on an Atlantic voyage to England were more interested in the column next to the warning. It was the departure timetable of the Cunard Line *Lusitania*.

Completed in 1907, the *Lusitania* was the largest ship afloat when she set out on her maiden voyage. She was 30,396 gross tons and 45,000 tons displacement. Her length from bow to stern was 787 feet. Her height from the waterline to the top deck was a distance of 80 feet. With this height, length, and narrowness of her beam, the *Lusitania* was similar to a canoe and this design enabled her to achieve great speeds.

This darling of the Atlantic was not fazed at all by the recent submarine warnings. The liner's speed gave confidence to both the passengers and crew. "We can outdistance any submarine afloat," one of her passengers, Alfred Vanderbilt, correctly boasted, for the *Lusitania* could cruise at speeds of 24 to 27 knots. This Cunard liner in fact won the Blue Ribbon of the Atlantic when she averaged 24 knots on a crossing. Even though six of her 25 boilers were not in service (the absence of manpower during the war resulted in shutting down some of them), this "Greyhound of the Sea" was much faster than any U-boat in the Kaiser's Navy.

Even if the *Lusitania* were to be attacked, she appeared to have a good chance of survival. Built as an auxiliary cruiser for the Royal Navy, the Cunarder was designed to shrug off damage. She was constructed with a double skin, or double layer of steel, throughout her hull. The liner was divided into eleven watertight compartments by longitudinal bulkheads. Coal was stored in some of these compartments to absorb the shock of enemy shells. Her boilers and stearing gear were placed below the waterline to protect them from damage during battle.

However, the designers of the *Lusitania* overlooked a few points. The first was that the coal bunkers were to be closed by the stokers during an emergency. Yet if a disaster were to occur, the "black gang" might panic and flee their posts before closing the doors. With the bunkers open, the ship would lose buoyancy and stability.

Another unforeseen danger was the chance that the coal would absorb water and become heavier and therefore result in a list. If one of these coal bunkers were exposed to the sea, the ship would list 7°. With two gone, it would list at least 15°, and with three or more flooded, the *Lusitania* might very well sink.

Abandoning ship in this situation would be difficult. Even with a slight list, the lifeboats on the side leaning towards the sea would hang a few feet from the deck. Another problem the crew would face would be lowering the boats on the other side. With a list of 22° or more, these would be impossible to launch.

There was another small but disturbing fact few took into account. With a list of 7° or more, the water would rush into any open portholes in F deck. To overcome this problem, the bridge was equipped with a control panel to close off this area. Any crew member trapped there could escape by means of a manual override system. There was, though, no explanation given to the passengers on the use of this system. Thus if an emergency developed and if no member of the crew was around, any passenger down in this area of the ship would be unable to flee to safety.

Yet despite these flaws, the *Lusitania* was one of the safest liners of her day. Nothing in her early career hinted that there were any faults with her design. She had successfully crossed the Atlantic Ocean 201 times without any serious trouble.

Now, Saturday, May 1, 1915, the "Greyhound" was to depart from New York for Liverpool on the eastbound leg of her 101st voyage east. The passenger roster listed 157 Americans, including Alfred Gwynne Vanderbilt whose assets of $100-million made him one of the wealthiest men in the world, theatrical producer Charles Frohman, playwright Charles Klein, and Elbert Hubbard, the author of *Who Lifted the Lid Off of Hell*. Hubbard was especially enthusiastic about this voyage for he wanted to see the war firsthand.

Most of the passengers were not that eager, however. Some of the steerage travelers were Persians returning to Turkey to learn the fate of their relatives in the aftermath of news of recent massacres. Other third class passengers were emigrants returning home for a visit. For the most part, the majority of the 1,257 passengers were traveling either on business or visiting relatives.

The *Lusitania*'s cargo consisted of sheet brass, copper, machinery, beef, cheese, lard, bacon and 205 barrels of Long Island

Sound oysters.* Later, it was revealed that 42,000 cases of rifle ammunition and 100 cases of empty shrapnel shells were also stored below in the stowage space. Although the United States was then neutral, it was perfectly legal to transport such supplies.

With the illness of the *Lusitania*'s regular master, Captain "Paddy" Dow, the Cunard Line looked for a suitable replacement. Captain William Thomas Turner was chosen. "Bowler Bill" Turner, as he was called because he often wore a bowler hat, was the regular captain of the *Aquitania*. This sixty-year-old, tall, broad-shouldered man had been at sea for many years and was one of Cunard Line's most capable master. Unfortunately, he was stubborn and inflexible. He took the submarine peril too lightly. This attitude would have tragic consequences.

Aboard his new command, Captain Turner found many faults with the engines, lifesaving equipment, and seamanship. Cunard quickly corrected most of these defects, including replacing lifeboats. There was little the steamship company could do regarding the inferior quality of the crew since most of the more experienced seamen were serving in the Royal Navy at the time.

With improvements made, the *Lusitania* departed from New York for Liverpool as a dockside crowd waved goodbye. A few spectators, conscious of the warning published by the Germans, wondered if this would be the last voyage of the *Lusitania*.

During the voyage, a boat drill was conducted in which eight men and an officer participated. The officer gave an order and the group of men strapped on their life jackets and boarded one of the lifeboats. The officer then ordered the men out of the boat and dismissed them. Not one of the 1,257 passengers participated. It was, as one observer stated, "a pitiable exhibition."

A few concerned passengers talked to the captain about the boat drill. They asked Turner to hold another one with everyone aboard taking part in it. Turner reassured them that "a torpedo can't get the *Lusitania*. She runs too fast." Nevertheless the passengers insisted that another drill be conducted. The captain agreed to their request but did not follow through. The grim lessons of the *Titanic* disaster had apparently been lost on Turner.

By Friday, May 7, one week out of New York, the *Lusitania*

*Rumor had it that gold was also aboard but there is no proof of this.

encountered dense fog. To adjust to the arrival schedule and for safe navigation through the fog, "Bowler Bill" reduced speed to 18 knots. This sacrifice of speed was dangerous since there was a definite possibility of the *Lusitania* coming upon a U-boat, but the "Greyhound" was still faster than any submarine which could at the most make seven knots submerged and 15 knots on the surface. Besides, the fog would make the Cunarder a very difficult target.

By 11:00, the fog finally cleared. Twenty five minutes later, Captain Turner received a wireless warning from the Admiralty stating: "Submarine active in southern part of Irish Channel, last heard of 20 miles south of Coningbe Light Vessel."

A submarine was indeed active in the southern coast of Ireland. U-Boat 20, under the command of Kapitan-Leutnant Walter Schwieger, had been patrolling this area for the past few days. Schwieger, who was ruthless in dealing with enemy vessels, had earlier come across the *Earl of Lathom*. He stopped the vessel and ordered the crew to abandon ship. He then sank the captured ship by gunfire.

Later, U-20 met and attacked the fleeing *Candidate*. Schwieger forced the vessel to stop by firing a few shots from the deck gun. After allowing the crew to take to the boats, Schwieger sent a boarding party to search the ship. An hour later, the men returned to their submarine and sent a torpedo into her. Seeing this was not effective, Schwieger fired a dozen rounds from the deck gun into the ship. With this, the *Candidate* finally gave up her struggle and sank.

That same day, the U-boat met with the *Candidate*'s sistership, the *Centurion*. Without warning, Schwieger torpedoed her. After she refused to sink, a second torpedo was fired. About an hour and half later, the *Centurion* joined her sister ship at the bottom of the Atlantic.

By 12:40 on the afternoon of May 7, another warning was relayed to the *Lusitania*. This one reported submarine activity south of Cape Clear and proceeding west. To Captain Turner, this posed no danger to his command. He did order the watertight doors closed and had the lifeboats prepared, but otherwise he was determined to carry on as in peacetime. To Turner, submarines could not inflict very much harm to a modern liner, for their reputation during past wars had shown them to be too slow and impotent to be of any threat. He was wrong. The submarine in 1915, still underdeveloped (at least by today's standards), had made great strides by the early 20th century. It was faster than the Davids of the American Civil War and now was equipped with a dangerous weapon—the torpedo.

With the clearing of fog, Turner decided to survey the landscape of the Irish coast to get a better idea of his position. From his charts the captain found he was at Old Head of Kinsale. To determine exactly how far he was from the shore, he began a four-point bearing, a method of establishing a fix with a steady course and speed.

By doing this, Turner was violating two rules under submarine alert: he came too close to shore and he failed to zigzag. This did not seem to worry the captain as he continued with the four-point bearing.

Not far away, Kapitan-Leutnant Schwieger was scanning the horizon for more prey. He had only three torpedos left and he intended to spend two on the return voyage. He would soon have to return home for a variety of reasons including fog, the presence of enemy destroyers and a dwindling supply of fuel and torpedos.

Then, in his own words: "Ahead and to starboard four funnels and two masts of a steamer with course perpendicular to us came into sight." Schwieger wasted no time. He quickly dived and set course for the unknown steamer.

To his pilot he described the steamer as a four funnel 30,000-odd ton passenger liner. From *Jane's Fighting Ships* and the *Naval Annual*, the pilot identified the ship as either the *Lusitania* or her sistership the *Mauretania*. Both Cunarders were auxiliary cruisers for the British Navy.

With this information, Schwieger decided it was time to perform his duty. At 2:10 PM, he aimed for the forward boiler room and fired a torpedo. From his periscope he watched the torpedo travel toward its target he judged to be "700 meters" away.

Aboard the *Lusitania*, many passengers were relaxing, unaware of the danger they were in. The ship was soon to dock in Liverpool and many of the passengers were taking full advantage of the "Lusy's" comforts before they would have to leave her.

Among them was Mme. Florence Padly. She was seated comfortably in a deck chair when someone near her noticed a "porpoise."

James Brocks, a businessman from Connecticut, also saw something. The outline did not appear to be a porpoise at all. It looked more like a torpedo.

Oliver P. Bernard, a scenic director of London's Covent Garden Theater, also knew what it was. From his seat on the promenade, he saw the U-boat's periscope. Suddenly, he saw a long white streak of foam making its way to the starboard side of the ship. "Is that a torpedo?" someone asked him. Bernard, fully aware that it was, covered his eyes, corked his ears and waited for the explosion.

Robert Rankin, a mining engineer, was standing on deck talking to two passengers when he saw a periscope.

"That looks like a torpedo!" Rankin exclaimed.

Sixteen-year-old W.G.E. Meyers, who was on his way to join the Royal Navy, was enjoying a game of quoits with two other boys on the upper deck. One of his companions glanced over his shoulder and shouted, "There's a torpedo coming straight at us!" Meyers rushed to the railing and observed a streak of bubbles coming in the direction of the liner.

On the starboard forecastle head, lookout Leslie Morton spotted a torpedo heading straight for the *Lusitania*. He shouted through his megaphone, "Torpedo coming!" to the bridge. Then without waiting for an acknowledgment, he fled his post and began looking for his brother who was also a member of the crew.

High in the crow's nest, Seaman Thomas Quinn also spotted the track of the torpedo. "It came abaft the foremast," he later explained. Immediately he shouted his observation to the bridge.

The torpedo struck the *Lusitania* starboard side and exploded. The explosion shock the entire ship. Then suddenly a second one rocked the huge liner. Within a few seconds after the second detonation, the ship developed a 15° list to starboard.

Through his periscope, Schwieger observed, "Unusually great detonation with large cloud of smoke and debris shot above funnels. In addition to torpedo, a second explosion must have taken place (boiler, coal or powder?) The ship stops . . . leans to the starboard, at the same time sinking at bow. It looks as though she would capsize in a short time."

On the bridge, Captain Turner had been informed by Second Officer Heppert of the warning from the crow's nest. No sooner had Turner rushed to the starboard bridge wing than the liner was rocked by two explosions. Turner checked the indicator to see which bulkheads were still holding. To his horror, the instrument revealed the forward compartments were flooded.

Overcoming the shock of the explosion, Meyers rushed down to the boat deck. There he noticed water and debris "flew all around us," and he hurried on below to grab his lifebelt.

The steam and coal dust Meyers saw knocked James Brocks off his feet. Fortunately a wind blew the steam and coal dust away before he suffocated. Brocks got to his feet and ran to the lifeboats.

In the second class dining room, Archibald Donald was startled by the sound of shattering glass. He was tapped on the shoulder by the Reverend Gwyer who said, "Let us quiet the people." The two men went about reassuring the diners that all would be saved and advised them to leave in an orderly fashion.

The speech worked. The passengers moved quickly but calmly out of the room. One woman fainted as she neared the exit. Donald helped carry her up the slanting staircase and out on the second class deck.

Fred Gauntlett, in the first class dining room, was interrupted in his conversation with a shipboard friend by a loud explosion. He realized at once that the *Lusitania* was under attack. Before he could react, the ship developed a frightening list to starboard. Gauntlett shouted to the others to close the portholes. He then rushed to his cabin and strapped on his life jacket.

Charles Lauriat was casually chatting with Elbert Hubbard and his wife on the portside when suddenly he heard "a heavy rather muffled sound." A split second later, there was a second explosion which sounded "quite different" from the first. Perhaps, he thought, a boiler exploded.

Lauriat quickly suggested to the Hubbards that they go to their staterooms and get their life jackets. Hubbard remained where he was with his arm around his wife. Lauriat left the two and hurried to his cabin to fetch his life jacket.

Certain that his command was doomed. Captain Turner climbed up to the navigation bridge to see if the lifeboats could be launched. He noticed that the *Lusitania* was still moving forward. This was putting a strain on the bulkheads as well as making it impossible to lower the boats. Turner summoned staff captain John C. "Jock" Anderson and told him not to lower any lifeboats until the ship had stopped.

Meanwhile, the list began to increase. On the advice of the staff captain, Turner ordered the flooding of the portside trim tanks to counteract the list. His order was in vain for the crew stationed at the flooding valves had already abandoned their posts.

In desperation, Captain Turner decided to beach his command in the nearby shallow water. He attempted to carry this out when he discovered the *Lusitania*'s bow was already submerged and her rudders were practically out of the water. All hope of saving the *Lusitania* was now gone.

In the wireless shack, Senior Wireless Operator Robert Leith relayed out, "Come at once. Big list. Ten miles south Old Head of Kinsale." He was able to make contact with several ships including the tanker *Narragansett*, the steamer *City of Exeter*, and the freighter *Etonian*. Leith urged them to, "Send help quickly. Am listing badly."

A short distance away, Kapitan-Leutnant Schwieger recorded in his log book, "There is great confusion on board. Boats are cleared and many of them lowered into the water. . . ."

The confusion Schwieger referred to was the launching of the boats. The Cunard liner carried 48 lifeboats, 22 which were the conventional wooden type and were suspended by davits, while the remaining 26 were collapsibles that were placed on the deck instead of being attached to davits. This meant the crew had to first lower all of the 22 conventional lifeboats, haul up the ropes, attach them to the collapsibles, and then lower once more. This procedure was too time-consuming to evacuate the ship in the few minutes the crew had.

Moreover, some of the conventional lifeboats were suspended over 18 of the collapsibles. During the confusion, a few of the boats on the portside were released by panic-stricken davit men and fell on the collapsibles beneath them. One by one they fell; boats No. 2, 4, 6, 8 and 10 came crashing down on the collapsibles and slid towards the bow.

Staff Captain Anderson and Junior Third Officer Bestic managed to restore some order to the portside boat stations. However, most of the remaining lifeboats also were improperly lowered too quickly. The stern dropped and practically all aboard were thrown into the water. A lifeboat came loose and tumbled down on them.

Lifeboat No. 14 met a similar fate. The davit men lost control and the boat toppled on top of No. 12. Some of the occupants climbed back on board boat No. 14 but it was too damaged to float and sank under their feet.

A seaman stationed by No. 18 intended to cut the fall and release the pin when the boat became level with the water. Then passenger Isaac Lehmann appeared on the scene with a handgun. "I don't know whatever possessed me," he later explained. He demanded to know why the lifeboat was not being lowered away. The seaman with the ax tried to explain the captain's order not to lower the boats but Lehmann apparently was not concerned with Turner's commands.

"To hell with the captain. Don't you see that the ship is sinking. And the first man who disobeys my orders to launch the boat I shoot to kill," Lehmann said with his revolver drawn.

Obeying, the seaman knocked out the pin. The lifeboat came crashing down on Lehmann's leg. Lehmann survived but witnessed to his horror the thirty or so occupants of the lifeboat being crushed to death.

The situation on the starboard side was somewhat better. With the exception of lifeboat No. 5 which was destroyed by falling water and debris, the boats on this side were undamaged. Also the list did not present as much difficulty since this was the "low side." Under the supervision of First Officer Jones lifeboats Nos. 9 and 11 were lowered safely away with a handful of passengers and crew in each. No. 13 was successfully lowered off with sixty-five people. With Jones in command, boat No. 15 pulled away from the doomed liner with over eighty aboard. Discovering No. 1 drifting empty, Jones transferred some of the passengers to it.

There were still some mishaps. Twelve occupants of lifeboat No. 19 fell to the water when one of the davit men lost control. Fortunately, the boat reached the water safely. In all only six of the twenty-two conventional boats were successfully launched.

Charles Lauriat meanwhile was handing out life jackets to those who needed them. He worked his way toward the bridge where he overheard a woman passenger ask, "Captain, what do you wish us to do?"

"Stay right where you are, madam," Turner assured her, "She's alright."

"Where did you get your information?" she inquired.

"From the engine room, madam," was the firm reply.

Hearing this, Lauriat and the woman began to reassure the other passengers. Lauriat knew, however, the *Lusitania* would remain afloat only for a few more minutes. He decided therefore to take time out and retrieve some of his personal possessions. If the ship was going to sink, he thought, he might as well save what he could.

On his way down to his stateroom, he noticed many of his fellow passengers were wearing their life jackets improperly. Some had them were around their waists, some upside down and some around their necks. Lauriat took time out to help them attach their jackets properly and then continued on to his cabin.

Oliver Bernard, the scenic director, was busy handing out life jackets to the woman passengers. He ran into Alfred Vanderbilt who was holding what appeared to be a jewel case. To Bernard he seemed to be "amused by the excitement."

Down below, Charles Lauriat was working his way to his cabin where he discovered the lights to be inoperative. He reached for the box of matches he had taken along in case of emergency and lighted one. Lauriate was able to find his passport and other valuable papers, then he quickly returned to the boat deck.

There he proceeded to the starboard lifeboats. He climbed aboard one of them and began to cut the ropes with his pocket knife. He knew he didn't have much time, for the boat was already afloat.

Then suddenly the boat capsized, dumping Lauriat and the other occupants into the water. An excellent swimmer, Lauriat swam away from the sinking liner, then turned to see if the others had followed him. Unfortunately, most stayed where they were, petrified.

By 2:23, thirteen minutes after the torpedo struck, Quartermaster Johnston reported to the captain that the *Lusitania* was now listing 25°. "Then save yourself," Turner called back. Strapping on a lifebelt, the quartermaster stepped into the water, which was by now level with the bow, and floated away.

Archibald Donald was not wasting time. Carefully, he put his watch in his trouser pocket and, with the help of a steward, fastened his life jacket securely. Then he summoned all of his courage and leaped overboard, plunging into the water which was by now only ten feet below.

Oliver Bernard realized the ship's inevitable fate. He climbed up to the Marconi deck, removed his coat and tie, and dove overboard, swimming as fast as he could away from the doomed liner.

Robert Rankin also realized that the ship was doomed. He waited until the water was within a few feet of the deck and then jumped. He was picked up by one of the starboard boats.

Junior Third Officer Bestic had resigned himself to the hopelessness of the lifeboats and directed his efforts to helping some of the passengers. He found many of them standing around, seemingly unaware of the danger they were in. Alfred Vanderbilt and Carl Frohman were tying life jackets to baskets containing infants. Bestic tried to warn them that they had only seconds to save themselves but the two continued with their work. Frohman, according to legend, shrugged, "Why fear death? It is the most beautiful adventure in life."

Suddenly, a bulkhead collapsed and No. 3 boiler exploded. The ship rolled over on its side. Seconds later, the *Lusitania* plunged to the bottom of the sea.

Charles Lauriat got himself entangled in the ship's wireless antenna and was dragged under. He "kicked" free and swam to the surface. To him the experience reminded him of "Susy the Mermaid" in which the older boys at camp would dunk the younger ones under the water to instruct them how to swim.

James Brooks also was caught in the antenna, but managed to wiggle free, cutting his hand in the process. He turned and witnessed the sea closing over the *Lusitania*. The terrible rumbling sound that accompanied the foundering resembled, he thought, a building collapsing during a fire.

Brooks swam to a collapsible floating nearby. With the aid of a seaman and another passenger, he assembled the canvas boat.

The three were joined by Charles Lauriat. Together they began to pull survivors out of the water.

Seaman Leslie Morton and his brother swam clear of lifeboat No. 3 as it was dragged to the bottom, still fastened to the *Lusitania*. Along with a few passengers, they assembled a floating collapsible and set out to pick up some of those struggling in the water. In all they saved thirty-four lives.

Junior Third Officer Bestic was fortunate enough to have a stream of water carry him off the sinking liner. Lying on his back, he heard the cries of the infants in the baskets die out one by one as the life jackets came loose. Bestic himself wanted to unfasten his jacket and join them but he lacked the strength.

Not far away, Captain Turner was also lucky enough to be thrown clear of his sinking ship. This was not to be his only terrifying experience during the war. Two years later, in command of the *Ivernia*, he was again torpedoed and set adrift. Given shore duties, he remained on land for the duration of the war. He was promoted to Commadore of the Line in 1921 but he could never escape the memory of the last eighteen terrible minutes of the *Lusitania*. Turner lived in seclusion until he died of intestinal cancer in 1933.

Beneath the water, Schwieger viewed the sinking through his periscope. He spotted the golden letters of the ship's bow proclaiming her *Lusitania*. Satisfied, he set course for home. The deed was done. Two years later, Walter Schwieger, in command of U-38, was killed in action.

The result of Schwieger's deed was appalling. Of the 1,959 passengers and crew who took passage, 1,201 of them were lost. Of those, 124 were Americans including Alfred Vanderbilt, Elbert Hubbard and Carl Frohman. With 708 saved, about 62 percent of the *Lusitania*'s complement perished.

Seeking the sympathy of the neutral nations of the world, the British took full advantage of the diplomatic capital of the sinking. "Teutonic bestiality," they cried. Terms such as "Prussian barbarism" and "Hunnish brutality" were coined to take full measure of the tragedy.

The coroner's verdict pulled no punches. "This appalling crime," it read, "was contrary to international law and the conventions of all civilized nations, and we therefore charge the owners of the submarine, the German Emperor and the Government of Germany, under whose orders they acted, with the crime of willful and wholesale murder."

The findings, however, of the Official Inquiry conducted by Lord Mersey stand out from the rest. "What was the cause of the loss of life? The answer is plain. The effective cause of the loss of life was the attack made against the ship by those on board the submarine. It was a murderous attack because it was made with the deliberate and wholly unjustifiable intention of killing the people on board."

The German government repudiated these charges. The passengers of the *Lusitania*, they pointed out, had been clearly warned of the danger by the newspaper advertisement. They further countercharged that the liner was an auxiliary cruiser of the British Navy. The Germans also insisted that the Admiralty with using the Cunarder for transporting contraband of war and Canadian troops.

The British government of course denied these charges. Although the *Lusitania* was in fact an auxiliary cruiser, it was not, according to the British, armed. Nor was she carrying contraband or troops. She was just an innocent passenger liner, they maintained.

However, there are many unanswered questions which linger to this day. In the early 1970s, a sensational book was published which alleged that the *Lusitania* actually was armed and carrying munitions and Canadian troops on her last voyage. The author of this book goes as far as to claim that the Admiralty, under the supervision of the First Lord, Winston Churchill, had deliberately allowed the liner to be sunk in order to draw the United States into the war.

Under close scrutiny, however, these theories do not hold water. There is no evidence, for instance, to support the claim that the *Lusitania* was armed on her last voyage. It is true there were plans made for the installment of twelve 6-inch guns. But there is no evidence that the *Lusitania* was provided with such armament. Photographs taken of her on her last voyage reveal no trace of any guns. Furthermore, none of the passengers reported seeing naval cannons.

Nor is there sufficient evidence to conclude the *Lusitania* was transporting Canadian troops. There were Canadians aboard, such as W.G.E. Meyers, who intended to enlist when they reached England, but there is no indication that a large body of troops was on the ship. Indeed many of the Canadian passengers were women, children and elderly men who could not have provided service for the Allied cause. It seems doubtful therefore that the *Lusitania* was acting as a troop transport on her final crossing.

The question of contraband is not as easily resolved. The Cunarder was carrying large amounts of foodstuffs on that fateful trip, and sometime earlier, the British themselves declared that food would be treated as contraband. Several German-bound ships carrying food were seized by the British Navy. By Britain's own definition then, the *Lusitania* was transporting contraband.

It has been theorized that the *Lusitania* was carrying munitions of war as well. In actuality the liner, as previously mentioned, had 42,000 cases of rifle ammunition and 100 cases of empty shrapnel shells stored in her cargo holds, but there is no evidence that anything other than that was aboard.

Yet there are many who have asked what had caused the second blast. Those inclined to think the *Lusitania* was carrying contraband maintain it was caused by exploding munitions. They overlook the fact that the torpedo struck more than a hundred feet from where the cargo was stored. There were two, possibly three, bulkheads to absorb the shock. The second explosion then was not munitions going up but rather a bursting boiler.

The most absurd theory advanced concerning the *Lusitania* was the one which holds the Cunarder was deliberately allowed to be torpedoed in hope that it would bring the United States of America into the war on the Allied side. It originated shortly after the event by the pro-German element in this country and was advanced again in the early 1970s.

The basis of this theory is the May 7 conversation between Colonel House, an advisor of President Wilson, and the King of England, just a few hours before the *Lusitania* met her doom. House was asked, "Colonel, what will America do if the Germans sink the *Lusitania*?"

Another point raised is why there was no escort provided for the Cunarder. It seems suspicious to some that the Admiralty would allow a liner with a large number of passengers to enter an area unprotected where there was submarine activity unless she was deliberately allowed to be sunk.

What the proponents of this theory overlook is that the Admiralty had sent wireless messages to the *Lusitania* warning her of the presence of a U-boat in the Irish Channel. One of the messages stated, "Make sure *Lusitania* gets this." Had the Admiralty intended to have the liner sunk, it would not have gone out of its way to warn her.

Nor would the British be foolish enough to divulge their plan by asking such a direct question to Colonel House. More than likely the King wished to know what America's position would be if a large liner would be sunk. The British may have wanted to prepare their diplomatic strategy for such an occurrence. The mention of the *Lusitania* as an example was merely a coincidence.

The absence of an escort most likely was due not to any conspiracy on the part of Churchill but instead was the result of the shortage of warships. Although the British had the largest navy in the world at this time, they were unable to provide protection to every civilian vessel. Ships were needed to enforce the blockade of Germany and for other operations. Therefore many vessels would have to be on their own.

Ironically the fact that the *Lusitania* was a passenger liner may have been partly the reason why she was not given an escort. The Admiralty may have believed the Germans were incapable of attacking a ship carrying innocent passengers. If nothing else the force of world opinion might deter them from sinking passenger liners without giving the conventional warning. Thus to provide warships for protection not only would have been unnecessary, but would have given the enemy justification under international law to sink the vessel. The British evidently did not consider the rash judgment of a U-boat commander.

Another reason why the Admiralty may not have offered the *Lusitania* protection was her speed. As previously mentioned, the Cunarder was capable of at least three times the speed of a submerged submarine. With this speed it seemed as if the *Lusitania* did not need an escort. Indeed, had Turner followed his instructions and zigzagged, it is safe to assume that his command would have reached Liverpool unharmed.

The biggest flaw in this theory is the fact that the British in

May of 1915 did not need or want the United States in the war. Many Allied leaders at the time believed the war would be won even without American intervention. To carry out a scheme such as this would have risked driving the United States in the Central Power camp if her leaders discovered the plot.

Actually to bring America into the war at this time would have hurt the Allies more than helped them. The United States at the time had a modest army which was unprepared to fight in Europe. To have raised and equipped a sizable army would have drained some of the supplies the British were buying for their own forces.

If it was not a deliberate plot on the part of the British, there could be no doubt there was a great deal of negligence. Captain Turner had entered a war zone with a light attitude toward the submarine peril. He came too close to the shore and failed to zigzag. Had he followed the instructions the Admiralty had given him, his command undoubtedly would have reached Liverpool safely. During the inquest, Turner blamed the loss of the *Lusitania* on "the fortunes of war." Had he exercised better judgment however, the fortunes of war would not have been so tragic.

Some of the blame naturally rests with the Cunard Line. Although the company provided ample boats for the ship's company, they failed to install the necessary number of davits. The crew did not have time to lower the conventional boats and haul the ropes up and attach them to the collapsibles. Nor did the steamship line adequately train the crew in the lowering and handling of the lifeboats. Cunard's failure to do so resulted in the loss of hundreds of lives.

Neither was the Admiralty completely without blame. One shipmaster recalled a conversation with a representative from the Admiralty in which he asked what was meant by zigzag course.

"To tell you the truth, I don't exactly know," the Admiralty representative replied. When the shipmaster mentioned that his speed was 17½ knots, the Royal Navy officer stated flatly, "You need not worry about submarines. You are immune going at that speed."

Turner, it must be remembered, was doing 18 knots when he was torpedoed. It is possible that the failure of the Admiralty to adequately explain zigzag tactics led Captain Turner to regard the submarine peril lightly. Even Thomas Bailey and Paul Ryan, in their book, *The "Lusitania" Disaster*, while absolving the Admiralty of deliberately allowing the liner to be sunk, concluded,

> With the benefit of hindsight we can see that the Admiralty should have spelled out with diagrams, as it later did, and probably also with demonstrations precisely how zigzag tactics worked with optimum effectiveness.

Another development in the *Lusitania* case was presented by authors Des Hickey and Gus Smith in *Seven Days to Disaster*. In it, they allege that a crewmember of the U-20 drew a revolver against Schwieger while the *Lusitania* was sinking. This writer doubts this story, for Schwieger did not record this event in his logbook.

Whether it was a plot by the English or not, the effect was the same. Many across the United States of America were stunned by the sinking. The torpedoing was "hellish" and "damnable" cried one prominent American. Former President Theodore Roosevelt called the action an act of piracy and demanded that Woodrow Wilson act.

Nor did the warning printed in the newspaper help the German cause. "The Blackhand sent its warnings," said the *Saturday Evening Post*, "so did Jack the Ripper write his defiant letters to the police. Nothing of this prevents us from regarding such miscreants as wild beasts, against whom society has to defend itself at all hazards."

Judge Julius Mayer, who in 1918 presided over the law suits between some survivors and the Cunard Line, concluded bitterly,

> The cause of the sinking of the *Lusitania* was the illegal act of the Imperial German Government acting through its instrument, the submarine commander, and violating a cherished and humane rule observed, until this war, by even the bitterest antagonist.

In many ways the Germans were the recipients of the same bitterness and outrage as the Soviets later were after the 1983 Korean airliner incident. Before the sinking of the *Lusitania*, the American public had been bombarded with stories of atrocities committed by the "huns." British newspapers carried accounts of German soldiers torturing Belgian children and other barbaric actions. It was the sinking of the *Lusitania* that gave these stories credibility. From May 7 of 1915 onward, the American public began to believe the stories of crimes committed by the Germans.

The sinking was important for another reason. President Wilson sent a stern protest to Germany, for the first time shaking a fist rather than waving a finger. As Germany continued her deadly submarine activity, the United States took a stronger stand and relations between the two countries rapidly worsened.

The question of justification of the attack is not easy to resolve. This is a moral question, not a historical one. The Cunarder was carrying ammunition and may have been used at a future date as a troop transport. The Germans may not have had another chance to sink her.

The war militarily came to an end on November 11, 1918. On May 7, 1919, four years to the day after the *Lusitania* was sunk, the German representatives were handed the terms of the peace treaty. Among the provisions were reparations and a war guilt clause. The Germans may have wondered whether it would have been better if Schwieger had allowed the *Lusitania* to complete her voyage.

11 ■ AUGUST 19, 1915

The *Arabic*
". . . Appearance of Sharp Diplomacy"

CAPTAIN WILLIAM FINCH of the White Star liner *Arabic* was keeping careful watch. It was around 9:15 on the morning of August 19, 1915. The weather was clear but there was a slight swell. His ship was about 50 miles southwest of the Old Head of Kinsale or about 50 miles from where the *Lusitania* had been sunk some three months earlier.

Finch's command was one of the most important ships of the White Star Line. Built in 1903 as the *Minnewaska* for the Atlantic Transport Line, the vessel was purchased by White Star and renamed the *Arabic*. The liner was 15,801 tons gross and measured 600 feet 7 inches in length. Her twin screws were driven by quadruple expansion engines, producing 10,000 horsepower. The ship spent her first seven years as a cruise ship to Egypt and Palestine. A few years prior to the war her First Class was eliminated and she was turned into a two class liner.

There were 423 people making this voyage, 261 of them passengers. Among them was Stella Carol, English prima donna, on her way to a New York singing engagement. Also aboard were actor Kenneth S. Douglas and a vaudeville acrobatic team known as the Flying Martins. In addition, the liner was transporting 2,813 bags of mail on this trip.

Although there was a war on, many of the passengers were in a relaxed mood. One of them, J. Edward Usher, who served as a

wireless operator, discussed with other passengers the possibility
of being torpedoed. He concluded that there was only one chance
in 100 of being "submarined."

The ship was under excellent care. Captain William Finch was a
well seasoned seaman. He had served on the Pacific mail service
for a number of years. For more than six years, he commanded
the *Arabic*. Finch was offered promotions to larger liners but he
declined them for her as he refused to part with the *Arabic*.

The crew under Finch's command was competent. The ship's
surgeon, Dr. D.W.S. Muir, had seen many years of medical service. The liner's purser, H.L.T. Templeton, and the chief steward, A.H. Less, had been at sea for many years, mainly on the
Canadian service.

Finch had taken precautions against U-boat attack. Sand bags
were placed around the wheelhouse to protect the steering gear
from shell fire. The lifeboats were loaded with provisions and
swung out, ready for lowering. Lifebelts were placed on deck as
an extra precaution.

A lifeboat drill had been conducted the previous night. Finch
was observing a lights out policy and was avoiding headlands as
he zigzagged at the liner's top speed of 16 knots.

Finch doubtlessly worried, for there were rumors that the
Germans intended to sink the *Adriatic* and *Arabic*. On the previous
voyage, the *Arabic* carried several tons of war goods, making her a
tempting target. On that trip, detectives discovered two sticks of
dynamite under a settee in the woman's retiring room. The
slightest concussion could have set them off. It was never determined who placed them aboard the ship but German saboteurs
could not be ruled out.

All of this happened on an earlier crossing. So far nothing had
happened since the liner left Liverpool at 2:34 the previous
afternoon. Finch seemed to have everything under control.

Then the *Arabic* unexpectedly came upon the British steamer
Dunsley. Finch and his officers could tell something was wrong, for
the two of the *Dunsley* lifeboats were waterborne. She was under
attack by U-24.

Suddenly, Finch saw an object under the water 30 feet away
and heading at a right angle from the north. There was no doubt
about its identity—torpedo! Finch at once ordered the engines

stopped and put astern but it was, as he recalled, "then impossible to escape it." The torpedo struck the starboard side of the ship about 100 feet from the stern.

The next instant, he heard a "terrible explosion." It was "so loud I never heard anything like it." Presumably, the ship's boilers exploded. A large amount of water and debris was blown in the air, reducing one of the starboard lifeboats to splinters. Immediately the vessel developed a list to the starboard.

The liner's bugler saw it coming. "By the time the torpedo reached us," he later explained, "we had moved on a couple of hundred feet but so well was the speed calculated by the submarine's commander that the torpedo struck us about 100 feet from the stern and near the engine room." Hearing "a tremendous explosion," he sounded his bugle as loud as he could.

J. Edward Usher was on the promenade deck when he heard a woman seated next to him shout, "Here's a submarine!" Before he got out of his chair, he felt a "terrible jar" and heard an "awful roar."

Joseph G. DeLorimer and a friend saw a white line in the water. His companion shouted, "We are gone." Quickly, DeLorimer rushed to his cabin to get his lifebelt.

Playwright Zillah Covington and his wife were in their cabin putting on their lifebelts. The couple had seen the *Dunsley* and felt they were in danger. Suddenly, they heard a terrific explosion. They instantly realized that they were in a precarious situation.

Overcoming the shock of the explosion, Louis Bruguiere ran to his mother's cabin. He found her breakfasting in bed. Bruguiere quickly fastened lifebelts around both her and the maid and led them to the promenade deck.

Captain Finch reacted immediately. He was unable to send an S.O.S. since the wireless was destroyed. He ordered the crew to prepare to abandon ship. There were ten lifeboats with a total capacity of 945 persons. In addition, there were a few rafts increasing capacity to 1,147. Although this was more than enough for all aboard even though one of the lifeboats was wrecked, the ship was sinking at an alarming rate and the starboard list would hinder the lowering of the boats.

The crew did its best in launching the nine remaining boats. Two of them capsized while being lowered. Fortunately, six successfully became waterborne. Through it all, the majority of the crew and passengers behaved, in Finch's words, "splendidly." Passenger Charles Pringle agreed. "The crew kept cool heads," he recalled.

Some could not make it to the boats. Louis Bruguiere came on deck with his mother and her maid only to discover the lifeboats were gone. He noticed his two bulldogs were on deck. He quickly threw them in a lowering boat. "There comes the water up the deck," his mother called out. Bruguiere grabbed her and dove overboard.

From a lifeboat, J. Edward Usher saw the *Arabic* dip by the stern. He caught a glimpse of Captain Finch on the bridge. "His face was calm and pale as if he was facing death with the grim resolve not to desert his post," he noticed.

The White Star liner began to sink deeper in the water. The liferafts tore from their fastenings and floated away. Usher heard, "a sizzing roar." Then nine minutes after the torpedo struck, the 15,801-ton *Arabic* disappeared from sight.

In the water, Louis Bruguiere was swimming with his mother on his back. Then without warning he bumped his head on a piece of wreckage. Bruguiere went under but soon resurfaced. His mother, unfortunately, broke loose and was never seen again.

Not far away, a woman passenger was screaming for her life. Two seamen swam to her and assisted the terrified woman on to a raft.

Meanwhile, Captain Finch was also struggling in the water. One of the lifeboats was "banging the life" out of him, but he clung to it although he was too weak to haul himself aboard.

Two firemen drifted by. The captain helped them aboard the lifeboat but again was too exhausted to pull himself into the boat. Later a woman and her baby floated by and were assisted by Finch into the lifeboat. Fortunately for Finch, a wave also swept him in.

For more than an hour, the lifeboats drifted over the *Arabic*'s grave. The choppy water tossed and turned the boats, in the words of J. Edward Usher, "like corks." Many of those in the water managed to cling to the liferafts that floated away. A few boats came by and picked up some of the survivors.

The first sign of hope came when the patrol boats *Primrose* and

Mongolian arrived on the scene. They quickly fished the survivors such as Louis Bruguiere from the water and brought them ashore. The survivors were taken to Queenstown where they were cared for by the White Star Line.

The news of the sinking of the *Arabic* quickly spread throughout the world. It was learned that of the 423 people aboard the liner, 44 perished in the disaster. Two of them were Americans.

The crew of the *Arabic* received praise. Captain Finch declared, "They [the engine room staff] were all heroes a thousand times over." One passenger stated, "It was marvelous how so many boats got afloat. It spoke well for the discipline of the crew."

The performance of Finch and his men was in marked contrast to that of the crew of the *Lusitania*. Unlike Turner, Finch traveled at top speed and avoided headlands. The evacuation was much more organized than on the *Lusitania*. As a result about 90 percent of those aboard the *Arabic* survived compared with only 38 percent on the Cunarder. This is especially impressive considering that the crew of the White Star liner had only nine minutes to abandon ship while that of the *Lusitania* had twice as much time. Their success was due in part to the superior boat drill.

The reaction in the United States was one of hostility towards Germany. *The New York Times* bitterly stated in an editorial:

> But Americans look to the President to uphold the nation's dignity and self-respect and to keep its binding engagements for the protection of the rights of Americans by whatever measures the undertaking may demand. "Peacefully, if we may, forcibly, if we must," is a principle of action not unworthy of the most pacific of nations, and one which where its rights are involved, no nation can disregard without menace to its future peace and security.

Likewise the *Chicago Tribune* blasted:

> It has been established that the *Arabic* was torpedoed without warning and that three (sic) Americans were drowned by the German submarine. The case comes directly under the phrase of President Wilson's note, "a deliberate unfriendly act." Furthermore, the case is outside of the defense given by the Imperial German government for the sinking of the *Lusitania*.
> There is no room for the excuse that the ship was carrying

British troops or war supplies. The ship was sailing *from* England to America. On top of this the torpedoing comes at a time which gives every appearance of sharp diplomacy.

President Woodrow Wilson upon hearing the news of the *Arabic* summoned his Secretary of State, Robert Lansing, to the White House for consultation. It was 29 days since the President's last note to Germany in regard to the *Lusitania* and he wasn't certain whether this attack was Germany's response. The President had stated in that letter that attacking ships with Americans aboard would be viewed as "deliberately unfriendly." Now Germany had committed such an act.

The Germans explained that the commander of U-24, Lt. Commander Schneider, mistook the *Arabic's* zigzag course as an attempt to ram him. He fired the torpedo in self-defense.

Through diplomatic pressure, Wilson forced the German government to refrain from sinking unarmed passenger liners without warning and provisions for the safety of those on board "provided that the liners do not try to escape or offer resistance." Yet six months later, the Germans attacked without warning the ferry boat *Sussex*. Then in January of 1917, the German government announced it would conduct unrestricted submarine warfare. With the threatened sinking of American ships, the United States was drawn into World War I.

The pent up American hostility toward the Kaiser's government was finally unleashed.

12 ■ NOVEMBER 21, 1916

The *Britannic*
". . . Wonderfully Constructed Vessel"

ONE DAY IN 1907, a Mercedes tonneau pulled up in front of the house of Lord Pirrie, the head of Harland & Wolff shipbuilding firm. There, White Star Line President Bruce Ismay and his wife dined with Lord and Lady Pirrie. After dinner, the wives excused themselves while Ismay and Pirrie discussed business.

Ismay had come to the right man. As head of Harland & Wolff, Pirrie had produced many a fine ship. It was for this reason the White Star Line made an agreement to contract a new ship only with that firm. In exchange, Harland & Wolff agreed not to construct a vessel for a line in direct competition with White Star. Now the White Star Line needed an "answer" to Cunard's *Lusitania* and *Mauretania*.

Out of this discussion came the plan to construct three super liners. Each would be half again the size of the *Mauretania*. The three would boast the finest accommodations afloat. They would be named *Olympic, Titanic* and *Britannic*.*

The keel of the third ship, the *Britannic*, was laid on November 30, 1911. By March of the following year, she was framed to the

---

*Legend has it that the third ship was to be called *Gigantic* but was changed after the *Titanic* sank.

height of her double bottom. Shortly after the news of the *Titanic* disaster reached the shipbuilders, alterations were made to make the *Britannic* safer. Her double bottom was extended all the way to the top of the hull. As a result, the 92.5 foot beam was extended by two feet.

Two years later, on February 20, 1914, the new liner was ready for launching. During the ceremonies, an official of Harland & Wolff boldly declared, "Even in the light of the unfortunate and tragic loss of the *Titanic*, I cannot foresee any event that would cause this wonderfully constructed vessel to founder." After all of the speeches were delivered, a bottle was broken on the bow and the ship slid majestically down the ways and into the water.

The *Britannic* was towed to the fitting-out basin. There, for several months, the shipyard workers prepared the liner for service. As Henry Concanon, the joint manager of the company, remarked, "Neither thought nor money has been spared, and when you see the finished article we feel sure that we shall have your approval, as we have had your good wishes today."

When completed, the *Britannic* was very impressive. She was 882.5 feet in length and was 48,158 gross tons. Like the *Olympic* and *Titanic*, the *Britannic* had twenty-four double ended and five single ended boilers. The liner was equipped with two sets of quadruple expansion engines and one set of turbine engines. With triple screws, the ship could make at least 24 knots.

Like her sisterships, the *Britannic* boasted luxurious accommodations. Similar to the *Titanic*, the forward end of the "A" deck promenade was glassed in. While the *Olympic*'s hull was white, the *Titanic*'s was black, and the *Britannic*'s a dark gray.

One of the most interesting features of the new liner was her lifeboat arrangement. The davits were crane-like contractions designed to handle numerous boats. Both of the forward davits lowered a motor launch, two emergency boats and three lifeboats. Fourteen boats were placed amidship and two groups of twelve boats were situated by the forward funnel. The davits were supposedly capable of handling the boats even if the vessel developed a pronounced list. All told there were more than enough boats for her legal capacity.

A White Star Line brochure described the arrangements:

The vessel is equipped with the latest and most approved type of electrically-driven boat lowering gear, by means of which a very large number of boats can, one after the other, be put over the side of the vessel and lowered in much less time than was possible under the old system of davits. . . . One of the advantages of the new system is that the passengers take their places in the boats expeditiously and with perfect safety before the boats are lifted from the deck of the vessel, and the gear is constructed so that the fully laden boats are lowered at a very considerable distance from the side of the ship, thus minimizing risk in bad weather. Moreover, the whole of the boats on board can be lowered on either side of the vessel which happens to be clear, and the gear has been kept so far inboard as to give a wide passage at either side of the ship for promenading and for marshalling the passengers in the event of an emergency.

Plans were made to deliver the *Britannic* to the White Star Line in early 1916, but in the summer of 1914, the First World War broke out. The Admiralty called nearly all of Britain's large liners for service as either troop transports or hospital ships. The *Britannic* was chosen for conversion into a hospital ship.

Thus the shipyard workers prepared the liner for her duty. The first class dining salon was converted to the main hospital. The reception room was made into the Emergency Operating Room. The staterooms were constructed for the officers. The doctors and nurses were given rooms on the upper decks in order to be close to the patients.

The liner's hull was painted white. A huge red stripe was painted along the entire length of the ship below "E" deck. Large red crosses were placed between the second and third funnels below the after mast and just below the forward mast. In addition, two large red crosses were painted on the boat deck and were illuminated at night by bright lights. Hopefully, the Admiralty thought, the *Britannic* would be unmistakenly seen as a hospital ship.

After all of these preparations were completed, the *Britannic* was, on November 17, 1915, ready for duty. She was officially turned over to the Admiralty. Her war career began.

The crew of the new hospital ship went to work. The engineers and stokers lighted the boilers and checked the machinery. The doctors and nurses made the hospital ready. On the bridge, the deck officers were preparing the navigational equipment for service.

This splendid crew was under the command of Captain Charles A. Bartlett. In his distinguished career, Bartlett had served the White Star Line for many years, steadily rising to the rank of Commodore of the Line. He had commanded the *Olympic* and thus was the natural choice for captain of the *Britannic*.

On December 23, 1915, the *Britannic* set out on her first mission. She docked at Mudros on December 28. There she took on 3,300 wounded and arrived at Southampton on January 9, 1916.

After two weeks in Southampton, the *Britannic* departed for another trip. By spring of that year, the hospital ship returned to Belfast. There she was turned back to her owners. Then on August 28, the Admiralty retook possession of the vessel and again employed her as a hospital ship.

On November 18, 1916, the *Britannic* left Salonika, Greece, on a voyage to Mudros. It was her sixth voyage as a hospital ship. She was once more under the command of Charles Bartlett. The liner had no sick or wounded aboard, which was to prove fortunate. However, the ship was carrying 22 surgeons, 77 nurses, 290 orderlies. Altogether there were 1,065 people aboard this fateful trip.

By 8:00 in the morning of November 21, 1916, the *Britannic* was cruising about four miles west of Port St. Nikolo in the Zea Channel. The weather was clear and the sea was calm. There was no sign of any enemy warships.

To Captain Bartlett, this was a relief. There had been reports of German submarines in the region. He wondered if a U-boat would attack his command. While his vessell had unmistakable signs of a hospital ship, the Germans had already sunk such liners as the *Lusitania* and *Arabic* in violation of international law. Would the enemy respect international law in this case?

Suddenly at twelve minutes after 8:00, the *Britannic* was shaken by an explosion. Something had occurred on the starboard side forward, near the bulkhead between the Nos. 2 and 3 holds. Smoke, debris and water shot up and landed on the bridge and boat deck. Some witnesses claim to have heard a second explosion but this has never been confirmed. Almost at once the ship developed a list to the starboard.

Captain Bartlett reacted immediately. He ordered the wireless operators to transmit an S.O.S. He then decided to beach his command by the shore which was a mere four miles away.

The huge hospital ship swung around and headed for land. Unfortunately for Bartlett, the steering gear failed. Water continued to cascade into the forward compartments. Reluctantly the captain stopped the engines.

Bartlett turned his attention toward abandoning ship. He ordered the lifeboats filled and lowered. Quickly the crew prepared the boats. The nurses, doctors and crew calmly entered the boats. There was no panic. The two motor launches and several conventional boats were successfully lowered.

When all of the crew had abandoned ship, Captain Bartlett "walked off his ship, into the water . . ." He floated in the water for several minutes until he was picked up by a motor launch.

A crisis developed when three lifeboats came too close to the liner's stern. As the *Britannic* dipped down by the head, her starboard propeller rose above the water and smashed the three lifeboats. Some of the occupants were lost. Captain Bartlett ordered the two motor launches to pick up the survivors.

After these people were fished out of the water, Bartlett began to consider his next course of action. With some of his crew injured, the captain decided to send the motor boats to Port St. Nikolo. There his crew could receive medical attention.

Soon in response to the *Britannic*'s S.O.S., the British warships *Heroic*, *Scourge* and *Foxhound*, along with a French tug, arrived on the scene. When all of the survivors were taken aboard, the tug's captain suggested towing the crippled liner to the shore. By this time, however, the *Britannic*'s bow was down and the ship had a pronounced list. Such a plan was out of the question.

Those aboard the rescue ships watched helplessly as the liner's bow dipped under water. The bulkheads collapsed and the *Britannic* slid down into the bottom of the Aegean Sea 620 feet below. Numerous explosions occurred as the boilers blew.

It was not the last time, though, that the *Britannic* was seen. In 1977, Jacques Cousteau, the famous sea explorer, visited the *Britannic*'s grave and discovered the lost liner in fairly good condition.

One question unanswered to this day is whether the *Britannic* was torpedoed by a German U-boat or struck a mine. At the time, many assumed that since the *Lusitania* and *Arabic* were torpedoed, the *Britannic* was similarly attacked. Thus there was a worldwide uproar. London's *Daily Chronicle* stated bitterly:

> Those who calculate the seriousness of these crimes by their actual results alone may think less of such a case than of the *Lusitania*, but if wickedness is to be measured as it is reasonably to be expected, the results of this crime must exceed even that ghastly massacre and take rank at the very top of German achievements in infamy. Those of our friends in America who have been suggesting that Germany has learned her lesson and changed her bad heart for a better one will forgive us if in view of such sustained and reiterated atrocities we remain of different opinion.

Some of the survivors claimed to have heard a second explosion. The Germans seized on this and concluded, "The *Britannic* was transporting fresh troops and munitions to aid in battle . . ." However, there is insufficient evidence to support this theory. It is possible that the second explosion, if there was one, was a bursting boiler.

The question of whether it was a torpedo or mine which doomed the *Britannic* is difficult to resolve. Some witnesses claimed to have seen a periscope and the wake of a torpedo but false reports are not uncommon. The U-73 under Lt. Commander Siehs had laid mines in the channel. Although the area was previously cleared of mines, the day after the *Britannic* sank two were discovered not far from where the great liner met her doom. It is this author's (qualified) opinion that the hospital ship did strike a mine.

In any event the Allies suffered a terrible loss. The *Britannic* was the largest ship sunk in World War I. The White Star Line's dream of a trio of luxury liners serving the North Atlantic was as dead as were twenty-one crew members of the *Britannic*.

13 ■ NOVEMBER 12, 1928

The *Vestris*
"A Change From the Conventional"

By AGE sixty, Captain William J. Carey had served the Lamport & Holt Line for four decades without serious accident. With the exception of the World War I casualty *Titian*, he had never experienced a shipwreck. Already he had been made Commodore of the Line. His prospects were looking brighter with his new command, the *Voltaire*, awaiting him at Buenos Aires.

Carey was not to have such thoughts as he stood on the bridge of the 511-foot-5-inch-long *Vestris* (the *Voltaire*'s sistership) on November 10, 1928. He was to take his twin screw command to Barbados, Rio and finally Buenos Aires on her Christmas voyage with 128 passengers and 6,000 tons of cargo aboard. Actually he was carrying some 200 tons more than was permitted but the Lamport & Holt Line felt the *Vestris* would still make her Brazilian port safely even though she was a foot over draft.

Many of the more observant spectators by the pier noticed something else peculiar about the *Vestris*. She gave the appearance of listing slightly. A few women friends of Carlos Quiros, an Argentine consulate official, jokingly told him, "You will have to walk on one side." Quiros also noticed the list but thought nothing of it. He was certain the *Vestris*, advertised as "a change from the conventional," was safe and dwelled more on his visit to his mother than on the vessel's slight list.

What was unknown to Quiros and his friends was that the ship had several leaks, notably in the starboard ash ejector discharge. Captain Carey was aware of the problem but did not think it warranted serious concern. It seemed doubtful, Carey reasoned, that either the ship or the passengers would be in any danger. It was the first of many fatal blunders he was to make on this voyage.

Within hours after departing from New York, the clear weather deteriorated. A strong northeast wind swept into the path of the *Vestris*, causing the placid ocean to become rough. Although Carey did not record it as gale force, it was sufficient enough to toss and turn the 10,494 ton vessel considerably.

By Sunday morning, the day after sailing day, the *Vestris* was listing to the starboard by some 5°. Paul Dana, a South American representative of the Radio Corporation of America, recalled, "I had never seen quite such a list. It looked bad," though he dismissed the situation. They were, after all, in the midst of a terrible storm. Besides the crew was reassuring everyone that all would be well. So he, like most of the passengers, simply relaxed as much as one can in a storm and enjoyed the ship that was said to be so unconventional.

Correspondent William Davies was not so easily convinced. He was also told that the list would be corrected in an hour or so. Still, he could not help but feel the situation was "alarming."

Carlos Quiros rang up a steward and ordered a meal of consommé, eggs and fruit. He attempted to enjoy his dinner when the ship gave a violent roll and both he and his food fell to the floor. This made Quiros "realize for the first time that the situation was serious."

Quiros at once ventured into the salon dining room only to find it a shambles. Numerous tables and chairs were piled up towards the starboard side of the ship. Quiros also noticed some women who appeared to be seasick.

The consul made his way back to his stateroom for half a bottle of champagne and some fruit. His steward could not find champagne in the disorderly pantry but was able to salvage some grapes, gin and water. Quiros asked if there was any indication of danger. The steward politely replied that the crew was manning the pumps and that the ocean was calmer now. Quiros was content with the answer and turned in around 9:30.

A few diehards attempted to brave out the list in the dining room. Among them was Edward Johnson, a Standard Oil Company attorney, who joined Chief Engineer Adams at his table. The two attempted to eat their dinner but were constantly interrupted by sliding furniture and finally by a waiter falling on their table.

This was too much for William Davies. He gathered a plate of cold meat and retired to his cabin to finish his meal. En route, the correspondent was assured by a crewman that the ship was in no danger.

Not all was well. The list, now 20°, caused three automobiles stored in the cargo hold to crash through a bulkhead and into the crew's quarters. By late evening, all unfastened furniture slid over to the starboard side. Practically no one was able to sleep that night.

Through it all, Captain Carey remained confident. At midnight, he was informed by Chief Engineer Adams that the pumps were "holding the water" although the bulkheads were leaking. Still, Carey was not alarmed. Instead he wired his Lamport & Holt employers that he was "lying hove-to," meaning bow first and engines stopped. Actually, Carey had his ship's engines pushing the *Vestris* at her full 15-knot speed.

His risky action was in accordance with the line's policy:

> . . . in the case of serious disaster happening to one of the vessels of this line, whilst at sea, the master must in the first instance carefully consider the actual amount of peril there may be for the lives of those under his charge and then judge whether he will be justified or not, in fighting his own way unaided to the nearest port. His being able to succeed in this will always be considered a matter of high recommendation to his skill as a master.

In this case the policy was to prove costly.

At 4:00 A.M., Carey decided to personally inspect the engine room. He found the *Vestris* in far worse condition than he had anticipated. To remedy the problem, the captain ordered three ballast tanks pumped dry. Again Carey blundered. Instead of correcting the list, this action worsened the ship's stability.

Monday morning brought more disturbing occurrences. As

Paul Dana, the RCA representative, opened his eyes, he noticed water seeping through the port. He called this to the attention of a steward, who explained it as a "leak."

In another cabin, William Davies found looking out of his porthole was like "looking at the bottom of a well." The list was so great he could not even see the horizon.

Dr. E. Lehner was awakened by a shipboard friend, H.C.W. Johnston. Johnston had traveled many times before at sea and he could sense when something was wrong. "Look here, Lehner," Johnston said to him, "I think you are very much safer on deck. You had better get up and get dressed."

"Well, I am sleeping quite comfortably here, thank you," the half-awake Lehner replied. With that said, Johnston went topside and Lehner went back to sleep. An hour later, Lehner woke up and saw the light. He gathered up his passport and notebook and ascended to the boat deck.

On the open deck, Lehner found the *Vestris* to be listing about 30° to 35°, he judged by his geological knowledge. He quickly found Johnston, who was discussing with two other passengers whether they should talk this matter over with the captain. "Well, I think we ought to go and ask the captain what the devil is the matter," Johnston said solidly. Lehner advised against it. The captain knew what he was doing, he asserted. Johnston and the others agreed to allow the captain to run his ship as he saw fit.

Argentine consul Quiros did go to the bridge to ask Carey if there was any danger. "No danger at all," he received for an answer, "we shall have this trouble over soon."

Quiros did not share Carey's optimism. He had already come across a group of seamen bailing out water with buckets. "Afraid and cautious," Quiros returned to his cabin for his life preserver.

Finally, Captain Carey belatedly decided to send a call of distress. At 8:37 A.M., he ordered Chief Wireless Operator Michael O'Laughlin to send "CQ," meaning "stand by." He did not authorize an S.O.S.

Elsewhere, a few members of the crew were struggling to throw items of cargo overboard. Standing by, Paul Dana observed "bales of cloth and such stuff" being thrown overboard. "They couldn't get rid of the heavier things like automobiles."

Dana by now had suspected that he would have to abandon the

Vestris by the end of the day. He tried not to show his fears so that there would be no panic. He and several others did what they could to enlighten the ones in despair. A few officers helped by going about cheering everyone up with words of hope.

Not everyone was careful to conceal their evident fate. Dana overheard one man casually say, "Well, anyway, we've got a nice day to be wrecked on." It was a low comic remark but it proved to be prophetic.

Dana decided if he was going to leave the *Vestris* at least he could save the money he had in his trunk. So he returned to his room to get it but found that the trunk was by now under water. So he gathered his passport and some cigarettes and hurried back to the boat deck.

At 10:00, all illusions of safety the captain had were gone. He again ordered O'Laughlin to send a wireless dispatch. This time the message had a tone of urgency. "*Vestris* in distress . . . !" the message read. She gave her position about 240 miles east of Norfolk.

A number of ships in the 150-mile vicinity picked up the message from "HWNK" (the *Vestris* call letters). The S.S. *Berlin* of the Hamburg American Line, the Puerto Rico Line *San Juan*, the Grace Line *Santa Barbare*, the Coast Guard cutter *Davis*, the battleship *Wyoming*, and the *American Shipper* of the United States Line, along with numerous other ships, acknowledged the call for help and set course for the endangered liner. Even the air dirigible *Los Angeles* was dispatched despite the poor flying conditions.

With high hopes that rescue was at hand, Captain Carey decided to ready the lifeboats but not lower them. Other ships were on the way and it did not make much sense to Carey to put the lifeboats out in the turbulent sea. Instead, he decided to fill them with the women and children and then wait.

Again Carey made a fatal error. In addition to delaying the lowering of the boats, he had the women and children huddled into the weather boats which were high above the water rather than into the boats which were closer to the water. This seemed especially foolish in light of the wrecks of the *Empress of Ireland* and *Lusitania*.

Nevertheless, the crew obeyed. The women and children were

loaded into the weather boats, which were discovered to be lacking provisions. Second Steward Duncan solved this problem by distributing bananas, Fig Newtons and crackers.

At 11:30, the captain felt he could wait no longer and he gave the order to cast off the lifeboats. Boat No. 8 couldn't be immediately lowered because it had a hole in it. Quickly the crew set out to repair it.

The davit men at boat No. 10 also had problems. After loading the boat with Edward Johnson, Dr. Lehner and about fifty others, one of the men working the davit became careless and had his hand crushed against the ship's side. The rest of the crew members were able to lower the boat only to find the ax provided was too dull to cut the davit rope. A passenger quickly produced a jackknife and was able to slice through the hemp.

With boat No. 10 adrift, another problem arose. Of the fifty or so individuals aboard, none were seamen. Dr. Lehner proposed that a passenger by the name of Sinclair take charge. He seemed to Lehner to be the most level-headed of the group. The others didn't take his advice. So lifeboat No. 10 drifted away with no one in command.

Meanwhile, a crewman was able to repair the damaged No. 8 with a tin plate and nails. It was a far from comforting repair job but it would have to do. Quickly the boat was loaded with ten women, two children, Stewardess Clara Ball, and RCA's Paul Dana and was lowered away. As it dropped down to the sea, the list caused it to bang against the side, stowing a hole in the keel.

Cline Slaughter, a traveling auditor for International Harvester Company, and his tall, gray-eyed wife climbed aboard No. 4 with about fifty others. The boat bumped down the side when a heavy spar suddenly came crashing down, splitting the boat in two. Most of the occupants were crushed or drowned. In the confusion, Slaughter and his wife were separated.

Quiros watched the scene in horror. He believed that "this ship would not survive another roll." Nevertheless he decided not to board a lifeboat. It seemed to him to be safer to remain aboard the ship and wait for rescue than to venture in a small wooden boat.

Captain Carey also decided to stay with his command. Without cap, unshaven, and according to some survivors, a broken man, Carey paid no attention to Second Steward Duncan's pleas to save himself.

"Well, Captain," Duncan tried, "here's a belt for you!"

"Never mind about me, Duncan,'" Carey said flatly, "Take the belt yourself and go!"

And he did.

Chief Wireless Operator Michael O'Laughlin also refused to abandon his post. For hours, the thirty-year-old Irishman tapped out the distress message Captain Carey had given him. At one point, he wired, "It's the devil's work with this list." Through his efforts, O'Laughlin managed to contact numerous vessels.

The situation only worsened with time. At one point, he wired desperately, "Oh, please come at once! We need immediate assistance!" Finally, wireless operators MacDonald and Verchere persuaded O'Laughlin to leave before it was too late. O'Laughlin took the advice and wired "Now taking to the lifeboats. Goodbye to WSC," and followed his two companions to the boat deck.

Quiros, the consul, experienced a twist of fate. Before him was a bewildered Spaniard whom he recognized as the very man he earlier had turned down for a visa on the grounds that he lacked the proper credentials. Later, Quiros decided to approve the passport so he could visit his family. Now the man was on a sinking ship.

"There," Quiros approached him, "aren't you sorry I gave you that visa?" The man did not say a word. He just remained where he was, unable to grasp what was happening to him. The man subsequently had survived, for Quiros saw him on one of the rescue ships.

Quiros had no more time for him. "Stay with me," he told correspondent Davies, "I'm going to live." When asked why, Quiros replied, "Because of my mother." It seemed an odd answer but the consul was somehow certain that his visit to his mother was destined to happen.

By 2:00, the *Vestris* had sunk deeper. The end was near. "Time to go!" Quiros called to Davies. The two men shook hands and leaped overboard.

First Officer Johnson was about to jump into the water when he heard his captain shout, "My God! My God! I am not to blame for this!"

Finally at 2:36 on the morning of November 12, 1928, the agony of the Lamport & Holt Line *Vestris* ended. The ship that was "a change from the conventional" disappeared from sight.

Over the *Vestris*'s grave, Carlos Quiros swam for a nearby lifeboat. He managed to reach No. 13 and was pulled in by the crew. Quiros helped organize the boat and returned to the scene. By the end of the day, he had helped rescue Steward Duncan, Chief Engineer Adams and fourteen others.

H. C. Johnston, the General Manger to the Trinidad Lease-holds Ltd., also was fortunate to make it to a boat. He and the others aboard rowed to the crowded No. 10 and took a few of the occupants into their own boat.

One particularly brave man was Lionel Lucorish, the black quartermaster. Lucorish, in charge of lifeboat No. 14, found that he and his men were short of oars. He dove into the water and swam from boat to boat borrowing a few oars. On several occasions, he picked up several helpless nonswimmers. In all, he saved between sixteen and twenty lives.

Not all were able to make it aboard a lifeboat. Paul Dana found himself in the open water when his boat, No. 8, sank under his feet. It was the one that had sustained a hole when it banged against the *Vestris*'s side. Rough water did not help matters. The boat's company tried to righten it but a wave reduced it to splinters.

Dana and Stewardess Ball were left clinging to a piece of wreckage. At a time like this, Dana managed to notice that Mrs. Ball carried an extra pair of shoes in her life preserver and he asked her why. The woman explained that her feet were of an unusual size and the shoes were made especially for her. She did not wish to lose them.

William Davies had a different experience. He later explained:

> I supported myself, by clinging first to a chair, then to part of a hatch, on which I scrambled, next to a piece of heavy timber which offered good support. In this boiling and seething mass of water and wood, I caught sight of my friend, Mr. Koppe, who was clinging to what looked like a small raft, but this may have

been the top of a hatch. A heavy wave came along and I was hurled off the board to which I was clinging when it collided with a tightly wedged mass of heavy wreckage. . . . I was able to look around me and I saw numbers of people swimming in the water, but most of the boats were standing off, apparently feeling that they had their full complement. I saw two boats were cruising around the wreckage but they did not come very near. I found that I had time to shift from one piece of timber to another, until finally I reached a broken overturned boat. It was lying completely upside down in the water, and I managed to scramble on top of it, and from this position to look around. . . .

Davies tried to hail one of the boats but there was no response. He called for another boat. It came within 20 feet of him but could venture no further in fear of smashing against the timber. So Davies jumped into the water, swam to it and was pulled in by a crew member using a boat hook.

For hours, the boats and swimmers drifted about. Night came and the occupants of the lifeboats made numerous tries, most of them unsuccessful, to fire flares. Others were occupied with the task of bailing out water in their boats.

A squabble broke out in lifeboat No., 13. Carlos Quiros was awakened from slumber by a healthy kick. The angry consul let loose a few expletives. "No, man," the perpetrator of the incident said fearfully, "don't swear just now. Please, man, don't swear!"

Paul Dana and Mrs. Ball weren't as mindful. They spent the night freely "cussing out Captain Carey for not getting those radio messages out earlier."

Around midnight, the survivors were aware of a searchlight scanning the area. Numerous flares were sent off in hope of attracting the rescue ships' attention. In lifeboat No. 13, one of the complement would count to three when all aboard would shout for help.

By daybreak on the 14th, virtually all of the survivors were picked up. Among those rescued were Chief Engineer Adams, William Davies, Carlos Quiros, Edward Johnson, Dr. Lehner, H.C.W. Johnston, Second Steward Duncan, and Mr. and Mrs. Cline Slaughter.

One near oversight was Paul Dana and Mrs. Ball, who were both still clinging to a piece of wreckage. Dana suggested that they had best swim for the battleship *Wyoming*. Ball began to stroke towards the large warship when Captain Cummings of the *American Shipper* noticed them (the "pluckiest pair," he described them). Within minutes the two were safely aboard.

The world was stunned by the news of the *Vestris*. It was later learned that of the 325 who sailed on that fateful voyage, 110— almost one-third of the passengers and crew—were lost, including Captain Carey and wireless operator O'Laughlin. The 215 rescued were predominately men. None of the children and only a handful of women survived. Most of the men who survived were members of the crew. In fact three-quarters of the crew were saved while less than one half of the passengers were rescued.

In fairness to the crew, most acted bravely with the safety of the passengers in mind. The evidence clearly supports this assumption. The first few boats lowered contained passengers. Also Quartermaster Lucorish's bravery and Wireless Operator O'Laughlin's sacrificing his life in order to perform his duty would indicate that this was so. It was a combination of circumstances, one of them that many of the passengers, notably the women and children, were placed into the weather boats that led to a proportionally high loss of life.

The fault lies not with the crew in general, but squarely on the dead captain who, to his credit, did remain aboard his command until the end. Still his actions by all accounts were disastrous. He delayed in sending an S.O.S. when all was obviously not well. The Court of Inquiry believed, "His (Captain Carey's) conduct in connection with the boats is open to some criticism." The captain, the court concluded, should not have lowered the weather boats. Only one weather boat survived while most of the remaining conventional boats were successfully lowered.

A wireless operator tried to defend Carey by pointing out that the sending of an S.O.S. is a "serious" undertaking. He stated the undeniable fact that a master should do his best at his end before involving other ships. Yet the condition of the *Vestris* was beyond this situation. The leaks, the automobiles smashing through a bulkhead, and the incredible list of the ship definitely warranted an S.O.S.

Nor was the Lamport & Holt Line without blame. The company had seriously overloaded the *Vestris* on her last voyage.

Strangely the company was fined only $2,500. This was an extremely light penalty when one considers the devasting results of the overloading. In addition, the company policy may have led Carey to delay the sending of an S.O.S.

In the end, beyond question, the root cause of the disaster lies in human error. As was the case sixteen years earlier, man had put too much faith in modern shipbuilding and too little emphasis on seamanship. Once again the danger of the sea had been greatly underestimated.

14 ■ JULY 26, 1956

The *Andrea Doria*
"A Living Testament to Beauty"

WITH THE END of World War II, the shipping
companies of the world were able to resume transporting cargo
and passengers without concern for torpedoes and mines. In fact,
the use of ships not only was resumed, but more passengers and
cargo made ocean crossings than in pre-war days. It was at first
thought that the airplane would replace the ship for travel after
the war and in a sense it did. However, the trade and tourism
during the postwar period surged to the point where even with
airplane competition, shipping lines actually gained business.

Many European nations took full advantage of this surge,
including Italy. That country needed all available business to put
it back on its feet after its wartime defeat, and shipping would be
one of these available opportunities that she could use. Consequently, the Italian Line began at war's end to build a large
merchant fleet.

One of the liner's most impressive ships was the luxury liner
Andrea Doria. Completed in June of 1951 and embarking on her
maiden voyage in January 1953, the *Andrea Doria* was one of the
biggest and most comfortable passenger liners to cross the Atlantic. With limited resources, the Italian Line was forced to build its
passenger ships smaller and slower than the liners of its British
competition. Instead, the company concentrated on providing the

143

1,250 possible passengers of the *Andrea Doria* with beauty and luxury. All three classes were provided with swimming pools and other recreation facilities. There were also daily movies in handsome theaters for all three classes, sports events, lovely paintings, music and air conditioning for the entire ship. She was so beautiful that the Italian Line described the *Andrea Doria* as "a living testament to the importance of beauty in the everyday world."

Although the liner was not as large as some of the British ships, she nevertheless was one of the largest passenger ships in the world. Registered at 29,100 gross tons, the *Andrea Doria* was only some 2,000 tons smaller than the *Lusitania*. She was eleven decks in height and measured 697 feet in length and 90 feet in width.

Equally impressive were her powerful engines. The *Andrea Doria*'s twin turbine engines were capable of turning the double 16 foot propellers 134 revolutions per minute. At Full Speed Ahead, this ship could achieve 23 knots. A great deal of fuel was required to operate these engines, with approximately 2,200 tons of oil used per Atlantic crossing. In fact, the *Andrea Doria* consumed between 10-11 tons of oil in one hour.

This vessel also featured the safety standards of the 1948 International Conference of Stability. Divided into eleven watertight compartments, the *Andrea Doria* would remain buoyant with any two of these compartments flooded, but like the "safety design" of the *Titanic*, the bulkheads separating the compartments did not extend to the top deck level. If three or more adjacent compartments were flooded, the ship would list enough for the water to overflow, fill the remaining compartments and ultimately sink.

However, the *Andrea Doria* seemed immune from this disaster because of two factors. The first was that the ship's radar system could reveal the relative position of icebergs and other ships. Even in dense fog conditions, the officer in charge could guide the ship safely on her course.

Second, the master of the *Andrea Doria*, Captain Piero Calamai, was an experienced and cautious seaman. At 58, he had served 39 years at sea. During his career, he had won the War Cross for Military Valor in both world wars. He had served on 29 different ships between the wars and finally received his first command of the *Andrea Doria* (a different ship). After World War II, he was given command of the postwar *Andrea Doria* and became the youngest captain of a first-rate ship on the Italian Line.

Through his long career, "Little Peter" was said to have developed a "sixth sense" in predicting fog. Actually he was simply a cautious mariner who was concerned with the safe navigation of his ship. He feared, with justification, fog conditions. He had faced mist off the coast of Nantucket on many of his voyages aboard the *Doria*. After all of these numerous experiences, Calamai was able to study the sky and foresee the coming of fog.

On July 25, 1956, on the last leg of the westbound portion of the *Andrea Doria's* 51st voyage, Captain Calamai's "sixth sense" didn't fail him and he began to notice the telltale signs of fog. For safety's sake, all ships encountering fog were to reduce speed. Rule 16 of the "Regulations for Preventing Collision at Sea" (commonly called "the rules of the road") states that all ships in fog shall "go at a moderate speed."

On the other hand, the passengers had been traveling nine days and had been held up by a storm. Any further delays might mean missing train, bus and plane connections on docking. Also there were longshoremen who would have to wait hours longer by the dock on salary. This put Calamai in a dilemma.

The key in rule 16 was no mention of the degree of the speed reduction. This was generally based upon the discretion of the ship's master. For the most part the Atlantic crossings at this time were conducted at top speed or nearly top speed even in the worst fog conditions. The business of the shipping companies after all would be hurt by delays. Besides, the modern ship by 1956 was equipped with radar. It did not seem that there was an untoward risk in running a liner at top speed in even the worst visibility conditions.

So the captain decided to cut his speed from 23 knots to only 21.8 knots. This was accomplished by reducing steam pressure in the boilers, a less expensive and less fuel-consuming method than reducing the number of nozzles feeding high-compression steam from the boilers into the turbines. At the same time, this cost the *Andrea Doria* power and maneuverability because it would take much more time to build up boiler pressure than to open closed turbine nozzles.

Other measures also were taken. The fog whistle was activated at 100 second intervals, the watertight doors were ordered closed, and the lookout in the crow's nest was stationed near the bow in order to overcome the poor visibility caused by the heavy water particles. As an added precaution, one of the two radar sets was manned by an officer to scan the 20-mile vicinity.

About 100 miles west of the *Andrea Doria*, the Swedish-American liner *Stockholm* was on an eastbound course to Copenhagen and Gothenburg from New York. Her master, Captain H. Gunnar Nordenson, was as cautious a mariner as Captain Calamai. A veteran of the sea for forty-six years, Captain Nordenson was well aware of the potential danger of collision in fog. It was for this reason he left standing orders that he be summoned to the bridge in case of fog. The *Stockholm* was traveling in a region where fog was common, but so far this night her officers hadn't encountered any such visibility problems. So Nordenson decided to remain in his quarters.

At 8:30, Third Officer Johan-Ernst Bogislau August Carstens-Johanssen (referred to as Carstens by his friends) reported to the bridge for his 8:30 to midnight watch. Second Officer Lars Enestrom, the officer on watch, turned the bridge over to Carstens and retired for the night. With the captain not present and the second officer retiring, Carstens was now in control of the ship.

Carstens was rather young to take charge of the bridge of a 12,163-ton ship. He was only twenty-six and had been at sea for just six years. He had been assigned to the *Stockholm* a mere two months before.

On the other hand, the enormously large third officer had many impressive points. He had decided to devote his life to the sea at a very early age. At nineteen, in 1949, he was hired by the Brostrom Concern, the largest shipowning company in Sweden. Three years later, he went to Sweden's Nautical College where he earned both his officer's license and master's license at the age of twenty-two. In the next three years, Carstens had served on various cargo ships and one passenger liner. Then in May 1956, he was assigned to the *Stockholm*.

Now on the night of July 25, 1956, he was in charge of the ship. He was instructed to call Captain Nordenson in the event of fog or the sighting of the Nantucket Lightship. So far he encountered none of these sights. He had everything under control. The weather was clear and the ocean was peaceful. The young officer had no reason to believe a disaster would soon occur.

But the officer was to keep on the alert tonight. He was responsible for the safety of the ship for the next three and half hours. He had three men, Peder Larsen, Ingenar Björkman and Sten Johansson, under his command to aid him in the navigation of the *Stockholm*. The three were alternates, one to act as lookout, one as the helmsman, and one to stand by.

Both Captain Nordenson and Carstens may or may not have known that each ship was traveling on a "recognized track" set aside by the North Atlantic Track Agreement. This voluntary agreement was established among shipping companies of Great Britain, the United States, Belgium, France, and the Netherlands to prevent collision. Neither the Swedish-American Line nor the Italian Line was under this agreement.

After checking the new course in the chartroom, Carstens found the ship's position by use of the SAL log, an instrument that records the mileage of the ship by means of a brass tube projecting from the bottom of the vessel. With the *Stockholm*'s position marked, he returned to the bridge.

The *Stockholm* usually passed two or three ships on the first night of embarkation from New York. So far this night Carstens found no need to take action for oncoming ships. To break the monotony, he switched the range of his radar from 15 miles to 50 miles. After observing many geographical points of interest on the Eastern seaboard, the third officer switched it back to 15 miles and resumed his watch.

At 10:30, Carstens took an RDF (Radar Direction Finder) reading to locate the lightship from his present position. He found the *Stockholm* to be two and three quarters miles off course.

"Steer eighty-nine," he instructed helmsman Johansson.

"Eighty-nine, yes sir," the helmsman replied.

Ten minutes later, the crew was rotated. Peder Larsen took over as helmsman. Johansson relieved Bjorkman in the crow's nest and Bjorkman went to the standby room to rest.

Carstens kept a sharp eye on various activities on the bridge. He would occasionally look up at the crow's nest to check on Johansson, and would examine the radar set every two or three minutes to see if there were any ships in the *Stockholm*'s path. Carstens once in awhile would also observe Larsen at the wheel. The third officer was well aware of the helmsman's wandering attention.

Some 50 miles east of the *Stockholm*, the *Andrea Doria* was cruising on her New York voyage. Unlike the Swedish liner, the *Andrea Doria* had three officers on watch instead of one. Captain Calamai himself was one of them. Staff Captain Magagnini had offered to take his place for this night but Calamai would have no other man run his command during fog conditions.

The captain had sufficient help from the other two officers on the bridge. One of them, Second Officer Franchini, was well experienced. At the age of thirty-six, he had spent nearly two decades at sea. The other, Junior Third Officer Giannini, had served only seven years at sea but he had the proper training and held a master's certificate. Both of these officers were trained in the use of radar.

Captain Calamai, like the *Stockholm*'s third officer, kept careful watch over the various activities on the bridge, checking the course in the chartroom and often walking out to the bridge wing to see if any ships were visible. Occasionally, the captain would glance at the radar scope.

Around 9:30, Giannini, manning one of the radar sets, reported that he had picked up an object. Observing the radar screen Captain Calamai concluded they had at last reached Nantucket Lightship. The lightship was expected at about this time. Franchini took an RDF reading and not only confirmed it was the lightship but found the *Doria* was on a collision course with the anchored ship.

For safety's sake, Calamai ordered a six degree change in course to the port. Franchini took over the radar watch for the approach to the lightship. By 10:20, the *Andrea Doria* safely passed the anchored ship. It was all routine.

Less than a half an hour after passing the lightship, the radar picked up another object. Second Officer Franchini at first thought it was a small, slow ship being overtaken by the *Doria*. Then it dawned on him that it was a vessel coming towards them.

"It's a ship!" he called, "I can see a ship coming against us!"

"What's its bearing?" the captain asked.

"She's 17 miles away, four degrees to the starboard!"

Gathering around the radar set, the three officers observed the "pip" move closer to the *Andrea Doria*. It seemed so small and slow that no one on the *Doria* bothered to plot the speed of the oncoming vessel. The captain thought the "pip" most likely represented a slow fishing trawler headed for Nantucket Island. He was not aware that the ship was closing in on his command two miles every three minutes.

Some 17 miles west of the Italian liner, the *Stockholm*'s third officer was engaged in finding the Swedish ship's present course. He knew the *Stockholm* was drifting farther to the north. Shortly after 10:30, he found the liner was off course by 2¾ miles. To correct this, Carstens ordered a 2° turn to the starboard.

As helmsman Larsen turned the wheel to 91°, Carstens noticed a "pip" on the radar scope. It was a ship about 12 miles to the port of the *Stockholm*. Carstens adjusted the set for added brightness to improve the focus but the object remained small. He decided to wait until the oncoming ship was within ten miles of his vessel to plan his action.

Carstens knew he had to be careful in plotting his maneuvers. He was well aware the ship's radar was not totally accurate, giving not an exact position, but a relative one.

Soon the "pip" of the other ship was within a ten mile range. Carstens quickly plotted the new course for a safe passing. He would have to arrange for a passing with a margin of one mile in accordance with Captain Nordenson's standing orders to never allow a ship to come within one mile of the *Stockholm*.

Some ten miles away, Second Officer Franchini of the *Andrea Doria* did not bother to go through the long mental process of trigometry to find the course and speed of the "pip" on his radar screen. Instead he relied on a method commonly used by most seaman. He simply studied the angle of the other ship to his with the rule that if the angle of the radar bearing on the other ship increased, there would be a safe passing. Although this shortcut saved time and work, it was not as accurate as plotting by pencil and paper. To Franchini's strained eyes, the angle appeared to be increasing.

To make certain that the two vessels would pass each other without danger, Calamai decided to make a turn to the port to increase the passing distance. Actually the Rules of the Road state that all ships meeting head on or nearly head on should turn to the starboard to have a port-to-port side passing. Only under certain circumstances when a port-to-port passing would be dangerous is a starboard-to-starboard passing permitted. With the crowded shallow water on his right and the open sea to his left, Calamai felt a left turn was in order.

By 11:03, Third Officer Carstens had his maneuvers planned. The radar screen showed the ship to be about four miles away. He was somewhat puzzled by the fact that he could not see the lights of the other ship. It did not occur to him that a patch of fog might be obstructing the view.

Suspicious, Carstens had a feeling he should summon the captain, but then decided not to bother Nordenson. The visibility was after all not poor enough to warrant this action. Besides, he had his maneuvers already planned and the *Stockholm* with her diesel engines had 100 percent backing power compared with ships with steam turbines which have only 30-60 percent backing power.

By 11:06, the other ship was less than two miles away from the *Stockholm*. From the crow's nest came the shout, "Lights to the port!"

Confident he had everything under control, Carstens ordered helmsman Larsen to turn to the starboard for the standard port-to-port passing.

A short distance away, Captain Calamai was also taking measures to insure his ship's safety. He order the helmsman, Seaman Visuano, "Four degrees to the left . . . and nothing to the right." Now, he thought, the *Andrea Doria* would have a larger passing distance without wasting fuel or getting too far off course.

Still the captain was disturbed. He couldn't hear the other ship's fog whistle, nor could he see its lights. Along with Junior Third Officer Giannini, Calamai stood by the bridge wing peering into the foggy night. Giannini with his younger eyes and aided with binoculars spotted a haze of light. The young officer began to study the lights curiously. Something, he knew, was wrong. Suddenly, he realized that the mysterious ship was turning towards the *Doria*!

"She is turning! She is turning!" he cried.

In a flash, Calamai also saw what was happening. He hesitated. After a moment of indecision, he gave the order, "Tutto sinistro" (All left).

The captain also kept the engines at Full Speed Ahead. He knew that the *Doria* with 40-60 percent backing power could not possibly stop in time. His only hope was for the liner to outrace the mysterious ship.

A short distance away, the *Stockholm*'s third officer also realized both ships were on a collision course. Instantly, he pulled the levers of the engine telegraph to "Stop" position and then to "Full Speed Astern."

"Hard-a-starboard," he shouted to the helmsman. He then waited . . . and hoped.

On board the *Andrea Doria*, Captain Calamai stood on the bridge wing watching in shock as the *Stockholm* came closer to his ship. It soon came clear to him that the *Doria* could not turn in time. Terrified, he whirled back into the bridge.

A few seconds later, the double skin bow of the 12,165 ton *Stockholm* pierced the hull of the Italian liner. The *Andrea Doria* shook violently. Then with the damage inflicted, the Swedish liner separated from the *Doria* and drifted away.

The crew and passengers of both ships felt the jar. Aboard the *Stockholm*, passenger Dr. Pettit watched through a porthole as the two ships drew closer together. He warned his wife, "We're going to crash." While his wife braced herself, the doctor remained by the porthole to witness the collision.

In a cabin near the *Stockholm*'s hospital, Nurse Karin Claesson had been drinking a cup of coffee at the time of the collision. Suddenly the cup flew in the air and she fell backwards. Getting up, she quickly put on her lifebelt and raced to the cabin door when she realized that she was undressed. She slipped into her uniform and rushed to offer her help.

Her help was needed. In cabin 4M, crew member Alf Johansson was hurled about in the room upon impact. Both his legs were broken and his skull was fractured.

In the *Stockholm*'s radio shack, Third Radio Operator Sven Brick Johansson was occupied with a message to Gothenburg when he was hurled through the air. After he got back to his feet, he wired back to Gothenburg apologizing, "Sorry, we have collided."

Aboard the *Andrea Doria*, actress Ruth Roman kicked off her shoes and ran for her double cabin. She awakened her son Richard and told him they were to embark on a "picnic." Gathering lifejackets and blankets, she and her son abandoned their cabin.

In the card room just behind the Belvedere Lounge, Father Richard Wojcik and two other priests were interrupted in their game of Scrabble by a "jarring of the ship." Wojcik noticed the ship developed an ominous list on the starboard. At first he thought the ship was making a sharp turn but the liner did not right itself. The priest soon realized it was something more serious.

Ferdinand M. Theiriot, business manager of the *San Francisco Chronicle* and his wife had the misfortune of being in deluxe first class suite 180. They were both killed instantly in the crash. About 50 feet away, their 13-year-old son Peter had survived the terrible collision. He was awakened by the jar but did not know what had happened to his parents.

Walter G. Carlin, an attorney and political leader from Brooklyn, had also survived. Brushing his teeth in the bathroom of his cabin, he suddenly was thrown to the floor. When he reached the main section of the cabin, he saw that his wife and most of the cabin furniture were gone.

In cabin 56, Mrs. Thure Peterson found herself unable to move in the wreckage. She soon noticed she wasn't alone. Nearby in cabin 54, Mrs. Camille Cianfarra was also trapped. Mrs. Cianfarra was more concerned about her family than herself. Her husband, she knew, was already dead. She feared that possibly her two daughters Linda Morgan (from her previous marriage) and Joan in the next cabin may also have been killed.

Lilianna Dooner was in cabin 641 thinking about her reunion with her husband when suddenly she heard a crash. It reminded her of the World War II bombing raids she experienced, only this was louder. Mrs. Dooner was thrown to the floor. When she got up she noticed various portions of her cabin falling apart.

Overcoming the shock of the collision, Father Wojcik jumped to his feet. His attention was drawn to a steward who told everyone in the room, "Don't get excited, everything is all right!" A few seconds later, Wojcik heard another steward say, "Go to your stations and await further orders."

Hearing this, Wojcik and his fellow priests at the table rushed to their cabins. When Wojcik reached his, he was shocked to see it demolished. One of the walls was completely torn away. His bed was crushed into a pulp.

Wojcik wasted no time. He quickly grabbed his lifejacket. Turning off the light in fear of starting a fire, he then hurried to the promenade deck.

The most intense drama occurred on the bridges of the two ships. Aboard the Swedish vessel, Third Officer Carstens ran into the wheelhouse to seal the ship's nine watertight compartments. He evidently closed the doors at the exact moment of impact for he saw the sparks produced by the tremendous friction of the two liners.

Captain Nordenson was climbing the stairs to the bridge when he felt the jolt. He rapidly made his way to the bridge where he experienced another collision—with the third officer.

"What happened?" he demanded.

"Collision . . . we collided with another ship . . . she came from the port . . . from the port . . ." the shocked young officer answered.

"Shut the watertight doors!"

"They're closed!" Carstens assured him.

A glance at the control panel confirmed the fact that the doors were closed as Carsten stated. Nordenson hurried to the bridge wing to look at the vessel they had collided with. He saw the other ship but could not make out her identity.

As the mysterious ship disappeared in the mist, Nordenson turned his attention to his own ship. After first stopping the ship's engines, he checked the trim indicator and discovered there was a 4° list to the starboard. With other officers reporting to the bridge for an explanation, the captain ordered them to the forward section to inspect the damage. Fortunately, most of the reports revealed that, although the bow was badly damaged, the second bulkhead was still secure.

The situation on the *Andrea Doria* was far more serious. Within a minute of the collision, Third Officer Giannini reported a list of

18°. No sooner had the third officer called out his observation than the indicator needle jumped from 18° to 20°. This was shocking, to say the least. The *Doria* was built to meet the 1948 International Conference for Safety of Life at Sea which required a ship to list no more than 15°. Yet now the liner had a list of 20° and it was increasing.

What was surprising was that the damage the *Stockholm* inflicted, though serious, should not have been enough to doom the ship under ordinary circumstances. The *Andrea Doria* was designed to remain afloat with any two of her compartments ripped open. Only one of the eleven compartments was flooded and yet the ship was listing dangerously. What evidently had happened was the bow of the *Stockholm* had struck the five nearly empty fuel tanks on the starboard side while the five portside ones escaped damage. Thus with the tanks on the starboard side flooded and the portside tanks filled with air, the *Andrea Doria* listed much more than was provided for in its planning.

Within a few minutes after the accident, the liner was listing 22°. Unless something could be done, the *Andrea Doria* would sink. Yet there was little that could be done. The water began to seep up into the generator room. One by one, the generators had to be shut off. To conserve electricity, Chief Engineer Chiappori cut the air conditioning and instructed one of his men to shut off each generator only at the last minute. In spite of these measures, the crew of the *Andrea Doria* had less power for the pumps.

With these reports coming in, Captain Calamai decided to try one last desperate measure. During the war, he had saved the cruiser *Diulio* when it was torpedoed by running it aground. Calamai hoped this course of action might possibly work for this ship. With high hopes, he signalled the engine room to put the ship at Slow Ahead.

Unfortunately his plan did not work. After moving a few feet, the ship wobbled dangerously. Quickly, the captain moved the engine telegraph levers to Stop. With a 40-foot hole in her, the *Andrea Doria* could capsize. This movement would also hinder the launching of lifeboats. The only hope, Calamai now knew, would be rescue.

The captain ordered Junior Second Officer Badano and Senior

Second Officer Franchini to plot the stricken liner's present position. With this done, Calamai handed the position to Radio Operator Carlo Bussi with a few words added to the message to explain the situation.

A few minutes after the collision, the message, "S.O.S. de ICEH (the call letters of the *Andrea Doria*) S.O.S. Here at 0320 GMT at 40.30 N 69.53 W Need Immediate Assistance," was transmitted. Bussi was to launch the greatest sea rescue operation in peacetime history.

Ironically, the first ship to pick up the S.O.S. was the *Stockholm*. Second Radio Operator Ake Reinholdsson was in the process of sending a call to the ship they had collided with in the form of "SEJT (the *Stockholm*'s call letters) We have collided with another ship. Please—ship in collision—indicate" when he picked up the *Andrea Doria*'s plea for assistance.

There was little Captain Nordenson could do at the moment. He could not lower any of his lifeboats to help a ship in distress when he was not sure of his own ship's safety. Instead, he relayed back that he would help only after he was certain the *Stockholm* would not sink.

Fortunately, other ships were able to come to the *Doria*'s aid. Captain Rene Blanc of the tanker *Robert E. Hopkins* was only 45 miles away when he heard of the *Andrea Doria*'s condition. The daring seaman immediately ordered his ship to the scene at top speed. The freighter *Cap Ann* under the command of Joseph Boyd quickly did likewise when her radio man picked up the S.O.S. A few miles from the disaster scene, the Navy troop transport *Private William H. Thomas* set a new course for the stricken liner. Her master, Captain Shea, wired back, "We are seven miles south of Nantucket and proceeding your position."

Not every master of a ship in the nearby vicinity was swift to act. Fifty-three-year-old Baron Raol de Beaudean of the French passenger liner *Ile de France* was caught in a dilemma. The 44,500-ton ship, with a long history since 1926 of comfort for passengers and troop transport during World War II, was bound for Le Havre, France, when it picked up the distress call. Should he set course for the scene of the emergency and waste fuel or continue for France? The message really didn't mention anything about sinking and the *Andrea Doria* was a safe ship. In addition, many other ships were nearby to rescue her. On the other hand, suppose the *Doria* needed the *Ile de France?*

After a great deal of thought, Captain de Beauden decided he couldn't take a chance on human lives. He quickly set course for the position supplied to him by the distress message. He then took his place on the bridge to supervise the *Ile de France*'s rescue attempt.

As it turned out, the Italian ship *did* need the *Ile de France*'s assistance. Staff Captain Magagnini and the crew were experiencing difficulty in launching lifeboats. They were unable to get to some of the boats, for the passenger's baggage, piled up on the boat deck in anticipation of their arrival in New York, was blocking the path. Magagnini and his men were able to clear their way to the boats only to discover that the list made lowering the portside lifeboats impossible. He found he could lower the eight boats on the starboard side. However, because of the list, these boats had to be lowered almost empty. This meant the passengers and crew would have to climb down the side of the ship and into the boats.

The situation presented another disturbing problem. The sixteen lifeboats had a total capacity of little over 2,000. With half of them useless, the eight remaining boats could hold only 1,004. With 1,706 aboard the *Andrea Doria* on this voyage, at least 702 individuals would be forced to remain on the ship.

There were many other problems facing those on the passenger liner. Most found walking nearly impossible with the list and slippery floor. Many were forced to crawl to the boat deck.

Lilianna Dooner struggled in the wreckage of her cabin in an attempt to reach her three-year-old daughter Maria. The lights flickered on and Mrs. Dooner was able to see her way around. She pulled Maria out of the wreckage and crawled out of the cabin.

The cabin-class ballroom was a scene of confusion. The terrified passengers were too shocked to even get up out of their chairs. Many of them were without life jackets.

Out of the commotion, one man, Father Thomas Kelly, stepped forward and took charge. He called for volunteers to accompany him below to gather life jackets. Most of the men remained where they were but three offered their services.

They moved cautiously below deck with Father Kelly and began searching for life jackets. Their work was hindered by the acute list. Kelly and the other three made four trips, each time bringing up badly needed jackets. Then they were forced to give up out of sheer exhaustion and the fearful list.

Others were not as brave. Lilianna Dooner witnessed men running to the boats, pushing helpless woman and children aside. Some children were abandoned by their own parents. To Dooner, it reminded her of the cowardice of a man she had once seen rushing out of a burning house, leaving his wife and children to fend for themselves.

On the promenade deck, Father Wojcik was saying a prayer for help. He noticed an elderly woman shivering in fear. The Roman Catholic priest slowly crawled to her and offered to hold her hand. Gratefully the women accepted. While he was waiting on the promenade deck, it seemed to Wojcik he was seeing his entire life before his eyes. It did not flash all at once but rather it appeared very slowly. Life was sweet, he thought.

Thirteen-year-old Peter Thieriot was too occupied with locating his parents to think of abandoning ship. After being jarred awake, he began a fruitless search for his mother and father below deck, and then made his way topside. There he continued to look for the two but with no success.

Many other passengers were unable to reach the boat deck. Jane Cianfarra and Mrs. Martha Peterson were still trapped together down in cabins 54 and 56. Fortunately, Mrs. Peterson's husband had survived the collision. The tall, heavily built chiropractor had been awakened by the jolt and saw to his astonishment the *Stockholm*'s bow plowing into his cabin. He was knocked out for a short time, but regaining consciousness he managed to free himself and began to seek help.

He was in luck. Forty-eight-year-old Giovanni Rovelli, a cabin class waiter, volunteered his services. The thin Rovelli was able to maneuver through the wreckage better than the large Peterson. After hours of clearing obstacles, the two men finally freed Mrs. Cianfarra. Desperately, Peterson and Rovelli made their way for Mrs. Peterson. Only they reached her too late. At 4:25, she passed away.

A few miles away, Captain Nordenson was busily directing the repairs to his ship. His attention was suddenly drawn to the radar set. The horrified captain saw the "pip" representing the *Andrea Doria* was slowly drifting back towards the *Stockholm*.

Immediately, he pulled the engine telegraph levers to "Full Speed Astern" and ordered the helmsman to put the helm hard-a-starboard but the *Stockholm* refused to move. The engine room reported that the engines were working properly. A check with the wheel revealed it was not damaged. The floodlights showed the anchors not only were in place but were jammed into the side of the ship.

Unable to do anything, Nordenson and his men watched the *Andrea Doria* drift increasingly closer to the *Stockholm*. For a few suspenseful minutes, a second collision seemed certain. The *Andrea Doria* came within a third of a mile to the *Stockholm*; then, by a stroke of good fortune, it drifted away.

The captain demanded and received an explanation. The *Stockholm*, it was learned, was unable to move because the anchor chains had moored the vessel to the bottom of the ocean. It was later discovered that three seamen were dragged down to the ocean entangled in the chains.

With the new danger passed, the bridge sent a detail of men to cut the chains. While this was being done, Nordenson decided to raise the bow of his ship by pumping out the fresh water supply. His plan worked. With 90 tons of fresh water emptied the *Stockholm*'s bow rose and the pressure on the second bulkhead was relieved.

With the safety of his ship now secure, Captain Nordenson set out to help the *Andrea Doria*. He ordered all three motor boats and four of the eight oar-powered ones to be lowered to aid the Italian ship. The other four lifeboats were to remain aboard the *Stockholm* in case of an emergency.

Unknown to the captain, the *Stockholm* had already picked up a passenger from the *Andrea Doria*. Fourteen-year-old Linda Morgan, the daughter of Mrs. Cianfarra, was sleeping in cabin 52 on the *Andrea Doria* when the *Stockholm* struck. The bow crushed her eight-year-old sister Joan Cianfarra while she was catapulted from her cabin to the *Stockholm*'s bow. When she awakened, she was greeted by a Spanish crew member of the *Stockholm*, Bernabe Garcia.

Miss Morgan asked him in Spanish where her mother was. Surprised, Garcia, introducing himself as a "man from Cadiz," replied that he did not know. It wasn't until she noticed the new surroundings that she realized she was aboard a different ship. Miss Morgan was taken to the *Stockholm's* hospital where she was treated for her injuries. To this day, Linda Morgan is referred to as "the miracle girl" by seafaring men.

Valdemar Trasbo, an officer of the purser's department, found another passenger from the *Andrea Doria* in a much more gruesome manner. Encountering a body of a naked woman on the ship's bow, he began to crawl towards it in an attempt to recover it. He began to drag the body by the arm when to his horror the arm came off. Getting over his shock, Trasbo made another attempt to recover the husky woman, this time by grabbing her reddish hair. The head, like the arm, came off. Giving up, Trasbo crawled back to safety. From his description, the woman was later identified as Mrs. Walter G. Carlin.

By 12:30, many other passengers were aboard the *Stockholm*. With seven of the Swedish liner's lifeboats at the stricken side of the *Doria*, the ship's company were able to descend to them by means of ropes and ladders. It was a slow process. To speed things up, Captain Calamai, remembering troop transporting during the war, lowered nets over the side.

The rescue operation began to pick up with the arrival of the *Private William H. Thomas*, the *Cap Ann*, the *Robert E. Hopkins*, and other ships. The biggest lift in spirits occurred with the appearance of the *Ile de France*. Captain de Beaudean maneuvered his ship alongside the stricken liner and dispatched his lifeboats.

Aboard the *Doria*, a group of women hooked up a rope and began lowering children to the passing lifeboats. Lilianna Dooner decided to lower her daughter rather than wait. Slowly the child decended down the liner. When she was about two thirds the way down, the girl called out, "Mommy!" and began to slip out of the rope. In a matter of seconds she would fall into the water.

Quickly, Mrs. Dooner dove over. As she fell the 35 feet to the water, she began to wonder whether she could survive in the open sea at night. Fortunately as she surfaced, she managed to catch her falling daughter.

With Maria on her shoulder, Mrs. Dooner swam to a lifeboat

from the *Cap Ann*. She was pulled in by the boat's crew. A few minutes later, Mrs. Dooner observed a young girl being lowered. Since the lifeboat could not get near enough she again dove into the water and swam to the rope. Mrs. Dooner pulled the child to the lifeboat.

Father Wojcik careful crawled out from the promenade deck through a window and emerged on the boat deck. With the assistance of a few crew members he made his way down to a lifeboat. There he noticed the floodlights of the *Ile de France* focusing on the doomed ship. It reminded the priest of a Hollywood motion picture set.

As the boat departed from the *Andrea Doria*, Wojcik began to feel the accident was a "waste." He had just finished special studies and now it appeared as if it "was all going down the tubes." However, he was thankful that he had survived the terrible ordeal.

Young Peter Thierot was taken aboard one of the French liner's lifeboats. As it pulled away, he glanced at the mortally damaged *Andrea Doria* in hope of seeing his mother and father. What he saw instead was a large hole in the area where his parents' cabin was. There was now no doubt in the mind of the boy as to the fate of his parents.

By 5:30 in the morning, all but a handful of crew had abandoned ship. Among those who remained aboard was Captain Calamai. He refused to leave his command. The ship's master told Second Officer Badano that if he reached Genoa and saw his family, "Tell them I did everything I could." Instead of leaving his ship, the captain just stood by the rail and pondered.

Why leave, he thought. After all, the *Andrea Doria* was his command. He may not have known that the collision had killed forty-five aboard his vessel and five on the Swedish ship but he knew a number had died. Instead of abandoning ship by a lifeboat, he decided to remain aboard to the last and then swim to a nearby tug.

But his men would not have it. Staff Captain Magagnini called to Calamai to "come down."

"Go, go away. I remain," he called back.

Persistent, the staff captain climbed up and told him he and the others would not leave without him. With that said, Calamai boarded the lifeboat reserved for them and abandoned his post.

Meanwhile, the *Stockholm* was evacuating five who were injured beyond the ship's hospital facilities. With the use of a Coast Guard helicopter, *Andrea Doria* passenger Norma DiSandro, and *Stockholm* crewmen Lars Falk, Wilhelm Gustavsson, Arne Smedberg and Alf Johannson were rushed to a Nantucket Hospital. Four of the five were saved but seaman Alf Johansson died shortly afterwards. The death toll of the terrible collision was now fifty-one.

By daybreak, the *Andrea Doria* was still afloat. She was listing 45° to the starboard side. There was no doubt that the *Andrea Doria* would ultimately sink. In fact, the *Private William H. Thomas* reported "seaworthiness nil." It was now a question of time.

At 10:00, the *Andrea Doria* began to take her final plunge down to the deep. The ship began to turn on her side. It at first appeared that she would capsize but she remained on her side and sank deeper in the ocean. Some of the portside lifeboats were torn from the ship. Finally at 10:09 A.M. on July 26, 1956, eleven hours after the *Stockholm* dealt her death blow, the *Andrea Doria* sank 225 feet to the bottom at 40.29.4 north latitude, 69.50.5 west longitude (about two miles from the collision point).

The episode of the *Andrea Doria* was not over. Shortly after the sinking, the Italian Line sued the Swedish-American Line for $30 million, $29 million to cover the loss of the *Andrea Doria*, the remaining $1 million for freight and business damages. The Swedish-American Line in turn brought suit against the Italian Line for $2 million, $1 million of which was for repairs to the *Stockholm*'s bow with the additional $1 million for business losses.

To many around the world, this disaster seemed impossible. Many radar experts claimed this accident should never have happened. Both radars were in operating condition. The crew of both ships knew how to operate the radar sets. Yet the question remains: how was it possible for the *Andrea Doria* and *Stockholm* to have collided?

What many people failed to understand was this disaster, which was cited by journalists as one of the ten most newsworthy events of 1956, was due not to the fault of the radar itself but to the human factor. The officers on the *Andrea Doria* did not take time to plot the course of the oncoming ship. Instead, they used the easier but less accurate method of studying the angles of the radar bearing of the other ship. The Swedish-American Line assigned only one officer to a watch, which meant there was no one constantly monitoring the radar set at the crucial moment.

Another point misunderstood by the public was that the radar at that time was not totally accurate. It only provided the operator a relative position. This device was never meant to replace prudent seamanship. It was intended for ships as an additional precaution in the case of fog. Yet many mariners were going through fog at top speed depending totally on their radar sets.

Besides the use of radar, there was the question of the judgment on turns. From Carstens' point of view, the usual port-to-port passing was in order. To Calamai, the starboard-to-starboard passing seemed the safest course of action since he had the crowded shallow water on his right and the open sea on his left. The Rules of the Road state the portside-to-portside passing is the proper procedure although it made allowances for a starboard-to-starboard passing at the captain's discretion.

The sinking of the *Andrea Doria* revealed another weakness with the Rules of the Road. Rule 16 states that a ship in fog or other visibility problems is to slow down to a "moderate speed." It did not specify the speed. The only concession to Rule 16 was a token reduction of speed by sometimes less than a knot. In the case of the *Doria*, speed was reduced by only 1.2 knots.

The court never really established who was at fault. After arguments over helmsman Larsen's wandering attention, visibility conditions, radar readings, speed, and the *Andrea Doria*'s turn, both lines decided to settle out of court. The claims against each other were dropped and the two lines were to mutually pay liability claims against them.

One issue, unresolved to this day, is the conduct of the *Andrea Doria*'s crew. Many of the surviving passengers insisted that the first few lifeboats lowered were filled mostly with members of the liner's crew. Apologists have argued that they were stewards, cooks, etc., and not seamen. However, a large percentage of the crew in these boats was, in fact, seamen. While many of the crew behaved admirably and professionally, there was some cowardice among its ranks. As William Hoffer noted, it was "a tragedy within a tragedy."

With this issue settled, many improvements were implemented. The Swedish-American Line no longer depended on one officer during a watch. A more accurate radar was developed, and officers were better trained in its use.

This disaster had a profound effect on the captains in charge of the bridges of the two ships. Carstens-Johansen was assigned to a different ship. He never was able to live down the accident that broke the 1919-1956 passenger line safety record of collision during peacetime. Captain Calamai was never given another command. He was allowed to retire at the mandatory age of sixty. Heartbroken, he reflected, "When I was a boy and all my life I loved the sea: now I hate it!" Calamai died in 1972. According to William Hoffer his last words were, "Is it all right? Are the passengers saved?"

15 ■ JANUARY 30, 1959

The *Hans Hedtoft*
"A Revolution in Arctic Navigation"

For FORTY-SEVEN YEARS after the iceberg-shattered *Titanic* plunged to the bottom of the ocean with the loss of 1,502 lives, the shipping world was well aware of the danger of ice. Shortly after the catastrophe, the International Ice Patrol was set up to protect the ships of the world. Icebergs were shepherded out of the shipping lanes. Attempts were even made to destroy dangerous bergs. As a further precaution, the winter lane was shifted south.

Yet while others were taking these measures, one man, Johannes Kjaernoel, Denmark's Minister for Greenland, actually proposed to open a sea lane for passenger vessels to sail to Greenland during the winter months. He sincerely believed it was vital that Greenland be open the entire year to sea traffic. To accomplish this, Kjaernoel set out to construct small but sturdy ships that would be managed by the Royal Greenland Trade Department. The name of the first ship was *Hans Hedtoft*.*

Many were not in agreement with the Minister for Greenland. During the two years of construction, some members of parliament argued against the idea of sending a ship into Arctic waters during December and January. "These are the most dangerous months because of icebergs and gales," argued Parliament Mem-

---

*Hans Hedtoft was Prime Minister of Denmark.

164

ber Augo Lynge, "It is folly to build a passenger ship designed to service Greenland during these winter months." A colleague agreed. "The route laid out for the *Hans Hedtoft* is right up there where the big bergs are born," he said, "a very dangerous situation."

Despite this opposition, the *Hans Hedtoft* was completed and commissioned into service. Not forgetting the warnings of danger, the designers had the ship constructed to insure safety from the menace of icebergs. The 2,875-ton 383-foot-long vessel was constructed with an extra heavy skin plating, an armored bow and stern, a double bottom, and was divided into seven watertight compartments. Her single screw was protected by ice fins and an ice knife. As a further precaution,the vessel was equipped with radar.

Even if a critical situation developed and it was necessary to abandon ship, the passengers and crew could make use of the *Hans Hedtoft*'s life saving gear. She carried three metal alloy lifeboats, a motor launch, and several rubber dinghies or life rafts. Each one of these was equipped with an emergency radio transmitter.

As a further guarantee that the *Hans Hedtoft* would have a safe career, the Royal Greenland Trade Department chose Captain P. L. Rasmussen to command her. Rasmussen was a fine choice. At fifty-eight he had sailed the Arctic for many years and was said to have developed an ability to "smell" the cold breath of an iceberg before making visual contact with it. He was well able to sail the polar waters and was respected by many who had sailed with him.

Thus it would seem the newly completed *Hans Hedtoft* would have no problem in her Arctic trek. One government official boasted, "Now we can sail to Greenland all year round." Captain Rasmussen himself said, "This means a revolution in Arctic navigation."

One man at least found fault with the ship. Knud Lauritzen, a private shipowner, asserted that the steel plates of the *Hedtoft* should have been welded and not riveted on the frames. Riveting would not offer enough resistance to ice pressure the ship might encounter. His words were taken for personal chagrin that he hadn't built the vessel instead of the government.

On January 7, 1959, the newly completed *Hans Hedtoft* set sail on her maiden voyage from Copenhagen for Greenland. Aboard the diesel powered vessel were fifty-five passengers and a crew of forty. By the dock, cheering crowds bade farewell to the small ship as she embarked on her Arctic voyage.

The *Hans Hedtoft* safely crossed the ocean and laid anchor at Godthaab, Greenland's capital. She disembarked her fifty-five passengers and boarded another fifty-five. Among them was Augo Lynge, the very man who in Parliament had called the idea of the *Hans Hedtoft* a "folly." The ship was loaded with iced fish. Then with all aboard, the *Hans Hedtoft* embarked for Copenhagen to complete her maiden voyage.

The return voyage was not as peaceful as the first crossing. Shortly after the Danish ship set out, the weather became rough. The winds produced waves 10 to 15 feet high which pitched and rolled the small passenger-cargo ship as she pushed her way to the southern tip of Greenland.

When the *Hedtoft* set course east for Copenhagen, a blinding snowstorm swept in her path. Soon fog accompanied the snow, making visibility nearly impossible. Captain Rasmussen reduced speed but continued on course. Even though visual contact with ice was seriously handicapped, the captain did not doubt the *Hans Hedtoft* would complete her voyage safely.

By January 30, 1959, the *Hans Hedtoft* was 37 miles south of Cape Farvel. She was now more than 600 miles north of where about forty-seven years before the White Star Line *Titanic* had brushed against an iceberg and sunk. Visibility was restricted in that case but not nearly as poorly as with the *Hans Hedtoft*. The *Titanic* at least wasn't in a snowstorm or blanketed by thick fog. Nor had the British liner been in an area where the "big bergs are born."

There was one other notable difference between the two situations. The officers on watch of the *Titanic* had to depend totally on the lookouts in the crow's nest. Captain P. L. Rasmussen could depend on the ship's radar to aid his navigation. This, along with his ability to "smell" ice, gave the crew of the *Hans Hedtoft* confidence that they could sail on in the Arctic Ocean.

Yet at 11:30 A.M., without warning, the *Hans Hedtoft* struck a huge iceberg. The extent of the damage is not known for sure but it was apparently enough to doom the Danish liner.

This bit of information evidently wasn't immediately known to the captain, for the first message the stricken liner dispatched simply stated, "Collision with an iceberg." Then a half hour later, a more urgent message was flashed, "We are filling fast."

Immediate assistance was impossible. The scene of the wreck was several hundred miles north of most Atlantic traffic. The nearest vessel was the 650-ton German trawler *Johannes Kruess*. Her captain had already decided to return to port when the distress signal was picked up. Immediately the trawler pushed at top speed through the fog and ice to the *Hedtoft's* last reported position.

The Coast Guard cutter *Campbell* was some 280 miles away when her radio received the plea for help. The captain, Frederick Scheiber, altered course and raced to the scene. Scheiber, like the captain of the *Johannes Kruess*, was risking his own vessel in order to save the *Hans Hedtoft*. He knew that the people aboard the sinking ship would perish within seconds in that icy water. Scheiber had served in the Greenland Ice Patrol and had navigated through these dangerous waters before. He had complete faith in himself.

Soon other ships joined in the perilous search for the *Hans Hedtoft*. The German motor ship *Poseidon* and a few Danish ships were informed of the danger that the *Hans Hedtoft* was in and set course for the Arctic to offer their help. In the air, several planes were challenging the rough storm to locate the stricken liner.

Time was running out. The *Hans Hedtoft* wired, "We are taking a lot of water in the engine room." Finally, at 3:55 P.M., the Danish liner, after continuing to send out updated messages, transmitted, "Slowly sinking. Need immediate assistance." Nothing more was heard from the *Hans Hedtoft*.

The rescue ships pushed through the Arctic as fast as they could. The lookouts were keeping a sharp vigil for icebergs and wreckage. The radio men of the vessels were desperately trying to make contact with the distressed ship.

The *Johannes Kruess* was the first to arrive at the location. An extensive search was conducted by the trawler but nothing was found. "We have searched, nothing found or seen," the trawler reported, "no lights or lifeboats or ship. Plenty of ice from the northwest and we are becoming icebound." A bit later, the *Kruess* reported it could stay no longer. Her radioman wired, "We must go. It is dangerous for the ship and we can do no more." With that, the *Johannes Kruess* discontinued the search and headed for the nearest port.

The next day, the *Campbell* conducted a search of the area. Visibility was down to only one-half mile. To complicate matters 20-foot waves were constantly crashing around the sides of the cutter. The return of the *Johannes Kruess* and the arrival of the *Poseidon* was welcome news to Captain Scheiber.

Yet the search was unsuccessful. With the approach of night the search ships left the ice area to wait for daylight. With daybreak, the search fleet, this time reinforced, resumed looking for the *Hans Hedtoft*.

A ray of hope came to the searchers. The Danish ship *Umanak* picked up weak radio signals. Perhaps these signals came from one of the hand operated radios in the lifeboats. The weak signals were also heard by Coast Guard stations in Greenland. The *Campbell*, however, didn't hear such signals. Nor did any of the planes. The faint hope died.

Then another incident occurred to raise hopes. A pilot reported to have seen what resembled a white lifeboat with a black stripe. It is not uncommon for a false sighting to be reported during an air search, and visibility was poor. Moreover, none of the *Hedtoft*'s boats were white with a black stripe. Consequently the object was regarded as a piece of floating ice.

Throughout Denmark there was anxious waiting. In several churches, prayers were conducted. Some of these churches had models of the *Hans Hedtoft* on display.

By daylight the next day, the search was resumed. The visibility conditions continued extremely poor. The 40-foot waves rendered radar useless and maneuverability nearly impossible. Again the seamen's efforts were in vain.

By nightfall, the searchers returned to port. They had searched through fog patches and found only icebergs, growlers, floebergs and pack ice. Despite all efforts, no trace of the *Hans Hedtoft* or her passengers were found. The rescue was called off. The *Hans Hedtoft* and her ninety-five complement were presumed lost.

It is ironic that one of the lost was Augo Lynge. His words to his son before going on the *Hedtoft* was that in event of a crisis, "there is no rescue to be expected. This will be changed but it will take an accident." His words were tragically true.

Not very much information can be found on this tragedy because of the absence of survivors. With the available facts certain conclusions can be drawn. The *Hans Hedtoft* must have struck the iceberg around 11:30. The berg went unnoticed by the radar perhaps because of the waves hindering radar readings. The tone of the first message would indicate that the captain did not anticipate the danger his command was in for about half an hour. The lifeboats either were not lowered in fear of the turbulent water or were lowered and capsized by the waves. The ship foundered sometime around 4:00. The ninety-five passengers and crew were either drowned or froze to death in the terrible icy water.

Shortly after the disaster, the *Hans Hedtoft* was nicknamed the "Little *Titanic*." Indeed it is interesting to note the similarities between these two shipwrecks. Both were noted passenger liners of their countries. Both were constructed with a double bottom and divided into watertight compartments. Both were commanded by experienced captains. Both were on their maiden voyage. Both collided with an iceberg and foundered.

A nightmare at sea had been repeated.

16 ∎ DECEMBER 23, 1963

The *Lakonia*
"Absolute Freedom From Worry and Responsibility"

In 1963, MANY PEOPLE planned to spend the Christmas season away from home. On December 19, at Southampton, England, 653 decided to have their vacation at sea. So they booked passage on one of the most luxurious vessels in service.

Their choice was the Greek liner *Lakonia*. This 20,314-ton cruise liner offered movie theaters, tapestry-draft lounges and beautiful music. Those inclined for recreation were provided with swimming pools, a gymnasium, shuffleboard and tennis courts. It seemed like the perfect way to spend the Christmas vacation.

Most of the passengers were unaware of the liner's dark past. The *Lakonia* was originally the Dutch *Johan van Oldenbarnevelt* when it was built by the Nederland Shipping Company in 1930. During her maiden voyage of that year, the *Johan van Oldenbarnevelt* collided with another vessel. In 1951, six separate fires of suspicious origin broke out on her. Fortunately, they were extinguished before any serious damage occurred. In 1962, the *Johan van Oldenbarnevelt* again had a fire but it too was put out before the ship suffered much damage.

If any of the passengers knew of this, they showed little concern. After all, the vessel had experienced no serious accident since it had been sold to the Greek firm Ormos Shipping Company, Ltd. of London, the previous year. Everything was going along fine with the ship now that it was refitted and renamed the *Lakonia*. To her passengers, the thirty-three-year-old ship was "absolute freedom from worry and responsibility," as described by the brochures.

Richard Burca at least anticipated a voyage that met with that promise. The fifteen-year-old, along with his grandmother, was on his way to join his family on Madeira. He expected this to be "a holiday I'll never forget."

Mrs. Hazel Driscoll of Beavard-on-Sea, Sussex was also looking forward to a restful vacation. She and her six-year-old daughter Elizabeth were planning on spending Christmas in Las Palmas.

Also making this trip was Captain A. J. Campbell. The retired British Army officer was in his seventies and was eagerly seeking a peaceful voyage,

By far the most famous passenger was Sir Ivon Jennings of Cambridge University. Jennings was a leading constitutional authority of his time. He and Lady Jennings intended to spend Christmas in the Canary Islands.

Before the ship left harbor, her crew participated in a boat and fire drill. The performance was accepted by the representative of the British Sea Transport Department as meeting the standards of the International Convention for the Safety of Life at Sea. With this done, all port business was completed and the *Lakonia* departed.

On December 20, one day out of Southampton, a second boat drill was conducted for the passengers. Instructions were issued to each passenger on what they were to do in the event of an emergency. The ship's master, Mathio Zarbis, was satisfied with the drill.

The next day, the Greek liner was caught up in rough weather in the Bay of Biscay. The *Lakonia* pulled through and by the 22nd was proceeding on her course at 17 knots in clear weather.

Later that day, the passengers were more relaxed. The ship was now traveling in smooth water. In the lounge, several couples were dancing to the orchestra. Others were too tired and returned to their cabins for the night.

Some of the passengers didn't wish to retire so early. Richard

Burca disregarded "Granny's" wishes that he go to bed. Instead, he sneaked off to the movie theater. He wanted very much to see the Bob Hope movie *Call Me Bwana*.

It was at 10:00 P.M. when a steward noticed smoke coming from beneath the door of the closed barber shop. He quickly opened the door and was greeted by flames. The terrified steward ran for help. The fire spread unchecked throughout the hallway.

Sitting in the main salon, Captain Zarbis smelled the smoke and darted out of the room. Within a moment the fire alarm had sounded.

In the movie theater, Richard Burca heard the bells ringing. At first he thought it was part of the movie. After awhile when the ringing persisted, Burca realized it was the fire alarm. Quickly he and the rest of the audience rushed to the exit.

Outside the corridor, Burca encountered smoke and found it difficult to breathe. The teenager came upon a Coca-Cola machine and with an empty bottle he broke a porthole window. Next he tied his handkerchief over his mouth and nose, and then he ran to his cabin.

There he grabbed an orange, quickly put it in his pocket and hurried to find his grandmother whose cabin was next to his. Seeing she wasn't there he raced to the boat deck.

There he saw numerous passengers milling about. Some were clad in evening clothes while others wore nightgowns. Burca saw no sign of his grandmother. A woman near him shouted "Someone for heaven's sake get me a lifebelt." Burca took two life jackets from a nearby locker and gave one to the woman while strapping the other on himself.

In the radio shack, Radioman Kologridis was busy sending Christmas messages when he was suddenly interrupted by the bridge reporting, "We are on fire. Start emergency procedure at once." Kalogridis stopped sending passenger messages and tapped out a series of dashes at four-second intervals to notify all nearby ships to stand by for an important message. Then after attracting their attention, he sent out, "S.O.S. S.O.S. This is the *Lakonia*. We are on fire. Request immediate assistance." A few minutes later the radio man added the ship's position as latitude 35° north, longitude 24° west.

At once help was on the way. The Coast Guard cutter *Mackinac* was dispatched to the scene. The Argentine State Line *Salta*, bound for Buenos Aires, sped to the burning liner. The 5,000 ton British ship *Montcalm* also picked up the distress message and changed course for the *Lakonia*. They were joined by the French refrigerated cargo ship *Ville de Majunga*, the tanker *Gertrud Frizen*, the S.S. *Independence* and even the aircraft carrier *Centaur*. It was to be the largest sea rescue since the *Andrea Doria*.

Back on the buring vessel, radioman Kalogridis continued to update the rescue ships on the situation. Around midnight he tapped out, "We are leaving the ship. Please immediately give us assistance. Please help us." At 12:22 A.M, Kalogridis wired, "S.O.S. from *Lakonia* last time. I cannot stay any more in the wireless station. We are leaving the ship. Please immediate assistance. Please help."

Help was indeed needed. The burning *Lakonia*, by now, was a scene of confusion. People climbed aboard lifeboats only to find some of the davits were inoperable. Four of the boats were situated so close to the fire that the intense heat made it impossible for the davit men to lower them or even remain at their post. Some of the passengers gave up on the boats and jumped overboard.

During the confusion, someone instructed a group of passengers to go to the dining room. This did not seem logical to Richard Burca but he along with the others headed there. In the dining room they waited for further instructions. While he was there, Burca spotted his grandmother jammed against a wall.

A short time later, a steward entered and told everyone to report to their boat stations. Hearing this, the crowd quickly returned to the boat deck. On the way up, Burca was separated from his grandmother.

Burca dutifully reported to Lifeboat No. 17 to which he was assigned. However, he did not see his grandmother around. He discovered her instead at another boat. The boy persuaded her that it would be best if she go to her assigned station.

As it turned out it was fortunate he took his grandmother away from that boat. As it was being lowered, it capsized. Burca could hear the screams from those aboard sounding through the night.

When Burca returned to Lifeboat No. 17, he discovered another problem. To get aboard the boat it was necessary to climb over the rail. This was easy for young Burca to do but his seventy-year-old grandmother complained she could not do it. Burca and a member of the crew helped her over the rail and into the boat.

Then another problem arose. The davit men were unable to lower the boat because the pin was too tightly secured. "I began to get frightened," Richard Burca recalled, "Actually, I was frightened all the time but the thought that I might have to jump into the darkness and the deep water below frightened me most." Luckily, the boat was freed and safely lowered to the water.

Meanwhile, various members of the crew were helping those passengers who were still aboard. Some of the crew excelled in their efforts, such as Steward Ionnis Nimskikokas, who rushed into a burning room to save some passengers. Likewise Dimos Zilakos, the ship's accountant, darted into a burning stateroom to save an elderly lady and small child. Seaman Mantickos put his own life in jeopardy while hooking up rope ladders to save three helpless passengers.

Not withstanding these heroic actions, several of the passengers did not have high regard for the conduct of the crew. There were many accusations, some with the element of truth, that the emergency procedure was totally unorganized and the crew panicked to the point of endangering the lives of the passengers.

"There was unpardonable confusion of orders and counter orders," one of the passengers later complained, "The crew at one end of the ship didn't know what was happening at the other end."

Another man claimed there was a "shocking lack of experience of the crew." He went as far as to say the passengers had to take charge of the lifeboats. "They showed more ingenuity and calmness than the crew did."

Another passenger concurred. "There was no panic among the passengers. The crew appeared to be the panicky ones."

Some survivors told reporters of lifeboats being overturned because of the blundering of the crew. One story told of a lifeboat made for seventy-five being lowered away with only twenty aboard. There was one survivor who stated that when the rescue vessels came, the Greek crew "was the first up the ladder lowered for us!"

As harsh as these charges may seem, they were actually the milder ones. "We were left to take our chances," one man remarked. "I owe my life to a life jacket." One woman angrily reported, "I could not get into a lifeboat. The stewards got into them."

One woman went so far as to accuse a crewman of looting her cabin. A fellow passenger corroborated her story. He claimed to have seen, on his arrival ashore, a member of the *Lakonia*'s crew selling a piece of jewelry that was "obviously looted from a cabin."

These accusations were to come out after the rescue. Lifeboat No. 17 with Richard Burca and his grandmother aboard was drifting aimlessly. No one was in charge of the boat. There was one man in uniform who, according to Burca, "looked dazed." A seaman was also aboard but he sat there the whole time with his head down in his arms.

The boat drifted under a bilge injector. Water poured in until it was six inches deep. Those aboard began bailing the water with hands and shoes. No. 17 then came under a shower of deck chairs evidently thrown overboard to be used as rafts. "We've got to get out of this!" someone in the boat shouted. "The tanks will blow up and we'll be covered in flames." There then came shouts of "Row! Row! Everybody row!"

However, there was no one to supervise and hence they rowed in different directions. Richard Burca, who had rowed boats for years in Madeira, jumped up and sang out, "In—out—out." The man seated next to him called out, "Don't pay any attention to him, he's only a boy." Yet most of the boat's company followed Burca's directions.

From the lifeboat, Burca watched the flames mounting higher and higher on the ship. It reminded him of a big fireworks display with sparks shooting up and down. Burca also noticed the passengers and crew jumping overboard. He soon saw several bodies floating by but because of the darkness he was not able to determine whether they were dead or alive.

The first sign of real hope came when the *Montcalm* appeared on the scene. The captain of the British ship had his powerful searchlights focused over the surrounding water to locate swimmers and lifeboats. By daybreak, the *Montcalm* collected 240 passengers and crew from the fire-ravaged liner.

Lifeboat No. 17 made her way to the *Montcalm*. Ropes were dropped over the ship's side to haul up the women and children. After they were all aboard, the men were pulled up. One of the last to leave was Richard Burca. Burca felt proud in being classified as a man.

Soon other ships arrived to help the *Montcalm* with her work. The rescue was aided by the appearance of four C-54 airplanes, which flew over the area and dropped life rafts and life rings.

To one pilot the scene resembled a burning building. "The flames were creeping up through the superstructure," he reported, "there were people in the water around the ship. We sighted the *Lakonia* after we broke through the overcast from about 15 miles away."

For many the help had arrived too late. Several drowned or burned passengers floated in the surrounding water. One airman was especially disturbed when he saw a baby burn to death. Fortunately, most of the people were fished out of the water alive.

The rescue was not completed. About 100 people were still aboard the burning liner. Among them was fifty-three-year-old Captain Zarbis. He had served on the sea for many years now. He was determined to uphold the tradition of the master being the last to leave his ship.

The fire came closer to those at the stern until the heat become unbearable. One by one the last of those aboard jumped overboard. Seeing that everyone else was off his command, Captain Zarbis, his conscience clear, jumped from the *Lakonia*.

After all the survivors were safely aboard the rescue ships and sent to Madeira and Casablanca, an effort was made to tow the stricken liner to Gibraltar. Lines were hooked up to the *Lakonia* between the Dutch tug *Polzee* and the Norwegian salvage ship *Herkules*. They managed to come within 250 miles of Gibraltar when the charred *Lakonia* heeled over and began to sink. The salvagers were forced to abandon the project. The lines were released and the *Lakonia*, representing "absolute freedom from worry and responsibility" settled to the ocean floor some 2,000 fathoms below.

The story of the *Lakonia* was not over. The newspapers around the world carried the survivors' accusations of incompetence and cowardice of the crew. These charges were promptly denied by the captain. He at once phoned London and explained, "There was no panic aboard my ship, by neither the crew nor the passengers. And there was no drunkenness. I was the one who gave the order to abandon ship. It was my duty to do so."

The crew's conduct is controversial. Many of the charges stem from statements of the survivors. Researching this book, the author has found that often passenger statements and even those of crew members cannot always be taken as fact. In some cases. portions of the survivors' story have very little credibility. Much of the story was exaggerated greatly. Also, as was previously mentioned, some of the crew performed acts of bravery during the crisis.

Nevertheless, the operation was, as one crew member later reflected, "very unorganized." Part of this was due to the general confusion at the time. The language barrier between the Greek crew and the English-speaking passengers also hindered matters considerably. Moreover, the heat and smoke often interfered with the fulfillment of the boat assignments.

The official investigation also uncovered some faults with the ship's lifesaving and firefighting equipment. The *Lakonia* was equipped with 24 davits but many of them were almost impossible for the crew to operate. Also the *Lakonia* was not provided with automatic water sprinklers. Consequently, when the fire broke out, there was not a device to extinguish the conflagration until firefighting crews were organized. The time consumed to do this resulted in the loss of the *Lakonia* and the lives of 155 of the 1,041 aboard. Perhaps the most serious mistake was that the crew member who discovered the flames opened the door before a firefighting crew arrived at the scene.

Much of this was the fault of the owners. Although the exact cause of the fire is still unknown, there can be no doubt that the lack of efficient firefighting equipment proved fatal. Yet this lesson was to go unheeded for another two years.

17 ■ NOVEMBER 13, 1965

The *Yarmouth Castle*
"A Faded Beauty"

B Y THE SECOND HALF of the 20th century, the luxury liners began to fade away in the face of airplane competition. The days of the "floating palaces" such as the *Titanic* and *Lusitania* were numbered. The jet was infinitely faster than even the fastest passenger liners. By the 1960s, only a few passenger ships remained in service for those who wished to have a long leisurely vacation.

One such example was the *Yarmouth Castle*. Built in 1927 as the *Evangeline*, for the Eastern Steamship Company, this 5,002-ton cruise ship had served on the Boston-Yarmouth run and later on the New York-Bahamas service. For many years, this vessel was a familiar sight in the Nassau waterfront, for the *Evangeline* was one of the few liners small enough to be able to tie up at Prince George dock. She was once considered to be one of the most beautiful ships afloat with her white superstructure over a black hull and the yellow and blue markings of the Eastern Steamship Company on her single funnel.

This vessel had earned many honors for her owners. On more than one occasion she took part in rescue operations of freighters in distress. During the Second World War, the *Evangeline* served with distinction as a hospital ship and troop carrier. She helped the Allies in the Anzio landing. Later, the steamer was transferred to the Pacific theater where she transported troops to fight the Japanese.

In the years following the war, the *Evangeline* began to show signs of age. On a few voyages she failed to met her schedule. Incidents of bad luck began to plague her. In 1955, for instance, a whale was caught in her rudder. During Hurricane Betsy, she was torn from her mooring and collided with her sistership, the *Yarmouth*. Consequently, the once beautiful *Evangeline*, now "a faded beauty" as one observer described her, went through several changes of ownership and finally landed in the hands of the Chadade Steamship Company of Panamanian registry.

On Friday, November 12, 1965, the *Yarmouth Castle*, as she was now called, set sail from Miami, Florida, for Nassau. Aboard were 376 passengers and a crew of 176. Most of the travelers were from Florida. Sixty were members of the North Broward Florida Senior Citizens Club taking a pleasant retirement cruise.

It seemed like the voyage could very well be pleasant. The weather was clear and the sea was calm on the day of embarkation. The temperature was 80° F. However a light southeastern breeze of about five miles per hour would alleviate the discomfort of those who found the temperature too warm. The only problem the passengers may have experienced was the rolling of the vessel as she traveled her full 14-knot speed.

Many of the passengers occupied the first few hours of the voyage drinking at the ship's bar. Among them were Carole Pendleton and her mother, Mrs. John Kekelis. Pendleton in particular wanted to have a few drinks to help her forget she was aboard a ship. Earlier she and her mother had a sharp argument over how they should arrive at Nassau. Carole wanted to take an airplane while her mother preferred the *Castle*. At one point, the two women were so angered at one another they almost walked off the ship. Now, as the two enjoyed their drinks, things between them were softening up.

While at the bar, Carole and her mother struck up a conversation with a woman passenger who, like Carole, was trying to forget. Her problem was of a tragic nature. She, along with her son and his friend, was on this trip to put the recent death of her husband behind her.*

---

*This was most likely Mrs. Frank Wright, who survived. Unfortunately both her son and his friend were lost.

Also in the ship's bar were Malcolm Philbrook and his wife, Doris. They were having a conversation with a couple from New York. The husband was a retired policeman, which interested Philbrook, a police officer from Florida. They chatted for some time before bidding good night.

By 10:00 PM, some of the travelers began to turn in. "It was easy to fall asleep because of the beautiful moonlit night and the calm ocean," reflected Carole Pendleton. For her there was no difficulty in retiring for the night. After leaving the bar she had spent a number of hours studying her aviation books in preparation for her commercial pilot's license test. Mrs. Pendleton planned to pilot a plane for her husband's tool company.

Ebna Matias was not as eager to retire. She and her husband, Charles, were enjoying the last floor show. She wanted to stay up a little longer but Charles persuaded her that the party was getting "wild." So after a final drink, they returned to their cabin, stateroom 719, or "death trap" as Mr. Matias described it.

The *Yarmouth Castle* indeed could rightly be called a "death trap." A short time earlier, Congressman William Mailliard said at a hearing of the sub-committee on Merchant Marine and Fisheries that the *Yarmouth Castle* was "a shining example of a ship that is not in proper condition to engage in cruise trade." His observation was correct. The furniture, thick wooden paneling in the staterooms, and drapes made the ship a fire hazard. Moreover, one unoccupied room, 610, was packed with mattresses, damaged chairs, paneling and other items. There was no sprinkler outlet for 610 and the room was lighted by a "jury-rig" lamp cord type electric line with a "naked" light bulb.

This was not worrying the *Castle*'s master, thirty-five-year-old Byron Voutsinas. After all, his command was fitted with a dry-pipe automatic sprinkler system that extended to all staterooms, passageways, stairways and public places. This system was capable of pouring 300 gallons of water in 60 seconds. Also there were 46 fire hydrants, each capable of producing 400 gallons of water per minute, placed strategically throughout the vessel. Each one of these was provided with hoses 50 feet in length. Fire seemed to present no serious threat to the captain's command.

By midnight, seven hours after departing, things began to quiet down on the *Yarmouth Castle* as most of the passengers were sleeping or preparing to retire. In the engine room, Third Assistant Engineer Sotiriou, two oilers and two firemen were performing the task of blowing the boiler tubes to clear the exhaust carbon. On the bridge, along with two watchmen and the helmsman, Second Officer Jose L. Rams de Leon was on watch. Every so often one of the watchmen would go on security patrol for about 20 minutes, return to the bridge and relieve the helmsman. It was later learned that the watchmen did not follow their prescribed route and hence missed some of their stations. Among the areas they failed to cover was the port passageway on the main deck, where room 610 was located.

At 1:00 A.M., on November 13, 1965, the crew on duty in the engine room detected a strange odor. There was no doubt about its cause—smoke. A careful look revealed that it was seeping through the natural draft ventilation. The third assistant engineer sent an oiler to alert the chief engineer and a fireman to investigate the situation. He then informed the bridge of the problem by telephone. The time was 1:10.

On the bridge, the second officer immediately dispatched the two watchmen to patrol the sun and promenade deck. Then he informed the captain of the report from the engine room. Voutsinas replied, "Sound the alarm, I am coming up."

Meanwhile, the chief engineer was conducting a search of his own. He checked the galley to see if perhaps bread or cakes had overbaked. Seeing this was not the case, he proceeded to the main lobby where he met the night cleaner. From him the chief engineer learned of the presence of smoke in the men's toilet on the promenade deck. Together they searched this room but with inconclusive results.

The search party soon grew in number. Passenger Lloyd Lamn, the cruise director, the switchboard operator, the radio operator, the first officer and even Captain Voutsinas joined in the effort to locate the source of the smoke. By 1:15, the group arrived at the unoccupied room 610. The door was kicked open and flames leaped out.

Fire extinguishers were quickly employed but they were no match for the conflagration. Even one of the fire hoses proved inadequate in fighting the fire. The ship's sprinkler system, though operating, was ineffective in combating a blaze this size.

Seeing that the fire was out of control, Captain Voutsinas rushed back to the bridge. The chief engineer handed the hose to a crewman and hurried to the engine room. One by one, the remaining firefighters dispersed from the scene. The fire was now raging in the corridor uncontrolled.

Several of the crew went aft, hammering on the cabin doors to alert the passengers. The first officer rushed towards the bridge but the smoke and heat prevented him from going any farther than the entrance to the lobby of the forward stairway. Instead, he made his way to the promenade deck where he, with the aid of a few deck hands, began breaking windows and helping passengers out of their rooms. Nearby, other crewmen were preparing the fire hoses to combat the terrible conflagration.

Arriving on the bridge, Captain Voutsinas ordered, "Stop the engines." A minute later he instructed, "Close the watertight doors in the engine room." He instructed the helmsman to "turn to port." The fire by this time was raging in the chart room.

Realizing the *Yarmouth Castle* desperately needed help, Voutsinas ordered an S.O.S. hoping some nearby ships would come to the rescue. Neither the captain nor any of his bridge officers made an attempt to warn the passengers or give them instructions with the public address system.

Carole Pendleton and her mother were awakened by a shout of "Fire!" and the sound of running passengers. Carole's mother opened the door and was greeted by flames. It was at this point, according to Mrs. Pendleton, that "all hell broke loose."

The older woman ran out to the main lobby. Carole proceeded to follow her until she remembered her train case, and she quickly returned to the cabin to retrieve it. Gulping smoke, she again made her way to the main lobby, this time for good.

The news of the fire quickly circulated throughout the ship. There were no alarms or bells or sirens. But the passengers of the *Yarmouth Castle* learned of this situation by either shouts or by disturbing experiences.

Charles Matias was awakened by what he thought was "a bunch of drunks screaming and yelling." He wanted to go back to sleep but his wife Edna thought this to be unwise. "Charlie," she insisted, "there's something wrong."

To satisfy her, Matias decided to go outside to investigate. No sooner had he opened the door then he found himself immersed in smoke. His wife jumped up and rocketed out.

"Edna! Edna! Come back!" he shouted. It was the last Charles Matias ever saw of his wife.

Matias wasted no time slamming the door before the smoke suffocated him. He gathered his wallet and pants and exited through his cabin window. Soon he was safely on the promenade deck.

Arthur Gordon, like Charles Matias, thought the commotion "was just a couple of drunks." When the shouting continued, Gordon decided to check what was going on in the lobby. As he left his cabin he found himself "surrounded by flames."

Quickly he shut the door. He and his wife went into the bathroom and abandoned their cabin through the window. During the confusion on deck, Mr. Gordon was separated from his wife and did not see her again for many hours.*

Mrs. Morris Herman learned of the danger in a more curious fashion. She opened her door to see what was going on. She did not see flames or smoke but did witness a naked woman running by screaming, "My baby! My baby!"

In another room, Mary J. Hamilton, a recent widow, opened her door and witnessed "fire all over the place." She fainted.

Malcolm Philbrook and his wife were awakened by the sound of footsteps. Philbrook looked out of the window and saw a fire hose lying on deck. Some people came by and shouted "Fire, fire!"

Quickly the Philbrooks ran down the hall but were greeted by smoke. They turned and rushed the other way. This time they were able to make it to the boat deck.

It took time for others to learn there was a fire. Several of the passengers were still at the bar drinking when a young woman burst in shouting "Fire!" The crowd was left in a state of shock until another woman, this one badly burned, came in. This time the people at the bar went on deck to see what was happening, only to find panicky passengers running about in thick smoke.

Donald A. D'Elia was standing on the starboard side of the promenade with his wife when they both discovered the smoke.

*Both Gordons survived the disaster.

They were stunned to see passengers running about, some suffering from burns. One severely burned girl was just outside their cabin. Quickly, Mrs. D'Elia, a public health nurse, and her husband covered the injured girl with wet blankets, and then treated another passenger who had cut his wrist while breaking the window of his cabin.

Others were less fortunate. Dozens of passengers were killed in the staterooms on the boat deck as the flames, smoke and intense heat rose. Some sought escape through the windows but were unable to open them. Many of the passengers simply were trapped in their cabins as the fire raged.

Entering the main lobby, Carole Pendleton and her mother found two women, one badly burned. This stunned Carole, but she was certain the fire would be extinguished and order maintained. Still, she was concerned when she saw the fire hose "flat with no pressure" and that the sprinkler system where she was standing was "not working."

The problem with the firehoses was that there were more valves open than the pump could handle. To complicate matters, the valves to the swimming pool were open, reducing even more the pressure of the hoses. Thus the disorganized firefighters were unable to check the spreading fire.

Mrs. Pendleton remained calm throughout the ordeal. When a crewman gave her a life jacket, Carole passed it to an elderly lady. Later, five girls from Peru approached her for assistance. Carole assured them in Spanish that there would be no danger as she fastened their life jackets.

Carole herself believed that! The lifeboats so far hadn't been lowered. To Carole this was an indication that the crew would soon have the fire under control and that abandoning ship would not be necessary. Nevertheless, she and her mother were not going to take any chances. They found refuge behind the steel reinforced swimming pool in case the ship was a victim of explosions. There Carole suggested to the passengers to sing because ". . . we were in the dark section of the stern and I did not think we would be noticed." However, "that went over like a lead balloon."

It would seem that Mrs. Pendleton's prudence was wise. The

fire had swept the radio room before the radio operator was able to transmit a distress message. In desperation, the captain ordered an S.O.S. by use of the Morse lamp. Within only a few minutes after giving this order, Captain Voutsinas and his men were forced to flee the wheelhouse because of the intense heat.

Luckily for the *Yarmouth Castle*, the fire attracted the attention of a few nearby ships. Captain Lehta of the Finnish ship *Finnpulp* was awakened by the cry, "There's a ship burning!" Fearing his own vessel was aflame, Lehta rushed to the bridge where he learned that it was another ship that was on fire. Quickly, he radioed the Coast Guard for help and set course at full speed for the *Yarmouth Castle*.

Not far away, Captain Carl Brown of the Panamanian cruise liner *Bahama Star* was notified by an officer of an orange glow in the sky. At first, he thought it was the illuminated stack of a Cunarder. "It was the same sort of orange," he later explained. Suddenly, he realized the "faded beauty" was on fire. Immediately, he set his ship at top speed for the vessel in distress.

Back on the burning ship, Captain Voutsinas climbed aboard a lifeboat and abdicated his command. He had already vainly ordered the burners to be shut off and the ventilation blowers stopped. Now he was leaving his ship while hundreds of passengers and fellow crewmen remained aboard. He would later explain his action as an attempt to seek help.

Second Officer Rams de Leon viewed Voutsinas abandonment with anger. "Come back and help passengers!" he shouted to his commander. "Remember the penalty for this!"

Voutsinas continued to move away from the burning ship. He said the boat crew began firing distress flares in hope of gaining assistance from any nearby vessel. With the approach of the *Finnpulp*, the boat made its way alongside the Finnish ship. Voutsinas informed Lehta and his officers that his ship was in danger and requested they send a distress message. "We've already done that," he was told. With that Voutsinas returned to his command to offer help.

It was badly needed. Aboard the burning *Yarmouth Castle*, passengers were running to the lifeboats. Gerald A. McDonnel boarded a lifeboat only to find the boat could not be lowered because the recently painted ropes made working with the davits impossible. In distress, McDonnell climbed out of the boat and jumped clear of the ship.

George and Viola Brown climbed aboard a boat but, as Mr. Brown later explained, "They couldn't lower it. The winch wouldn't work." Growing impatient, he and his wife went aft to another boat. This one was to be lowered but there were no oarlocks and the crew were forced to row the boat like a canoe.

Others were also lowered. Malcolm Philbrook and his wife boarded a lifeboat. It was so crowded that some of the passengers were forced to stand. As the boat decended down the side of the ship, Philbrook noticed heads and feet sticking out of the portholes.

By now, Carole Pendleton no longer had any illusions of safety. She and her mother decided it would be best to jump clear of the *Yarmouth Castle* before the smoke and fire engulfed them. They headed towards a lower deck to make a more effective dive. The two were about to leap overboard when a few crewmen advised against abandoning ship without a boat for the water could be shark infested. Their argument worked. The two women decided to wait for a lifeboat.

Others descended ladders to the water regardless of this possible threat. A few crewmen abandoned ship through the port cargo door and the side pilot ports. Some were evacuated by the lifeboats which by now were being properly lowered. Many others did not wait for a boat or ladders but simply leaped overboard.

Nearby, Captain Brown of the *Bahama Star* viewed the scene with horror. The ship, he noticed, was "burning badly from the smokestack forward on the top deck and on the second deck." He saw that the radio room was already gone and the bridge was collapsing.

With a loudspeaker, Captain Brown called out to those aboard the *Yarmouth Castle*, "Listen to me. Our boats are coming for you. Go down the ropes hanging over the side or jump into the water. Be careful that you don't land on other people." The *Bahama Star*'s boats were soon alongside the burning vessel and began to haul in survivors.

Carole Pendleton and her mother climbed down to one of the *Bahama Star*'s lifeboats. "It was at this time," Mrs. Pendleton said,

"I realized the crewmen—who were left—were going to stay and make sure all the passengers were off the ship, so I handed up my lifejacket." Within minutes Carole Pendleton and her mother were safely aboard the *Bahama Star*.

Philbrook's boat came alongside the *Finnpulp*. Hauled aboard, he and the others were counted and fed. They were brought to the dining area where their names were taken.

One of the last to leave the *Yarmouth Castle* was her master, Captain Voutsinas. Black from head to foot from smoke, Voutsinas was a broken man. When he came aboard the *Bahama Star*, the only words he could say was "I'm very sorry."

At 4:00 A.M., almost three hours after the fire was discovered, the *Yarmouth Castle* was abandoned. To make certain that no one was overlooked, Captain Brown sent one of his boats to search the waters for survivors. The boat circled the dying ship but could find only deck chairs, air tanks from lifeboats and other debris.

The *Yarmouth Castle* by now was listing to the port as water accumulated from the sprinkler system, open fire hydrants, and damaged sanitary lines. As the list increased, the sea rushed through the open cargo side port. Gradually the ship began to roll over until she capsized. To onlooker Captain Brown, who had once served as an officer on the ship when she was the *Evangeline*, it was a "very sad sight." To Carole Pendleton, it was "a very strange sight."

Finally at 6:05, the *Yarmouth Castle*, "a faded beauty," was gone. Also lost were eighty-eight passengers and two crew members. A total of 475 survived the burning of the *Yarmouth Castle*.

Many factors led to this tragedy. One major cause was the long delay in discovering the fire. The *Yarmouth Castle* evidently was not equipped with smoke detectors. This along with the watchmen's failure to follow planned fire precaution exercises prevented early detection of the fire in room 610.

Once the fire started, it was able to spread quickly due to the flammable paneling and the mechanical exhaust system connecting room 610 with the toilet spaces on the main deck. The sprinkler system, though useful for small fires, could not extinguish a blaze of this size. Had there been an outlet in 610 and had the system been activated early enough, quite possibly the disaster could have been prevented.

Another factor in the large loss of life was the crew's failure to adequately warn the passengers of the fire. Although the captain and his officers would insist that they had sounded the alarm, not one of the passengers heard it. No attempt was made to notify the passengers with the public address system. Hence many did not learn of the fire until it was too late.

The basic origin of the fatal fire may never be known for certain. It is possible that the *Yarmouth Castle* was a victim of arson but the most likely cause of the fire was someone's failure to put out a cigarette or possibly a malfunction of the lighting circuit. The mattresses, broken furniture and paneling fueled this fire until it grew into a huge blaze.

If there was no intentional action that caused the disaster, there could be no doubt that there was negligence on the part of the crew in coping with the situation. In addition to the inadequate patrol by the watchmen and the failure to use the public address system, the crew was disorganized in fighting the fire. Had there been an organized firefighting attempt when the search party arrived at room 610, the conflagration may have been brought under control.

Captain Voutsinas in particular was guilty of negligence. While his command was on fire and hundreds of passengers and crew were still aboard, he had briefly abandoned ship, depriving the crew of badly needed supervision. Voutsinas always insisted that he quit the ship in order to insure the sending of a distress signal, and considering the fact that he returned after doing it, this may be so. Nevertheless, this still resulted in the absence of leadership as well as a violation of the tradition of the master being the last to leave his ship.

This tragic disaster might have been foretold. The *Yarmouth Castle* was indeed a "shining example of a ship that was not in proper condition to engage in cruise trade." Sadly, other ships with flawed fire prevention continue to sail the seas.

18 ■ NOVEMBER 10, 1975

The *Edmund Fitzgerald*
"Adequate to Weather
Any Storm"

O CEAN SAILORS often joke about the Great Lakes as being "millponds." Little do they know that the Great Lakes are capable of being quite violent, especially in the month of November. It is during this stormy month that many freighters make their final voyage before the winter weather moves in. More often than not these vessels complete their voyage without accident. Occasionally these ships succumb to the storms.

On November 9, 1913, for instance, the Great Lakes experienced a severe storm. No fewer than 18 ships and 413 lives were lost in that storm.

Forty-five years later, the freighter *Carl D. Bradley* became a victim. Built in 1927 at Lorain, Ohio, for the Bradley Transportation Line, the *Carl D. Bradley* was one of the largest freighters on the Great Lakes. She measured 639 feet from bow to stern. Her cargo space was capable of holding more than 18,000 tons of limestone. The *Bradley* in fact set a record on the Lakes in transporting the largest single cargo when it hauled 18,114 tons of limestone.

By 1958, the *Carl D. Bradley* was still in active service. She did have an accident when she ruptured one of her plates by scraping the bottom at Cedarville. The ship was repaired for her final voyage for the year 1958.

At 6:30 PM, on November 17, the *Bradley* left Buffington, Indiana. The lake was rough but not enough to suggest any danger. The old freighter had seen worse and survived.

That night the winds became rougher. By the next morning, the ships on Lake Michigan were told to expect severe weather. Many smaller ones heeded the warning. The *Carl D. Bradley*, however, continued on course.

The wind increased in speed until it reached 65 miles per hour. Waves 20 to 30 feet high were reported. The water temperature dropped to a cold 36°.

For hours it looked as if the *Bradley* would safely reach port. Late in the afternoon, the vessel was nearing the less dangerous waters at the strait of Mackinac. Around 5:00 Captain Roland Bryan, the *Bradley*'s master, reported to the owners that he would make port by 2:00 the next morning.

Then crises. At about 5:30, the captain and his first mate, Elmer Fleming, both watched in horror as two gigantic waves struck their ship fore and aft at the same instant. There was a thud throughout the vessel.

Bryan and the mate looked toward the stern and saw the ship breaking up. Quickly, the captain stopped the engines and sounded the alarm. As he did so another wave violently struck the ship.

"We're breaking in two," observed the captain grimly. He turned to the mate and ordered him to send a distress call. Quickly, Fleming reached for the radio phone and shouted, "Mayday!"

It was too late. A third wave doomed the vessel. Within minutes, the vessel was at the bottom of Lake Michigan. Captain Bryan and thirty-three of his men were lost. Only the first officer, Elmer Fleming, and crewman Frank Mayes survived the terrible disaster.

In spite of this loss, freighters continued to transport their cargoes in the month of November. One to do so was the *Edmund Fitzgerald*. Named after a prominent businessman, the *Edmund Fitzgerald* was the largest Great Lakes vessel when she was launched in 1958. The *Fitzgerald* had a length of over 700 feet, a width of 75 feet, and a depth of 39 feet. Her cargo hold was capable of carrying more than 26,000 tons of ore. She in fact set a few records in tonnage of transported ore. The *Fitzgerald* was huge and fairly sturdy. She was considered "adequate to weather any storm."

On November 9, 1975, the *Edmund Fitzgerald* was loaded with 26,216 tons of taconite pellets (a refined iron ore) at Burlington Northern Railroad Dock No. 1 at Superior Harbor, Wisconsin. Approximately 7,500 gallons of fuel were also loaded. It was, in the words of the Coast Guard report, "a routine loading and departure."

To her master, Ernest M. McSorley, all seemed well. He was to retire soon and command of the "Big *Fitz*" was the crowning of a great career. McSorley had served on the Lakes since the age of eighteen. He received his first command in 1951, becoming the youngest captain on the Lakes.

Also to retire was Edward F. Bindon, the first assistant engineer. By a strange twist of fate, Richard Bishop, the *Fitzgerald's* regular cook, was at home recuperating from an illness. Robert Rafferty took his place on this voyage.

A little after 2:15 PM, the *Edmund Fitzgerald* embarked on her final voyage for the year. Her 7,500 horsepower steam turbine engine drove the 19-foot six-inch diameter propeller to the top 16.3 miles per hour speed.* The weather was fair and Lake Superior was calm.

The weather was not placid for long. The following day, November 10, the *Edmund Fitzgerald* encountered a severe storm. The winds reached speeds of 60-65 miles per hour. Huge waves struck the freighter. It suffered some slight damage to the railing and vents, but the *Fitzgerald* still continued on course.

Since 5:00 PM on November 9, Captain McSorley had been in radio contact with Captain Jesse Cooper of the *Arthur M. Anderson*. McSorley casually mentioned the damaged railing and vents to Cooper. He also told Cooper that the ship was listing slightly. Notwithstanding this, the voice of the seaman of forty-four year's experience showed no signs of worry.

With both freighters heading to the Lake Huron Locks 100 miles away, McSorley and Cooper agreed to travel together for safety's sake. Since the *Fitzgerald* was 17 miles ahead of her companion, McSorley reduced speed.

*It is a custom to express speed in miles per hour on the Great Lakes.

Because of the bad weather, McSorley departed from the usual shipping lanes at the southern shore of the lake and headed northeastward. By 1:00, the *Fitzgerald* was about 11 miles northwest of Michipicoten Island. Captain McSorley radioed the ship's owners that his arrival time at Sault Ste. Marie was uncertain on account of the weather.

Not far from Michipicoten Island were shoals. Some of these shoals were only six fathoms deep. The *Fitzgerald* would still have nine feet clearance but the heavy seas could push the freighter down and cause her to scrape the bottom.

Around 4:20 on November 10, the *Anderson*'s first mate, Morgan Clark, picked up a radio message from the *Fitzgerald* indicating that her "radars weren't working." The freighter requested the *Anderson* to keep track of them and provide navigational assistance. The first mate assured the *Fitzgerald* he would do so.

Visibility was somewhat restricted by snowfall. However, the *Anderson* was still able to monitor the *Edmund Fitzgerald* with her radar. The first mate noticed the freighter was 15 miles ahead of his ship and "possibly between one or two degrees" to the right of the *Anderson*'s heading.

A half hour later the mate observed that the *Fitzgerald* was 10 miles ahead of the *Anderson*. The radar also revealed another object about 19 miles away. Clark radioed the *Fitzgerald* and informed her, "There is a target 19 miles ahead of us, so the target is nine miles on ahead." The voice at the other end asked, "Well, am I going to clear?" Clark responded that he would.

Before signing off, the mate asked, "Oh by the way, how are you making out with your problems?" "We are holding our own," came the reply. It was the last transmission heard from the *Edmund Fitzgerald*.

At around 7:30 the snow ceased and visibility improved considerably. The wheelsman on the *Anderson* caught a glimpse of a white light. He called it to the attention of the captain, who was unable to see it. Cooper believed the *Fitzgerald* might have had a blackout and instructed his bridge officers to look for a silhouette. But none was seen. Nor did the radar pick up the missing freighter.

Captain Cooper attempted to make contact with the *Fitzgerald* by radio but he received no response. Thinking the *Anderson*'s radio wasn't working, Cooper called the *William Clay Ford* at Whitefish Bay. When he received a reply the chilling thought that the *Edmund Fitzgerald* had taken "a nose dive" entered his head. Alarmed, Cooper notified the Coast Guard and explained the situation. With that done he set out to search for the missing vessel.

Numerous ships and planes joined the *Anderson* in the search. The *Naugatuck* left Sault St. Marie and headed for the scene. Another Coast Guard cutter, the *Woodrush*, was also dispatched. The *William Clay Ford* and the *Hilda Marjanne* left Whitefish Bay despite the severe weather.

Unfortunately the search force was reduced in size. The *Naugatuck* refused to go beyond the entrance of Whitefish Bay, for it was restricted from open water when the winds exceeded 60 knots. Other Coast Guard ships like the icebreaker *Mackinaw* and the buoy tender *Sundew* were undergoing repairs and could not leave port. The planes at Traverse City, which were to leave within a half hour notice, took a full hour to become airborne.

For hours, the ships and planes combed Lake Superior. Numerous fruitless attempts were made to radio the *Fitzgerald*. After hours of searching, the rescuers found only a few life rafts belonging to the *Edmund Fitzgerald*. Under close examination, the Coast Guard concluded they were not lowered but instead had floated away from the ship after she foundered.

After two days, the Coast Guard gave up the search for the *Edmund Fitzgerald*. The situation was considered "pretty hopeless." The water was at a temperature of 50° F. A man in this rough cold water could live for only a few hours at best. Thus, the twenty-nine men aboard the freighter were presumed lost.

Some time after the disaster, the Coast Guard located the wreck of the *Edmund Fitzgerald* at 46° 59.9 N. 85° 6.6 W. in 530 feet of water. The ship had split in two, with the bow section 170 feet from the capsized stern portion. The name plate revealed her to be the *Edmund Fitzgerald*.

Whatever caused the *Edmund Fitzgerald* to founder, it must have occurred swiftly. The crew of the ship evidently did not have time to send out a distress signal. The end must have come during the time it was invisible from the bridge of the *Anderson*.

Many theories have been put forward to explain the sinking of the *Edmund Fitzgerald*. Some say she broke up as the *Carl D. Bradley* had done. Others believe she may have capsized. The Coast Guard came up with the most likely cause. The board of investigation concluded that water entered through ineffectively sealed cargo hatches . . . finally resulting in such loss of buoyancy and stability that the vessel plunged in the heavy seas."

Some people have disputed this theory. Among them is Robert J. Hemming, author of *Gales of November*. According to Hemming, the *Fitzgerald's* charts were in error. The freighter entered the six fathom shoals near Michipicoten Island. A wave struck, causing the ship to scrape the bottom and rupture some of her plates. However, the Coast Guard discounted this theory, for "the distance between Michipicoten and the shoals is such that it appears that a delay in making the course change of upwards of an hour would have been required to cause *Fitzgerald* to have actually reached the shoals."

The investigating board also came to another conclusion: "The nature of the Great Lakes shipping, with short voyages, much of the time in very protected waters frequently with the same routine from trip to trip, leads to complacency and an overly optimistic attitude."

19 ■ MARCH 6, 1987

The *Herald of Free Enterprise*
"A Mainstay of the Townsend Thoresen"

SUSAN HAMES and her boyfriend Robert Heard drove their car to the pier. They were told by the person in the ticket booth to continue up the ramp. At 7:00 PM they were aboard the ferry. "How lucky we are," Susan remarked.

They were among the 460 or so passengers who were making passage from Zeebrugge to Dover on the *Herald of Free Enterprise*. Many of these passengers had followed the advice of a travel promotion that had appeared in British newspapers. They had spent their vacation on the continent and were now returning. At least 100 of them were soldiers of the Royal Army intending to spend their leave at home.

The ferry on which they had booked passage, the *Herald of Free Enterprise*, was one of the 22 owned by Townsend Thoresen, a subsidiary of the P. & U. Line. Built in 1980 by Schichau-Unterweser in West Germany, the *Herald* was registered at 7,950 tons, more than twice that of an *Oliver Hazard Ferry* class frigate. She measured 433 feet in length and had two vehicle decks which could accommodate 81 cars and 47 trucks or trailers. Triple screw, the *Herald*'s 12-cylinder, 24,000-horsepower diesel engines could drive the ferry at a speed of 22 knots.

The *Herald* was indeed "a mainstay of the Townsend Thoresen ferry fleet," as one writer later described her. She had two cafeterias and comfortable bunks to accommodate her passengers. The *Herald* was a beautiful vessel with an orange hull, white superstructure and blue funnels.

Susan Hames and her boyfriend Robert Heard were happy to have made it for the March 6, 1987, voyage. Susan was a thirty-three-year-old international auditor. Rob was a constructor. He was building their home in Coventry. They were looking forward to a pleasant four-and-one-half-hour voyage home.

Another passenger looking forward to going home was Brian Gibbons, an unemployed bus driver. He and a few others had landed jobs as truck drivers. They were now on their way home to tell their families of the good news.

Lance Corporal Philip Wilson intended to spend his Army leave at home. He took along his wife, Christina, and their two daughters, 18-month-old Angelina and nine-month-old Sabrina.

It would appear that the Wilsons and the other passengers were in good hands. The ferry's captain, David Lewry, had spent the last 17 years with the Townsend Line and had served as ferry captain for a decade. Lewry was respected by both his superiors and subordinates.

One problem he had, though, was the fatigue of the crew and himself. The *Herald of Free Enterprise* carried a crew of 80 per voyage who worked 24-hour shifts, or two round trips. They then would have 48 hours off while two other sets of crews worked. Needless to say, the crew, including Lewry and his officers, were often tired by the return leg of the second round trip.

This was not the captain's only worry. His vessel was a "Roll-on-roll-off," or "Ro-Ro" as they were called. These ferries were designed to be bow down in order to take on automobiles. It would take at least two hours to pump the ballast tanks to get the ship even. Six months before, Lewry wrote to other ferry boat captains, "The bow wave is well up the bow doors." The Marine Department was aware of this problem but took no action. Lewry was relieved to learn that new high speed pumps would be installed in the *Herald* on her overdue annual refit.

At around 7:00 PM, a few minutes before departure, the tired Chief Officer, Leslie Sabel, was completing his rounds. In the dim light of the automobile deck, Sabel saw a man in orange coveralls whom he took to be the assistant bosun, Mark Stanley. It was Stanley's duty to close the bow doors and Sabel surmised that these doors would soon be closed. Satisfied, Sabel returned to the bridge to report that everything was ready for departure.

Whoever the man in the orange overalls was, it was not Mark Stanley. Earlier that day, bosun Terry Ayling informed Stanley that he had no more immediate work. So Stanley went to his cabin to await the harbor stations call to close the bow doors. But it was near the end of the 24-hour shift and Stanley decided to relax in his bunk. By the time harbor stations was sounded, the bosun assistant was in deep sleep.

Thus a few minutes after 7:00 on the evening of March 6, 1987, the *Herald of Free Enterprise* edged out of her pier. Lewry was confident, as was Sabel, that the bow doors were secured. In a few hours, the ferry would safely arrive in her home port of Dover.

As the *Herald* began her voyage, Brian Gibbons decided to rest. He ate, showered, then climbed into his bunk in cabin No. 728 below the waterline. He didn't have a worry in the world.

Meanwhile, other passengers were enjoying the fine food of the cafeteria. Among them was Sergeant Brian Simpson of the Royal Army. He was eager to get back home. In the meantime he decided to quench his thirst with a drink.

Also in the cafeteria were Susan Hames and Robert Heard. After boarding the *Herald* at the last minute, Susan offered to treat Rob to dinner. Rob enthusiastically agreed.

At 7:20, the *Herald* passed the beacon on the inner breakwater. She then turned on to the main shipping channel. Lewry then sent Chief Officer Sabel to his dinner break and dismissed Second Officer Paul Morten. It was all routine.

As the *Herald* pushed through the channel at 15 knots, sea water began pouring through the bow doors. Initially, the spade, as the forward extension of the vehicle deck is called, impeded some of the incoming water. Eventually, however, water cascaded into the ferry at the rate of 200 tons a minute.

John Butler, a steward assigned to H deck, heard the water pouring in. He concluded that a pipe had ruptured. Butler telephoned the assistant purser, Stephen Homewood, and informed him of their predicament.

"Steve, we have a hell of a lot of water gushing down the stairs," he complained.

Homewood replied that he'd send the carpenter to attend to the matter. This was code for a general alarm that wouldn't disturb the passengers. Butler went to G deck where he heard the public address system page the ship's carpenter.

Then a few minutes later, at 7:27, the helmsman, Quartermaster John Hobbs, noticed the ship was not responding to the wheel. "I've got the helm on port and she's going to starboard!" he cried out in horror.

"What on earth is going on?" Lewry exclaimed. He quickly reversed the ship's engines.

It was too late. The ferry by now was listing 30° to starboard. In a matter of seconds, it was on beams end. It then settled on the bottom of the shallow water with its portside protruding out of the sea.

Sergeant Simpson was sitting at his table enjoying his drink when suddenly it slid off the table. He then noticed the entire ship began to list ominously.

"It was sheer murder," described James Bennett, "Passengers screamed, clinging to chairs and falling into water that was suddenly chest deep. The lights went out, and in the dark and pandemonium I recall telling myself, "This can't be happening."

Susan Hames and Robert Herd also noticed silverware and dishes sliding off the table. "What's happening?" Rob exclaimed. Then a woman fell on their table. Susan held the frame of the door behind her but Rob slid toward starboard. It was the last sight Susan had of her boyfriend.

"I must have swallowed half of the sea," Susan later recalled. She peeled off her two soaked sweaters and high-heeled boots. She then climbed up over the cafeteria bar. She heard a voice call out. "Is that you Rob?" she cried. But she received no answer.

Susan then noticed a man holding a girl about nine years of age. She pulled the girl up on the bar.

"Ah, you poor thing. What's your name?" Susan asked her.

"Claire."

"Are you frightened, Claire?"

"Yes, I am—very frightened. I don't know why I have to die. I've tried to be good. I never tell lies."

"You're not going to die, Claire, I promise you that."

The Wilsons were also in the cafeteria when disaster struck. As the ship began to list, Christina assumed that they had encountered rough weather. Phillip, who was by a porthole, noticed water rushing in. "Let's get out of here!" he cried.

The couple then attempted to flee the cafeteria, each holding one of their daughters. They climbed over tables and chairs. At one point, Christina noticed a man slide past her and crash through a window. The Wilsons reached a glass divider where a soldier smashed a hole. The opening was only large enough for Angelina and they passed her through the hole.

Assistant Bosun Mark Stanley was thrown out of his bunk by the list. Instantly, Stanley realized that he had failed to shut the bow doors. Quickly, he went to the passageway where he saw Bosun Ayling and other members of the crew.

Stanley and the others made their way to E deck where they heard the screams of the passengers. With an ax from one of the lifeboats, Stanley began smashing windows. Realizing that the people were 30 feet below the windows, the assistant bosun returned to the lifeboat for a rope. He then climbed down and began assuring the passengers that rescue was imminent.

Stanley soon realized that the rope was not enough to help these people. So he climbed up and was pulled through a window by two soldiers. After instructing one of them to get a ladder, he then lost consciousness from the prolonged exposure to the 37° water. He was covered with an overcoat and taken to safety.

At 7:36, the captain of the nearby *Sanderas* noticed that the *Herald* was on her side. Immediately he ceased dredging operations and set course for the ferry. He passed word to the harbor master who in turn dialed 900 and said, "Put the Zeebrugge plan into action. Rendezvous port control."

Operation Harbor Rescue was now set in motion. A key figure in the operation, Olivier Vaneste, the provincial governor and rescue coordinator, was informed by telephone of the development. Without saying a word in reply he hung up the phone and rushed to his car. Another important person involved in the plan, naval captain Jacques Thas, the provincial commander of West Flanders, was at an officer's ball when the news broke. Immediately he had a police escort take him to the harbor.

Lt. Commander Guy Couwenbergh, a diving officer, was at an officer's club when he was told of the disaster. "You mean hypothetically, as a part of the exercise?" was his response.

"No sir," came the grim reply, "it really happened. A helicopter is already on its way." At once Couwenbergh got his diving gear and boarded the helicopter.

Meanwhile, Dr. Conrad Haelterman learned of the predicament by an alarm. While his wife informed his patients to come back later, Haelterman rushed to his car and headed to the air base at Koksijde, where a helicopter was waiting for him.

Soon numerous tugs were on the scene. In the air, several helicopters were hovering over the wreck. Near the piers waited ambulances and paramedics. For the most part, Operation Harbor Rescue was working smoothly.

Lt. Commander Guy Couwenbergh and two other divers were hovering over the ferry in a helicopter. Couwenbergh climbed down a ladder over a passenger lounge. Seeing that the ladder ended about 13 feet above the water, Couwenbergh called to the other divers to get a rope. He then dove into the water.

In the water, Couwenbergh found himself surrounded by terror-stricken people dying of exposure in the 37° water. Quickly he began tying a rope around one person at a time to be hauled up. He knew that for some of these people it would be too late and was presented with the grim task of deciding whom he should rescue in time.

In the cafeteria, Susan Hames, standing in one foot of water, was holding both Claire and her younger brother Christopher. Knowing she couldn't hold the children for long, she tried to put them on a coat rack. Unable to do so, Susan called out, "Look, can anyone help me get these children up on that ledge and out of the water?"

A man made his way to her and literally fell on the coat rack. "Okay," he said, "let's have those kids up here." Susan handed him Chris and then Claire. Other women called to her to help with their children.

After three more children were lifted up, Susan saw a light in a nearby window. "Cover the children!" she shouted, "They're going to break that window." A window was then broken and a voice called down, "Hang on, we're throwing down a rope!"

A rope was lowered but too many were too exhausted to climb up. One woman attempted it but fell down. One of the passengers shouted, "Pull us up." Susan added, "Please, there are small children here. Can you lower something to take them out?"

In response to these pleas, a large wicker basket was lowered. People began shouting, "Send it over here!" Susan Hames managed to get it. "The children are going up first," she declared.

Chris was the first to be hauled up, followed by Claire. "See, Susan said to her, "I promised you'd get out of here."

"What about Dad?"

"He'll come soon."

"And you?"

"Yes, me too."

A few minutes later another window was smashed and a ladder was lowered. Susan watched breathlessly as Claire's father ascended. Within minutes, the people in the cafeteria were evacuated. Rob Heard was not one of them.

The crews of the nearby tugs did their part. The captain of the *Sea Horse*, Andre Pape, rammed the tug's bow onto the *Herald*'s stern. Then some seamen, including the captain's son, Patrick Pape, helped people cross over the *Sea Horse*. In all, 120 survivors were taken off.

The rescuers then began segregating the living from the dead. Dr. Haelterman and other medics began treating the survivors for bruises and other injuries. Many were suffering from hyperthermia, the cooling of the body. These people were treated with heated water and oxygen.

The dead were laid on the *Herald* with blankets over them. Dr. Haelterman did not wish to leave anything to chance. He checked to make certain they were dead. Miraculously, he discovered signs of life in two of them. Immediately they were rushed ashore for extensive treatment.

The rescue was not complete. In cabin 728, Brian Gibbons was stumbling in the darkness. He could hear the sound of water pouring in. He groped his way to the door and left his cabin.

Outside he saw three other truck drivers. Gibbons proposed that they move higher up to seek help. Two of the drivers were too seriously injured to make the venture, so Gibbons and the remaining truck driver began crawling up.

When they could go no further, Gibbons remained where he was while the other truckers decided to return below. A few minutes later, Gibbons heard a splash followed by screams.

"What happened?" he asked.

"It's the other lad," one of the drivers replied, "He's fallen into the water."

The truckers were unable to do anything but listen as the young man's screams died away.

Gibbons began tapping on a bulkhead. The sound was heard by one of the divers but he concluded it was wreckage banging. Then he noticed it was tapping at regular intervals. He tapped back on the bulkhead. "They're coming for us!" Gibbons triumpantly declared as he tapped. By the end of the night Gibbons and the two surviving truck drivers were evacuated.

In all, about 350 survived the terrible ordeal, including Susan Hames, Captain Lewry, and the Wilsons. No fewer than 190, thirty-eight of whom were crew members, had perished. It was one of the worst Channel disasters ever to take place. The survivors owe their lives to the brilliantly executed Zeebrugge Plan.

People around the world were shocked by the catastrophe. Prime Minister Margaret Thatcher flew to Zeebrugge to visit the survivors. "It has been a night of anguish for everyone but it has also been a night of great courage, great professionalism and concern on the part of the rescue service," she remarked.

The *Herald of Free Enterprise* was refloated the following month and towed to harbor. The British government established a board to investigate the disaster. It was clearly established that the root cause of the accident was the failure to close the bow doors before the ferry embarked on the voyage.

In a narrow sense, the blame for this circumstance rested on Assistant Bosun Mark Stanley for his dereliction of duty. Responsibility also lies with Chief Officer Leslie Sabel and Captain David Lewry for not making certain the bow doors were closed before leaving the pier. However, this probably wouldn't have happened if the Townsend Throesen Line had developed a more realistic work shift policy. After he had worked for nearly twenty hours, the possibility of someone like Stanley falling asleep on the job was more likely to occur.

Even with man's latest technology, the sea remains a dangerous adversary. The wreck of the *Herald of Free Enterprise*, along with that of the *Titanic, Vestris, Andrea Doria, Edmund Fitzgerald* and others could serve as a reminder of the potential hazards man faces when he ventures on the water.

Appendix

SELECTED CHRONOLOGY OF SHIP DISASTERS

1833, May 11 — *Lady of the Lake* bound to Quebec from England strikes an iceberg; 215 lost.

1850, March 29 — *Royal Adelaide* is wrecked off Margate, England; 400 lost.

1852, March 26 — *Troopship Birkenhead* is wrecked off South Africa; 454 lost.

1859, April 27 — The *Pomona* is wrecked off Ireland; 386 lost.

1859, October 25 — *Royal Charter* strikes rock off coast of Anglesea; 150 lost.

1860, September 8 — Excursion steamer *Lady Elgin* collides with lumber ship in Lake Michigan; 300 lost.

1865, April 27 — Steamer *Sultana* carrying released Union prisoners explodes near Memphis, Tenn.; 1,450 lost.

1878, September 3 — *Princess Alice* sinks in Thames after collision; 700 lost.

1880 — British sailing training-ship *Atalanta* disappears en route to England with 290.

1891, March 17 — Steamer *Utopia* sinks after collision off Gibraltar; 547 lost.

1898, July 4 — *La Bourgogne* sinks after collision with *Cromartyshire* off Nova Scotia; 560 lost.

1904, June 15 — Excursion *General Slocum* burns in New York City's East River; over 1,000 lost.

1912, March 5 — Steamer *Principe de Asturias* strikes rock off Sebastien Point; 500 lost.

1915, July 24 — Excursion *Eastland* capsizes in Chicago River; over 800 lost.

1916, August 29 — *Hsin Yu* sinks off coast of China; about 1,000 lost.

1918 — U.S. Navy collier *Cyclops* disappears with 309 men.

1921, March 18 — Steamer *Hong Kong* is wrecked on rocks off Swatow, China; about 1,000 lost.

1925, April 19 — *Raifuku Maru* sinks in heavy weather. Last message, "Now very danger. Come quick." 48 lost.

1927, October 25 — *Principessa Mafalda* explodes off Brazil; 326 lost.

1934, September 8 — *Morro Castle* catches fire off coast of New Jersey; 137 lost.

1947, January 19 — Greek steamer *Himara* strikes mine off Athens; 392 lost.

1948, June 11 — Danish ship *Kjoebenhaun* strikes mine off Jutland; 140 lost.

1961, April 8 — British liner *Dara* burns after bomb explosion; 212 lost.

1963, February — *Marine Sulphur Queen* sinks off coast of Florida; 34 lost.

1964, February 10 — Australian destroyer *Voyager* collides with aircraft carrier *Melbourne*; 82 lost.

1968, May 21 — U.S. nuclear submarine *Scorpion* is lost near Azores; 99 lost.

1969, June 2 — U.S. destroyer *Evans* collides with aircraft carrier *Melbourne*; 74 lost.

1972, February 1 — Tanker *V. A. Fogg* explodes in Gulf of Mexico; 39 lost.

1973, February 21 — Ferry boat collides with freighter in Rangoon Burma; over 200 lost.

1983, June 5 — Soviet ship rams railroad bridge across Volga River; 240 lost.

1986, April 20 — Bangladesh ferry sinks in rough weather; 300 lost.

1986, August 31 — Soviet passenger liner *Admiral Nakhimov* collides with freighter in Black Sea; 398 lost.

Acknowledgments and Selected Sources

I have consulted numerous sources in writing this book. In each chapter, I have employed at least one primary source.

Much of my information came from official investigations. Among them were *Loss of the Steamship "Titanic"* (Great Britain Board of Trade, 1912), the report of the British investigation and the testimony, *Court to Investigate the Loss of the Steamship "Titanic"* (Great Britain Board of Trade, 1912). The Senate report, *"Titanic" Disaster: Report of the Committee of Commerce* (Senate Report 806, 62nd Cong. 2nd sess., 1912) and its testimony, *"Titanic" Disaster: Hearing Before a Subcommittee on Commerce* (Senate Doc. 726, 62nd Cong. 2nd sess., 1912) were usefull in the study of the *Titanic* disaster. Lord Mersey's investigations into the *Lusitania* and the *Empress of Ireland* were also consulted. Other investigations include *U.S. Naval Court of Inquiry Upon Destruction of the Battleship "Maine," Report of Investigation into the Cause of the Wreck of the Steamship "Atlantic"* and *Loss of the Steamship "Vestris"* Two Coast Guard reports, one into the loss of the *Yarmouth Castle* and the other, the *S.S. "Edmund Fitzgerald" Sinking in Lake Superior on 10 November 1975 with Loss of Life* were useful.

General information was found in certain books. *Strange Adventures of the Great lakes* by Dwight Boyer (Dodd Mead, 1974) and *Guardians of the Eighth Sea* by Michael O Brien (U.S. Coast Guard) provided background on the Great Lakes. *The Atlantic Liners* by Frederick Emmons (Drake Publishers Inc., 1972) gave brief descriptions of the Atlantic liners as did *Passenger Ships of the World Past & Present* by Eugene W. Smith (George Dean Company, 1978). John Brinnin's *The Sway of the Grand Saloon* (Delacorte Press, 1971) was a brilliant job on the social history of the North Atlantic. *Fifty Famous Liners* by Frank C.

Braynard and William Miller (W.W. Norton & Co., 1982) contained information on the *Titanic*. Charles Hocking's *Dictionary of Disasters at Sea During the Age of Steam* (Lloyds Register of Shipping, 1969) and Jay Robert Nash's *Darkest Hour* (Nelson-Hall, 1976) had data on shipwrecks. *Road to War* by Walter Millis (Houghton Mifflin Company, 1935) revealed the friction between the United States and Germany during World War I. Bertraın Hayes' *Hull Down* (The Macmillan Company, 1925) provided background information on life on the liners during the turn of the century and during the First World War. *Naval Operations* by Julian Corbett (Longmans Green and Company, 1920) revealed the naval situation during the First World War.

Some sources provided background information on the Spanish-American War. Among them was *Dictionary of American Naval Fighting Ships* Vol. IV (Naval History Division, 1969). *Report of the Committee on Foreign Relations, U.S. Senate, Relative to Affairs in Cuba* (Government Printing Office, 1898) *The Martial Spirit* by Walter Millis (The Riverside Press, 1931), *The Journal of John Long*, edited by Margaret Long (Richard R. Smith Publisher Inc., 1956), and the papers of William McKinley. Two books about McKinley, *William McKinley and His America* by H. Wayne Morgan (Syracuse University Press, 1963) and *In the Days of McKinley* by Margaret Leech (Haper, 1959), provided insights into the *Maine* disaster. "The Needless War With Spain" by William E. Leuchtenburg for the February 1957 issue of *American Heritage* had some data on the events leading up to the Spanish-American War. *Bankers Magazine* and *The Wall Street Journal* were consulted for the business view of the war.

I found valuable background information on various shipwrecks in certain books. A.A. Hoehling's books *They Sailed Into Oblivion* (Thomas Yoseloff, 1959). *Great Ship Disasters* (Cowles Book Company, Inc., 1971) and *Epics of the Sea* (Contemporary Books Inc. 1977) provided important information on the *Vestris, Atlantic, Empress of Ireland*, and the *Cospatrick* and others. Hal Butler's *Abandon Ship!* (Henry Regnery Company, 1974) is a fine book on shipwrecks such as the *Atlantic, Lakonia* and *Hans Hedtoft*. *Great Storms and Famous Shipwrecks of the New England Coast* by Edward Rowe Snow (Yankee Publishing Company) was consulted for the *Portland* disaster. Snow's book, *Adventure, Blizzards and Coastal Calamities* (Dodd Mead, 1978) provided information on the *Atlantic* as did Irwin Forges' *Many Brave Hearts* (Chilton, 1968). Data on the *Atlantic* along with the *Arctic* was found in *Rivalry on the Atlantic* by William Mack Agnas (Lee Furman, 1939). Stories on collisions at sea can be found in Peter Padfield's *An Agony of Collisions* (Hodder and Stoughton, 1966). Some information on the *Maine* disaster was provided by Frank Meier's *Fathoms Below*

(E.P. Dutton & Co., Inc., 1943). *The Night Boat* by George W. Hilton (Howell-North Books, 1968) contained information on the *City of Portland*. *Majesty at Sea* by John H. Shaum Jr. and William Flayhart III (W.W. Norton Co., 1981) provided information on the *Britannic* as did *Damned by Destiny* by David Williams and Richard P. de Herbrech (Teredo Books, 1982).

Some books of course have been written about individual shipwrecks. I found Alexander Crosby Brown's *Women and Children Last* (G.P. Putman's Sons, 1961) useful in reconstructing the story of the *Arctic*. *The Coal Was There For Burning* by C.H. Milson (Instituet Marine Enginer, 1976) provided details of the *Atlantic* disaster. John Weems' book *The Fate of the "Maine"* (Henry Holt and Company, 1958) was valuable in the story of the U.S.S. *Maine*. I found important information on the *Empress of Ireland* in *Fourteen Minutes* by James Croall (Stein and Day, 1978). *Gales of November* by Robert J. Hemming (Contemporary Book, Inc., 1981) was useful for the chapter on the *Edmund Fitzgerald*. Two books on the *Andrea Doria*, *Collision Course* by Alvin Moscow (Putman's, 1959) and *Saved!* by William Hoffer (Bantam Books, 1979) were consulted. A.A. Hoehling and Mary Hoehling's *The Last Voyage of the "Lusitania"* (Henry Holt, 1956) was useful in the writing of the *Lusitania* chapter. The political history of the *Lusitania* is dealt with in *The "Lusitania" Disaster* by Thomas A. Bailey and Paul B. Ryan (Free Press, 1975). *The Maiden Voyage* by Geoffrey Marcus (Manor Books, 1969) is the complete story of the ill-fated *Titanic* from sailing day to the courts. *The "Titanic": End of a Dream* by Wyn Craig Wade (Rawson Wade, 1979) provided a wealth of information on the *Titanic*. Walter Lord's *A Night to Remember* (Henry Holt and Company, 1955) was a skillful narrative of the greatest and most moving chapter in the history of peacetime marine disaster, the story of the *Titanic*. Lord's book *The Night Lives On* (William Morrow and Company, Inc., 1986) provided new insights into the *Titanic* disaster.

Some books were consulted on rescues. *S.O.S. To the Rescue* by Karl Bearslag (Oxford University Press, 1935) contained excellent stories of rescue at sea by wireless. Captain Rostron's book *Home From the Sea* (The Macmillan Company, 1931) contains an interesting chapter on his part in the rescue of the *Titanic*. *The "Ile de France"* by Don Stanford (Appleton-Centuy Crofts Inc., 1960) provided interesting information on this liner and her part in the *Andrea Doria* rescue as did Raoul de Beaudean's account of the rescue in *Captain of the "Ile"* (McGraw-Hill Book Company Inc., 1960).

I also made use of numerous magazine articles. Ralph Whitney's article "The Unlucky Collins Line" which appeared in *The American Heritage* issue of February 1957 provided certain facts on the *Arctic* disaster and the Collins Line. Another article in this magazine, "Maiden Voyage" by Walter Lord in the December 1955 issue, contains interesting facts on the *Titanic*. The magazine's June 1955 issue contained an article on the *Lusitania* entitled "A Liner, a U-Boat and History" by Oscar Handlin which was consulted. The article "Sinking of the *Lusitania*" by Thomas Bailey which appeared in the October 1935 issue of *American Historical Review* revealed interesting facts. Cornelius Ryan's "Five Desperate Hours in Cabin 56" which appeared in September 28, 1956 issue of *Collier's* was useful to me in writing about the *Andrea Doria*. Two articles in *Sea Classics*, "No Survivors: The Tragic Loss of Steamer *Portland*"by Roger Freeman in September 1984, and "Triumph and Tragedy of the Collins Blue Ribbon Steamers" by J. Leeming in the May 1984 issue, were interesting. "False Call to War" by Thomas Fleming in *Military History*, April 1986, provided insights into the *Maine*. *"Britannic*—The Queen that Never Reigned" by John H. Shaum Jr. in the Spring 1967 *Steamboat Bill*, the quarterly of the Steamship Historical Society of America, contained important data on the *Britannic*.

I am not in agreement to all that has been written on these shipwrecks. For alternative views on the cause of the destruction of the *Maine* there is John M. Taylor's article in April 1978 issue of *American History Illustrated* entitled, "Remembering the *Maine*" and Hyman Rickover's *How the Battleship "Maine" was Destroyed* (Government Printing Office, 1976) should be sought. The conspiracy view of the *Lusitania* can be found in *The "Lusitania"* by Colin Simpson (Ballantine Books, 1972). Des Hickey and Gus Smith's *Seven Days to Disaster* (G. P. Putman's Sons, 1981) contains an account of the mutiny aboard U-20. *Gales of November* by Robert Hemming mentioned above presented an alternative version of the doom of the *Edmund Fitzgerald*. The alternative version of the *Californian*'s role in the *Titanic* disaster are provided in John Carrothers article "Lord of the *Californian*," in the March 1968 issue of U.S. Naval Institute *Proceedings*, and Peter Padfield's *The "Titanic" and the "Californian"* (John Day Co., 1965).

Some sources furnished technical information. Some old issues of *Shipbuilder* dealt with the construction and design of the *Titanic* and the *Lusitania*. The November 1956 issue of *Science Digest* provided data on radar as did *Radar* by Orrin Dunlop (Harper & Brothers, 1946). The safety of the *Titanic* was discussed in the spring 1972 *Steamboat Bill* article "Was the *Titanic* Unsafe At Any Speed?" by Colin Carmichael. Kenneth Barnaby's *Some Ship Disasters and Their Causes* (A.S. Barnes and Co., 1968) was interesting. Old *Engineering* magazine issues were consulted for the *Titanic* and the *Maine*.

Contemporary press was often inaccurate. One notable exception was *The New York Times*. This newspaper did a brilliant job on several disasters, especially the *Titanic*. Also consulted was *The Times* (London), the *Chicago Tribune*, and *Washington Post* and the *Boston American*. *Life* magazine provided information on the *Hans Hedtoft*. *Time* magazine had coverage of the *Hans Hedtoft*, the *Lakonia* and the discovery of the *Titanic*. *Newsweek* provided coverage of the *Yarmouth Castle* and the *Edmund Fitzgerald*.

Some of my important sources were survivors and their relatives. Many of them have long been dead. Nevertheless I was able to contact a few. I wish to thank Dr. Leonard Laufe for answering my correspondence. I am grateful to Edward Johnson for answering my telephone call. Carole Pendleton deserves thanks for mailing me a brief description of her experience on the *Yarmouth Castle* as did Malcolm and Doris Philbrook. Edwina Mackenzie furnished her experience aboard the *Titanic* when she was then Edwina Troutt. Louise Pope was helpful. Father Richard Wojcik related to the author his experience in regards to the *Andrea Doria*. Conrad Mangels informed me of the ordeal of his parents aboard the *Andrea Doria*.

When survivors could not be contacted, their published accounts were consulted. James Connally's article "Sinking of the *Republic*" in *Collier's Weekly* on February 6, 1909 is a sharp condemnation of the White Star Line. Jack Thayer wrote an interesting article of his survival of the *Titanic* sinking in the *Philadelphia Evening Bulletin* on April 14, 1932. Eva Hart's account of the *Titanic* disaster was found in the May 1980 issue of *USA Today*. Father Wojcik's interview in the *Independent Register* was useful. Likewise, Richard Burca wrote a fine article about his ordeal aboard the *Lakonia* in *Reader's Digest* issue of June 1964 entitled "A Holiday I'll Never Forget." Charles Sigsbee's article about the *Maine* appeared in *Century Magazine* of November 1898. Lilianna Donner wrote a fine article, "I survived the Sinking of the *Andrea Doria*" for the May 1984 issue of *Sea Classics*.

Some survivors wrote books about their experiences. Lawrence Beesley's *The Loss of the S.S. "Titanic"* (Houghton Mifflin, 1912), Colonel Gracie's *The Truth About the "Titanic"* (Mitchel Kennerley, 1913) and Charles Lightoller's *"Titanic" and Other Ships* (Ivor Nicholson & Watson, 1933) aided me immensely in my research. Jack Thayer's privately printed booklet, *The Sinking of the S.S. "Titanic"* was also useful. Charles Lauriate's *The "Lusitania's" Last Voyage* (Boston, 1915) was a brief account of his ordeal on the Cunard liner. Captain Sigsbee's book *The "Maine"* (The Century, 1898) is an invaluable account of the ship and her reception in Havana.

212 ► To the Bottom of the Sea

Some of my sources were non-printed material. The television documentary "*Calypso*'s Quest for the *Britannic*," which was broadcast November 22, 1977, was interesting as was the video "*Olympic, Titanic, Britannic*" by Spa films. Two records by Vantage Recording Company, *Titanic* and *Titanic II*, provided accounts by survivors as did the cassette "Remember the *Titanic!*" by 7 C's Press.

Government organizations provided assistance. The United Sates Coast Guard provided information and suggested leads. The United States Navy furnished information on the *Maine*. The British Ministry of Transport was helpful.

Private organizations also were helpful. The Mercantile Marine Service Association forwarded information on the *Californian*. The *Titanic* Historical Society and the Steamship Historical Society of America sent important data. Harland & Wolff was co-operative in my research on the *Titanic*.

Certain individuals have aided me in my research. James Cichcoh led me through the fundamentals of radar. The late William Tantum offered me useful advice. A. A. Hoehling recommended sources. Walter Lord furnished the names of *Titanic* survivors and helped in countless other ways. Edward Rowe Snow checked a lead for me. Dr. Robert Ballard had answered questions surrounding the discovery of the *Titanic*. The inter-library loan staffs at the James V. Brown Library, Lycoming College, Arkansas State University and the University of Akron and their unseen partners in other libraries were invaluable.

Other individuals closer to me have helped. James Revello had offered me sound advice. My uncle John Protasio and cousin Andrew Stack have offered me encouragement. Linda Hawkins had loaned me some of my earlier writing I had given her to examine. My brother Charles Protasio did important research. Mike Ertle, Gloria McFadden and Richard Morris read earlier drafts of this manuscript.

Glossary

Amidship The middle of the ship.

Beam A long piece of timber or metal used as horizontal support for decks.

Bow Forward part of the ship.

Bulkhead A wall that divides the ship into sections.

Collapsible A lifeboat with canvas sides.

Crow's Nest A small box or platform near the top of a mast for the lookouts.

Davits Pair of posts used to lower lifeboats.

Forecastle The upper deck in front of the ship often used by the crew to eat and sleep.

Funnel Smokestack.

Knot One nautical mile (6076.1 feet) per hour.

Port Facing forward (Bow) to the left side of the ship.

Rudder Broad piece of wood or metal attached to the rear of the ship used for steering.

Screw Propeller.

Starboard Facing forward (Bow), the right of the ship.

Stern The rear part of the ship.

Superstructure Part of the ship above the main deck.